A SYMPHONY OF SOLOISTS: THE STORY OF

Wakefern ❧ ShopRite

A SYMPHONY OF SOLOISTS: THE STORY OF
Wakefern & ShopRite

Jeffrey L. Rodengen

Foreword by Burt Prentice Flickinger III

Edited by Joseph Demma and Heather Lewin
Design and Layout by Elijah Meyer

WRITE STUFF

Write Stuff Enterprises, LLC
1001 South Andrews Avenue
Fort Lauderdale, FL 33316
1-800-900-Book (1-800-900-2665)
(954) 462-6657
www.writestuffbooks.com

The publisher has made every effort to identify and locate the source of the photographs included in this edition of *A Symphony of Soloists: The Story of Wakefern and ShopRite*. Grateful acknowledgment is made to those who have kindly granted permission for the use of their materials in this edition. If there are instances where proper credit was not given, the publisher will gladly make any necessary corrections in subsequent printings.

Publisher's Cataloging-In-Publication Data
(Prepared by The Donohue Group, Inc.)

Rodengen, Jeffrey L.
   A symphony of soloists : the story of Wakefern and ShopRite / Jeffrey L. Rodengen ; foreword by Burt Flickinger III ; edited by Joseph Demma and Heather Lewin ; design and layout by Elijah Meyer.

   p. ; cm.

   Includes index.
   ISBN: 978-1-932022-46-9

   1. Wakefern Food Corp.—History. 2. ShopRite (Firm)—History. 3. Food cooperatives—United States—History. 4. Supermarkets—United States—History. I. Flickinger, Burt. II. Demma, Joseph. III. Lewin, Heather. IV. Meyer, Elijah. V. Title. VI. Title: Wakefern and ShopRite

HF5469.23.U64 S56 2010
381/.456/413/065   2010925543

Completely produced in the
United States of America
10 9 8 7 6 5 4 3 2 1

TABLE OF CONTENTS

FOREWORD

BY

BURT PRENTICE FLICKINGER III

THE STORY OF WAKEFERN AND ShopRite is that of David taking on Goliath, and through tenacity, ingenuity, and genuine passion, this innovative group developed a proprietary model of cooperative business unmatched today in American enterprise.

As you will discover in the pages that follow, what eventually became the Wakefern cooperative in 1946, followed by the grocery stores that operated under the ShopRite banner beginning in 1951, began with a handful of owners of small food stores following World War II.

These individually owned stores were facing unprecedented profit and competitive chain store pressures largely due to the enormous presence of The Great Atlantic and Pacific Tea Company, known as A&P, which, because of its size, was able to secure lower prices from manufacturers. For perspective on A&P's national and international procurement power, A&P had 80 field buying offices and more than 60 manufacturing plants around the world to supply more than 4,000 A&P supermarkets when Wakefern started.

Because of this huge disadvantage in bulk purchasing, Louis Weiss, Sam Aidekman, Al Aidekman, Abe Kesselman, and David Fern—whose names and initials formed the word Wakefern—along with other founding members, Sam Garb and Albert Goldberg, formed a cooperative that would enable small grocers to compete with the industry giants.

To help understand the scale of the challenge, in 1950, Wakefern's co-op volume was $2.2 million. That same year, A&P reported record sales volume of $3.2 billion, with more than a 37 percent share of the U.S. food retail market (which, in comparison to today's U.S. market, would represent 175 percent of Wal-Mart's estimated 2010 food retail market share). When Wakefern started, A&P was bigger than the combined market share of Safeway, and Kroger, the Number Two, and Three national supermarket chains. A&P had higher global sales than both U.S. Steel and Standard Oil (i.e., Esso-Exxon). A&P was second only to General Motors in worldwide sales and was the largest privately held corporation in the world, spanning the entire United States and Canada from coast to coast.

A&P could sell a five-pound bag of sugar or flour for about 51 cents, the same price Wakefern members had to pay for it. A&P leveraged its procurement muscle, while at the same time Wakefern could not secure credit from manufacturers. Furthermore, A&P went on to make 10 major acquisitions to increase its tremendous size and scale. It was a genuine struggle for the co-op to survive against these overwhelming odds. When the members joined together under the ShopRite banner, they could participate in group advertising and marketing, and develop a highly regarded full portfolio of private-label brand products.

And, in one of the great retailing, branding, and marketing success stories in U.S. history—more than 60 years later—Wakefern and ShopRite today have the highest market share in the New Jersey–New York metropolitan area. ShopRite Supermarkets enjoy among the highest volume of food and drug superstore sales in the United States, or anywhere in the world for that matter.

As Wakefern moves into its seventh decade, its sales are 300 percent greater than all of A&P's seven operating companies, and ShopRite's sales and market share are higher than Wal-Mart's in Wakefern and ShopRite's primary markets—even though Wal-Mart has become the second largest corporation worldwide and largest global retailer.

At the heart of Wakefern's success, beyond hard work and determination, is the fact that its members are skilled multi-generational food retailers who dedicate many thousands of hours to voluntary committee membership at Wakefern, where they work in tandem with Wakefern's professional staff to deliver the best possible offerings to ShopRite's customers.

This unique grocery cooperative has had its share of challenges, from competitive to internal. In every instance, though, the leadership and the members rallied to further improve its bylaws, stockholders' agreement, and proprietary site selection process to emerge stronger and more efficient than ever. Today, Wakefern and its 46 members operate a total of 274 ShopRite and PriceRite stores in eight states. Together, Wakefern and ShopRite have 50,000 employees, 3.3 million square feet of warehouse space, and retail sales of $11.6 billion, placing them in an enviable position to continue their market leadership.

Wakefern has always been a fierce competitor, prepared to do battle with whatever came its way. Repeatedly, members have shown an unwavering commitment of support for each other and the cooperative structure. The food retailing industry has gone through great transition in recent years, with unprecedented mergers, consolidations, and a record number of bankruptcies. And yet, the Wakefern model crafted more than 60 years ago remains a successful formula, enabling it to compete with anyone far into the future.

The Wakefern membership thoroughly understands its markets, the communities it serves, shopping trends, and the power of customer loyalty. From its founding members in 1946, to David Silverberg, Jerry Yaguda, and Dean Janeway, to Tom Infusino and Joe Colalillo, Wakefern leadership is always exceptional. Each has been able to go beyond their individual business interests to consider the greater interest of the consumer, the greater interest of the co-op, and to take an innovative and proactive approach to solving problems successfully.

Having been privileged to observe and consult within this exciting and very dynamic industry for so many years, has made the accomplishment of Wakefern and ShopRite all the more dynamic, and all the more inevitable. For historical perspective on Wakefern and ShopRite's spectacular success—from its beginning as entrepreneurial stores —our Flickinger family has worked for five generations in the food industry. After coming out of a foster home after his mother's death, and being adopted by Burt Prentice's farming family, S. M. Flickinger gathered his brothers and expanded their retail farm stands to start independent food stores and multiregional food wholesaling.

Later, the Flickingers created retail franchising as well as the retail, independent chain movement nearly a century ago to help form Federated Foods private label manufacturing, IGA, and Red & White stores. After having seen so many of the famous retail chains, co-ops, and wholesalers that the Flickingers had worked with across the U.S. during the last 60 years, struggle and sometimes not survive, it greatly reinforces Wakefern's phenomenal accomplishments as one of the greatest success stories in American business, retailing, marketing, and strategic support services.

Wakefern's vision says it all: "We help small business succeed in a big business world." The next generation of membership is in active preparation to take the reins of leadership. If the past 60 years is any indication, the future of this passionate group is truly without limit.

ACKNOWLEDGMENTS

MANY DEDICATED PEOPLE assisted in the research, preparation, and publication of *A Symphony of Soloists: The Story of Wakefern and Shop-Rite*. Research Assistant Cort Smith conducted the principal archival research for the book, while senior editors Joseph Demma and Heather Lewin managed the editorial content. Graphic Designer Elijah Meyer brought the story to life.

Several key individuals associated with Wakefern and ShopRite provided their assistance in development of the book from its outline to its finished product. Special thanks to Mary Ellen Gowin, who provided project direction, research, and editorial assistance. Gratitude is extended to those serving on the book review committee: Joe Colalillo, Dean Janeway, Vincent Lo Curcio III, Karen McAuvic, and Joe Sheridan. Additional thanks to Karen Meleta, who provided writing assistance, and also served on the book review committee. Lisa Barry, Marvis Jackson, Marion Kelley, and Kathy O'Neill provided administrative assistance, while Alan Aront, Ann Burke, Joe Gozzi, Lisa Haley, Cheryl Macik, Christine Magyarits, Christine Rogers McMaster, Don Merrigan, Liz Mysak, and Jim Watson provided valuable research and background information. Jennifer Kline, and Shepard Rosenthal were key in the development of the Wakefern member profiles. Friends of Wakefern, Ron Gianettino, Shirley Anne Schultz, and Andrea Spinelli also contributed key historical details. A special thank you is also due to Shirley Aidekman, who shared her family's collection of ShopRite ads and photos from the earliest years. This resource was invaluable in piecing together and illustrating the early co-op history.

Appreciation is extended to the following Wakefern member families, past and present, for sharing their photos: Cingari, Colalillo, Gladstein, Infusino, Laurenti, Lo Curcio, Perlmutter, Romano, Sitar, Sumas, Szibdat, and Tully.

All of the people interviewed were generous with their time and insights. Those members who shared their memories were: Jeff Brown, Ken Capano, Sam Cingari, Rocco Cingari, Bob Clare, Ned Gladstein, Irv Glass, Terry Glass, Antoinette Lo Curcio, Tom Infusino, Joel Perlmutter, Steve Ravitz, Dominick V. Romano, Richard Saker, Tony Smutko, William Sumas, Jim Sumas, Perry Sumas, and Larri Wolfson. Others interviewed include: David Silverberg, former Wakefern president; Allen Bildner, former owner, Kings Super Markets; Dennis Block, senior partner, Cadwalader, Wickersham & Taft LLP; Dewey Cannella, Wakefern vice president, Industrial Relations; Kathleen DiChiara, executive director, Community FoodBank of New Jersey; Al Ferri, retired, vice president, Produce; Burt Prentice Flickinger III, industry analyst; Bob Gal, Wakefern, retired, senior vice president; Bill Noto, retired, Wakefern vice president, Business Development and Real Estate; Frank Rostan, Wakefern, senior vice president; Peter Rolandelli, vice president, Transportation; Doug Wille, Wakefern, chief financial officer; Jim Tracy, Wakefern, vice president, Wholesaling; Natan Tabak, senior vice president; and Tom Zaucha, chairman, National Grocers Association.

Finally, special thanks are extended to the staff at Write Stuff Enterprises, LLC: Elizabeth Fernandez, executive editor; Sandy Cruz, vice president/creative director; Roy Adelman, on-press supervisor; Lynn C. Jones and Martin Schultz, proofreaders; Mary Aaron, transcriptionist; Donna M. Drialo, indexer; Amy Major, executive assistant to Jeffrey L. Rodengen; Marianne Roberts, executive vice president, publisher, and chief financial officer; and Stanislava Alexandrova, marketing manager.

Ben Goldstein and his brother-in-law Julius Perlmutter started in the grocery business in a 500-square-foot store called P&G Market in Lakewood, New Jersey. Perlmutter stands in the doorway of the store, commonly known as Ben's Market, in 1928.

CHAPTER ONE

INTO THE LION'S CAGE

1946–1950

For we are but a group of small businessmen with big ideas, working collectively, not for individual benefit, not for individual prestige, and not for just a small group, but for each and every member, small or large.

—Samuel Aidekman,
founding member and president,
Wakefern Food Corp.[1]

IN THE EARLY 1940S, SMALL NEIGH-borhood stores were the ulti-mate in convenience. Located within walking distance of customers' homes, they catered to each neighborhood's needs by slipping customers a little extra flour or butter when they were hard to get during World War II. It was during this time that the chain supermarkets lost ground to mom-and-pop stores due to personnel and merchandise shortages, as well as the smaller grocers' ability to purchase cartel items for loyal customers.

Supermarkets first appeared in the 1920s as dry goods stores that began offering meat and produce under one roof and had been staking their own ground right up until the war began. A&P, Kroger, and Safeway stores began appearing, offering self service. In the 1930s, Michael Cullen, a former employee of Kroger, founded what is sometimes considered the first modern supermarket when he opened King Kullen, in a warehouse just outside New York City.[2] He emphasized volume sales rather than price, deemphasized decor, and sold merchandise from packing cartons, which helped keep prices low.[3]

After the War Ended

When wartime restraints on food rationing and price controls were lifted, consumers gained the ability to shop freely. Reflecting a new style of con-sumerism driven by convenience and price, consumers began relying heavily on large, self-service supermarkets. It enabled customers to pick items that lined the shelves themselves, rather than asking a clerk behind the counter for specific products. Customers were quick to sacrifice the personal service—and credit-buying privileges—that defined the small neighborhood grocer. Also, by bringing together grocery, produce, and meats under one roof, it made shopping more convenient—customers would visit just one store, rather than three. Chains began consolidating smaller stores into larger stores, offering more items at one location.[4] The chains regained their lost ground and more when these "modern" shoppers defected, driving some independent grocers out of business and creating a difficult business environment for those that remained.

Product innovation and the development of suburbs after World War II drove the introduction of "convenience products," a whole new product category, such as frozen TV dinners and pot pies, and

Seen in 1947, the Pioneer Super Market, owned by early Wakefern member Etorre Laurenti, was typical of the small independent grocery stores found throughout New Jersey in post–World War II America.

UNITED STATES OF AMERICA
OFFICE OF PRICE ADMINISTRATION

4 835359

WAR RATION BOOK No. 3 Void if altered   K   NOT VALID WITHOUT STAMP

Identification of person to whom issued: PRINT IN FULL

OP. As VA U.S. STAMP
and Sign

(First name)   (Middle name)   (Last name)

Street number or rural route ....

City or post office ....   State ....

AGE	SEX	WEIGHT Lbs.	HEIGHT Ft. In.	OCCUPATION

SIGNATURE ....
(Person to whom book is issued. If such person is unable to sign because of age or incapacity, another may sign in his behalf.)

WARNING
This book is the property of the United States Government. It is unlawful to sell it to any other person, or to use it or permit anyone else to use it, except to obtain rationed goods in accordance with regulations of the Office of Price Administration. Any person who finds a lost War Ration Book must return it to the War Price and Rationing Board which issued it. Persons who violate rationing regulations are subject to $10,000 fine or imprisonment, or both.

OPA Form No. R-130

LOCAL BOARD ACTION

Issued by ....
(Local board number)   (Date)

Street address ....

City ....   State ....

(Signature of issuing officer)

the previous year. For the same period, independent grocers realized a gain of just 12 percent. A trade journal at the time described the competition between chains and independents as "fast, furious, and unrelenting."[5]

Reacting to record sales posted by the chains, distributors were quick to adjust not only to higher prices—by the end of 1947, for example, prices were 118 percent higher than in 1939—but also to the demands of the largest food volume in history and passed along those price increases to their buyers.[6] This was another turn of the screw for independent grocers, who were already feeling the pinch.

United by Purpose

It was common for grocers to run into one another in the Newark wholesale food district, where they bought goods from different suppliers. In the summer of 1946, a small group of independent grocers in North Jersey gathered informally in Newark, not only to buy goods, but also "to drink coffee and complain about the chains" and discuss ways to cut costs to remain competitive.[7]

For independents, teamed together or not, the prevailing post-war sentiment was that they would fail: "At the time of its birth ... operating Wakefern—or any cooperative venture for that matter—was tantamount to doing a high wire act over a cage of hungry lions."[8]

The catalyst for these increasingly purposeful get-togethers, which went on for months, was Ed Casson, a young Del Monte Foods sales representative sympathetic to the independent grocers' concerns about being out-advertised and underpriced by the chains. At the same time, he hoped to land their business, although Del Monte wasn't a direct supplier (the products were handled by a broker).

"These retailers would sit around together early in the morning, at three, four, five o'clock," recalled David Silverberg, a Cornell MBA and economics instructor who joined the co-op in 1950 after being brought on board by his relative, General Manager Herman Wechsler. "They'd been doing this for years."[9]

cake mixes and other formulated products unheard of just a few years before. Larger chain stores had the room to merchandise the explosive growth of these new products, which the small mom-and-pop stores, short on space, could not.

The chains were simply better equipped to cope with these new shopping trends—as well as follow the great exodus of city dwellers to the suburbs in the late 1940s and early 1950s. In 1947, food prices and consumer demand rose, against all expectations, and chains reported a sales increase of $2.175 billion, the largest jump in history, to reach an all-time high of $8.44 billion. This represented a gain of close to 35 percent, compared with

Above: Ration books were crucial to shoppers during World War II, as the books kept a record of what consumers had purchased. Some stores even offered recipes based on what foods ration books allowed for purchasing. *(Image courtesy of Elijah Meyer and Maren Möller.)*

Right: Shown in this 1953 Wakefern Annual Year Book photo, Sam Garb was one of the "original eight" co-op members to engage in conversations with fellow founders Sam Aidekman and Abe Kesselman about the plight of the small independent grocer. The grocers met at Garb's house, sharing concerns and brainstorming possible solutions.

Right: Alex "Al" Aidekman, a founding Wakefern member in 1946, along with his brother Sam, ran the Uniondale Food Market in Union, New Jersey. In 1955, Aidekman became president and chairman of the Wakefern board and would later head Supermarkets General Corporation, which withdrew from the co-op and became a major competitor under the banner of Pathmark.

Below: Dru's Market, owned by Wakefern members Nick and Sara Drugach in Lake Parsippany, New Jersey, was typical of the neighborhood stores in the late 1930s and 1940s. They were small operations, often attached to the family's home.

Two of the grocers who began meeting were Abraham H. Kesselman and Samuel Aidekman. Kesselman, born in 1900, had opened his own butcher shop in 1933, which grew into a super-ette, Ideal Super Market, in East Orange, New Jersey. Aidekman, born in 1917, owned the "small but thriving" Good Deal Market on Old Mill Road in Irvington, New Jersey, which he established in 1938.[10]

Casson once again heard the independents' lament while calling on a small grocery store in Irvington, New Jersey. Familiar with the concept of retail cooperatives by now, he suggested to the grocer: "Abe, you talk just like Sam. Why don't you ... get together?"[11]

Aidekman recalled:

A Del Monte salesman came in and tried to sell me products, and up the street was an ACME. The ACME sold the products for less than Del Monte wanted from me. I worked and worked this fellow [Ed Casson], until one day somebody came around and either woke him up or got me the right numbers. Casson told me he had another account in East Orange who had the same complaint. I said, "Can you call him on the phone and let me talk to him?" [Aidekman, Kesselman, and Casson] sat down and talked a while, and ... the only way we figured we could be competitive to chains was to be one ourselves, but private.[12]

Promoting the idea of sharing, Aidekman and Kesselman convinced some of the other Newark-area independent grocers to participate in the informal and ongoing discussions. The first to join in was Sam Garb, the owner of a produce store.

"We called for a meeting, which was held at Abe Kesselman's house in East Orange," Aidekman

Whether selling groceries or produce, the independent grocers experienced similar purchasing difficulties. At the time, they could only purchase from independent wholesalers, lacking the volume to warrant direct sales from large companies such as Del Monte. As a result, the grocers often paid the same amount for some wholesale products that a chain, stocking the identical products, was able to sell at retail.

"Somehow, [Wakefern] got hold of a price book," said grocer Thomas Infusino, who later became a member of the cooperative. "Our cost was their retail."[14]

The eight men tossed around the idea of a retail cooperative with the notion to pool resources to remain competitive, as well as to try to expand the group to include more small grocers. They were united by the belief that they shouldn't continue "[paying] ridiculously high prices, buying their groceries on a tie-in basis [must buy certain products together], or being subjected to discriminatory activities on the part of wholesalers and manufacturers."[15]

Initially, they experimented with ordering in bulk and storing excess products at each other's homes and then in a storefront half of them rented on Miller Street in Newark, New Jersey—the co-op's first "warehouse," before they incorporated. The warehouse space consisted of several vacant stores and a basement.

"Just groceries, some paper, and [canned] goods," explained John Tully, the ninth member to join Wakefern. "In the real beginning, the amount each store was purchasing was very small."[16]

explained. "Before long, it was very simple: We had eight people signed up that day."

The other six grocers were Sam Garb; Sam Aidekman's brother, Alex Aidekman, co-owner of a small dairy-deli store; Abe Kesselman's brother, William Kesselman; Louis Weiss, operator of a superette; Albert "Kitty" Goldberg, owner of a produce store; and David Fern, who ran what was primarily a meat store. Although astute and successful small business owners, none had any experience running a co-op, except for Sam Aidekman, who had launched a short-lived produce co-op before World War II.

While the eight men immediately began to work with one another, they were virtual strangers. "We really didn't know each other," said Fern, owner of a store in affluent Millburn, New Jersey. "We had seen each other at the market, and even chatted together once in a while over coffee. But, basically, we were strangers. It was our [combined] purpose that soon made us friends."[13]

Above left: The inside of the Sitar family store in Carteret, New Jersey, is typical of what small grocers looked like in the 1940s, before self-service became widespread. Behind the counter (left) is John Sitar, an early Wakefern member.

Right: Sam Aidekman, one of the founding members of Wakefern, was one of the first grocers to consider the idea of a co-op.

"It was a buddy system," recalled Sandy Kessel-man, Abe's son. "When a shipment came in, some-one would come over and pay, and the next man would pay for the following order. They'd telephone each other, and each would send his truck to take what he could handle. Settlement was made at the end of the week."[17]

Through their hard work and trust, their friend-ships grew, as did their business acumen.

"When I first met Abe Kesselman, [he was] the nicest friend you'd want," Sam Aidekman remembered. "He was superb. He knew his business, and he was happy to share."

Sam Aidekman, who was very good with figures, was more than happy to repay him.

"[Abe] didn't know that I knew more about mathematics than he would ever know," Sam Aidekman said. "One day I took him aside and said, 'Abe, you're doing a lot for me, you're doing a lot for yourself, you're doing a lot for the company. I want to do something for you.' He said, 'What do you want to do?' I said, 'You taught me the meat busi-ness. I want to teach you how to buy it.' He looked at me like I was crazy. I said, 'Get your pencil out, and you start writing.'" Kesselman was soon mak-ing better purchases.

"Now, if you buy beef, if you buy the whole steer, you [may] think you're getting a bargain," Sam

Aidekman explained. "[But], if you're mathematically inclined, you'll find out how to [actually] get a bargain."[18]

Officially in Business

On December 5, 1946, the Wakefern Food Corp. was incorporated under New Jersey law. The name Wakefern was fashioned together as a loose portmanteau from four of the founders' names: the "W" from Weiss, the "A" from Aidekman, the "K" from Kesselman, the "E" to ease pronunciation, and "FERN" from Dave Fern. It is interesting to note that on the official papers filed to legally incorporate the co-op, the name was registered as Wakefern Food Corp., not Wakefern Food Corporation. Abe Kesselman was elected the first Wakefern Food Corp. president.

While each of the founders was quick to credit the others for launching the Wakefern co-op, saying it took a lot of courage as well as $4,000 in cash to

Above: Ann Buratin, one of Wakefern's first employees, is honored at a company dinner, with David Silverberg, Wakefern, immediate left, and Nick Sumas, Village, immediate right.

Right: One of the original eight co-op members, Louis Weiss, served as Wakefern's first treasurer. As his son, Larry, recalled, in those days "it was a post of dubious distinction," as the co-op didn't possess much in the way of finances.

begin the enterprise, there was considerably more involved. As a trade publication wrote of Wakefern at the time: "It takes the cooperation of sincere and honest people who aren't afraid to face a few setbacks in order to get the project off the ground."[19]

Actual operations commenced on January 1, 1947, in the Miller Street warehouse. The co-op's initial capital investment was $32,000—each of the eight co-op members put up $4,000, and a portion was earmarked to pay $105 per month to rent the warehouse. There were 200 shares of authorized stock, with no par value. The co-op was an ambitious venture, as the odds were decidedly against its success.

Some of the large food manufacturers, burned by co-ops in the past, predicted the nascent group wouldn't last six months.[20] At times, it appeared that they might be right.

A Meeting of Minds

One of Wakefern's early leaders who "wasn't afraid to face a few setbacks" was Fern, who made many 11th-hour saves when Wakefern was in desperate need of cash and whose strong leadership abilities helped Wakefern navigate through many crises. According to Joe Illard, an early co-op member (along with his brothers, Tom and Chuck Infusino) who managed a store in Union, New Jersey:

There was a soap powder shortage after the war, and I was told to go up to Dave Fern's store in Millburn, New Jersey, and get some. Dave had a connection with Colgate Palmolive. I went up there and met Dave. ... I picked up the soap powder and brought it to our store in Union. ...

Silverberg also had nothing but praise for Fern. Regarding Fern's affluent Millburn clientele, Silverberg said, "Dave catered to these people, and they all had a lot of affection and respect for him. ... He was totally unpretentious and ... he liked to help people. He contributed [to charity] and built up a wonderful reputation in this town."[21]

Aside from being well liked and well respected, Fern was very influential. The towns of Millburn and nearby Short Hills were home to a number of manufacturing executives whose wives shopped in Fern's store and came to know and like him. It wasn't long before Fern met these executives and explained the buying problems the fledgling co-op experienced.

Sam Aidekman said, "We couldn't buy the product as cheap as the chains because we weren't selling that much, But the door started opening."[22]

Another exemplary pioneer in the co-op's early years was John Tully, who started early in the grocery business. Just out of high school in 1933, he was offered a full-time job by National Grocery, a grocery store chain, for $10 a week. In 1937, after working with non-grocery outfits such as RCA, he bid on a small grocery store at auction. He bought the lease, fixtures, and goods for less than $500, of which he borrowed $300. As was common during the war years, he named the store after himself: Tully's Market.

"In the early days, we didn't have paper receipts. I wrote the sale amount on a paper bag and tied up the purchase with a string that came out of the ceiling," Tully recalled. "[The business] didn't take off too good. The first week I [only] did $200."[23]

"Sam Aidekman asked if I would join. The stock was $4,000 for A stock—some that hadn't yet been sold," Tully said. B stocks were around $2,000, and C stocks were even less. Tully did sign up, but his store did not experience much growth.

Business remained "very slow from 1947 until about 1951. Everyone was very hesitant about making changes," Tully said. "The exchange of ideas was

the biggest thing. There were lots of discussions on how to do things better. One of the reasons for meeting was to borrow money. We never had enough money to operate."[24]

Nick Sumas and John Tully were part of the second wave of four independent grocers to join Wakefern in 1947, which also included Harry Castroll and Joe Saker. Nick got his start in 1937 with the opening of a small produce stand in South Orange, New Jersey. He enlisted the aid of his brother, Perry, who came over from "the old country"—as had many of the early Wakefern families—which in Perry's case was Greece.

Living Day to Day

When Wakefern began, there was no vision among the members of what it might become. Rather, as Tully put it, "We were living day to day and just trying to do our best to keep our volume and not lose everything to the chains."[25] Oftentimes, members were forced to sell at a loss to match prices offered by chains, as well as use their own cash against shortfalls. Fern, whose financial resources were greater than those of most of the co-op members, was known for doing this more frequently to ensure that the co-op continued.

"My belief is ... that [Fern] really financially pulled the organization through the very early

Above: Shown here in a 1954 photo from the Wakefern Annual Year Book of that year, Dave Fern, one of the "original eight" founders, ran a successful store in the affluent Short Hills area of New Jersey, served on the Wakefern board of directors, and was head of the perishables division.

Right: Del Monte Foods, one of Wakefern's first major suppliers, is featured prominently in this picture of early Wakefern member Chuck Infusino, Sr., in front of his store in Newark, New Jersey.

DEEP ROOTS IN HISTORY

The Statue of Liberty, along with Ellis Island, has great meaning to many who would become part of the Wakefern/ShopRite legacy. *(Image courtesy of the U.S. National Archives & Records Administration.)*

IN THE LATE 1800S AND EARly 1900s, they came from Russia, Lithuania, Albania, and Latvia. They traveled from Italy, Greece, Ireland, and Scotland. Their journeys on boats, trains, and even donkeys could last from six weeks to three months to reach the United States. Sometimes husbands and fathers left their families in the "old country" and would secure their families' voyages to the United States later; others traveled together only to have Ellis Island agents try to deny siblings entry into the United States. Some changed their names, purposefully, optimistically, in hopes of a better life and opportunity. These were the future grocers and founders of Wakefern Food Corp.

Some began as laborers, others worked as pipefitters, shoe shiners, or butchers. Slowly small grocery stores began to dot the Northeast, along with fruit stands and produce shops. Some peddled wares door-to-door in horse-drawn carts, while others used Model T Fords. The grocers persevered, bringing family members into their businesses, sometimes from across the Atlantic Ocean—fathers, mothers, uncles, and children all worked side-by-side.

After World War II, soldiers returned to the United States and the environment became ripe for starting more grocery businesses. All these future Wakefern members shared a strict work ethic, were committed to their business, intent on exceeding customer satisfaction, and drew strength from family loyalty. These values allowed their businesses to grow and prosper.

These were the grocers whose vision led to the formation of Wakefern. They wanted to level what was becoming a difficult playing field as larger, more corporate entities were carving a niche within what had traditionally been a mom-and-pop market. These independent, entrepreneurial grocers were now competing against the chain stores. Regardless of their diverse backgrounds, their family work ethic and enthusiasm for the grocery business translated into a supportive effort to create a cooperative. Working together for the good of the business was not simply a theme—it had become a way of life, and these grocers, instead of being rivals, became colleagues.

To honor and celebrate those early grocers who had persevered through hard times and prospered, and continued in their quest for success, Wakefern/ShopRite held Wakefern's 50th anniversary celebration on Ellis Island as a reminder of the deep immigrant roots from which Wakefern/ShopRite has grown.

years," Silverberg said. "He was really an unusual type of guy."[26]

Sam Aidekman remembered one of the times Fern offered to help the co-op through a difficult financial circumstance. He drove to Fern's store to pick up the money, and Fern had him stand guard at the top of the basement stairs.

"[He told me to] 'be the eye,' so that no one came down to the basement as he went down and took a brick out of the wall. He took about $25,000, put it in a paper bag, and handed it to me," Sam Aidekman said. "I waited until he put the brick back and everything was done, and said, 'Thank, you, goodbye.' I took the money right back to Wakefern. He never charged any interest, never worried, and never said 'no.' "[27]

By August 1947, the combined store volume of the now 12-member co-op was about $22,000 per week, with total assets of $60,445. At the beginning, members could afford to buy only in small quantities, which meant they had no choice but to continue buying from a variety of wholesale grocers, such as Libby Products, S&W Products, and Royal

Dairy—and continue paying in cash. Tully, for example, whose store was in Hudson County, purchased goods from the Hudson Wholesale Company in Jersey City.

"We had a lot of difficulty in getting suppliers to sell to Wakefern in the early days," he said.[28]

Credit also remained a problem. In a sellers' market, manufacturers had no need for new distributors like Wakefern, and they remained wary of co-ops, having seen them fail in the New Jersey and New York markets. Unfortunately, in a catch-22 situation, Wakefern could not get credit because it had not established credit.

"Some suppliers wanted to sell only to businesses with good credit," Tully said. "And Campbell Soup was one of the ones that wouldn't sell to us." To make purchases, many co-op members were forced to sign personal guarantees.

Yet the ultimate solution to resolving the credit crisis was as simple as having a customer ask for a specific brand-name product. A woman shopping in Fern's store asked why he did not carry a Campbell Soup product. Fern explained that Wakefern had not established credit, and that Campbell wouldn't sell to him without it. The customer, it soon was revealed, was the widow of John T. Dorrance, a former Campbell chief executive whose family still owned the company. Within a few

This Nutley, New Jersey, market was owned by Vince Lo Curcio, his sister Rose Lo Curcio (far left), and Tom Infusino.

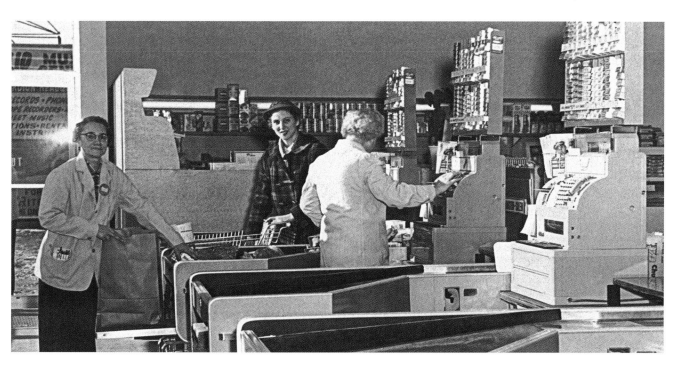

Left: David Silverberg (pictured in the 1956 Wakefern Annual Year Book), a Cornell graduate and former economics professor at Wayne University, became the assistant to General Manager Herman Wechsler in 1950. He purchased the co-op's first mimeograph, helped run its punch-card equipment, became a frozen food buyer, and eventually became a longtime Wakefern president.

Right: Albert Goldberg was running his own produce store when he was approached with the idea of becoming part of a grocer's co-op.

weeks of her initial inquiry, the co-op had access to Campbell products. This relationship with Campbell secured the co-op's entry into business with other manufacturers and wholesalers.[29]

Other manufacturers soon came on board, including Del Monte and Scott Paper—the result of the tireless efforts of members who would try to gain new contacts by any means possible, including attending events such as canners' conventions. As a producer and distributor of more than 15 products, Del Monte would supply the co-op's largest line of canned fruits and vegetables. Wakefern was off and running.

A Work Ethic That Worked

Although the work ethic fostered by the early co-op members was responsible for Wakefern's growth, the long and grueling work hours took their toll. Along with routinely putting in 40- to 60-hour weeks at their respective stores, members would devote more time to the co-op—often an additional 40 hours per week—attending meetings at night or working at the warehouse where, early on, there were no outside employees.

"That was one area [in which] our wives were very unhappy with us," said Tom Infusino, regarding the long hours. "We used to go and visit [competing] stores ad nauseam. We'd go at night. At times, we'd go to visit another member. One member held a class at his store on how to package lamb chops. But that's how you learned, you learned by doing, and learned by talking to people. I think the A&P was one of the greatest teachers we ever had. ... [We'd] visit, copy, and do better."[30]

Dan Solomon, an independent grocer who owned a store in Passaic, New Jersey, credits the other members for personally showing him how to transition from a small 2,800-square-foot market that didn't handle meat, to a full assortment, 5,200-square-feet successful ShopRite. Other members volunteered to let him work in their meat departments until he felt he knew enough, which he did. His volume quadrupled, and operating costs were reduced by half.

Members would retrieve merchandise at the Newark warehouse anytime, day or night, for their stores or for other members' stores. They used their own cars and pickup trucks, as they couldn't afford to hire truckers initially. They took turns paying for deliveries and keeping accounts, and assumed responsibility for certain product groups. In their efforts to make smart purchases for the co-op, they sometimes overbought. They sought each other's advice, as each knew some aspect of the business better than the others.

According to Tully:

The exchange of ideas and experiences ... has enabled all of us to benefit from the experience of each one of us. It means that new ideas, methods, and savings developed by one store were made available to all other stores.[31]

Hatching Plans and Hashing Problems

In 1949, with the Miller Street space bursting to the rafters, Wakefern moved its warehouse operation into larger quarters that it leased from the army. The 15,000-square-foot facility was located in Port Newark on Newark Bay, a major shipping area that provided the co-op with easy access to goods shipped from the West Coast by companies such as Del Monte. The facility also served as Wakefern's headquarters.

"We were showing progress," Alex Aidekman said. "But we still had a long, long way to go."[32]

Despite the long hours exacerbated by unrelenting uncertainties and frustrations, the spirits of the early members were never entirely dampened; they simply worked harder.

The business structure created in 1946 would have strong and long-lasting effects. The Wakefern bylaws uniquely stipulated that each member, whether he owned one store or multiple stores, was entitled to only one seat on the board. Also, if a member wished to open a new store, the co-op helped that member look for a suitable site. And when Wakefern made a profit, it sent the money back to the member stores.[33]

According to many of the founders, the most powerful tool the co-op possessed to wield against obstacles and help set initiatives was the general membership weekly meeting. Attendance at these Monday sessions was a consistent 90 percent—some members traveled as far as 50 miles to attend. At the meetings, merchandising plans were hatched and problems were discussed. To boost morale, there was often piano playing and spirited sing-alongs. When it came to decision-making, majority rule was king.

According to Tully, reaching a final decision at the meetings was never very hard. "Everyone had

In 1949, the Wakefern warehouse moved to Port Newark, New Jersey, which was a major shipping area.

the same goal—to try to do more business and make a profit," he said.[34]

Equally important were the Wakefern committees—a commanding voice at the meetings—set up to facilitate merchandising and pricing. The co-op's store products were eventually divided into seven groups or operating divisions—grocery, meats, produce, frozen goods and ice cream, dairy–deli, bakery, and non-foods. Each group was overseen and represented by a committee member who attended the weekly sessions with staff buyers.

"It's a major point in the success of the organization," Silverberg explained. "Decisions were never made by one person. You'd kick it around, and by kicking it around, I don't mean that we sat down formally and discussed it. You hollered out to three or four or five people in the place."[35]

In Wakefern's First Annual Year Book, members of the Wakefern Food Corp. were described as "among the most unusual group of men in supermarket merchandising."[36]

As the advantages of shared purchasing of groceries and produce became increasingly obvious, the activities of other supermarket departments were brought into "cooperative action" at Wakefern.[37] In 1948, the co-op created VeriBest Produce Company, the first of its type of ancillary cooperative, to supply members with fresh produce through a warehouse located on Miller Street in the Newark produce market.[38] VeriBest was the reincarnation of an earlier and short-lived attempt by Sam Aidekman to develop a produce co-op, which lasted just three days.

According to a Dun & Bradstreet Inc., credit report, VeriBest Produce Company was chartered on May 5, 1948, with an authorized capital of 500 shares of common stock. It was established to act as "a mutual purchasing organization for some fifteen members." VeriBest's headquarters was at 229 Miller Street in Newark,

Herman Wechsler, shown in a photo from the 1953 Wakefern Annual Year Book, was hired in 1950 as the co-op's general manager, joining a growing staff that included warehouse workers, buyers, and office personnel.

before moving in February 1949 to the Newark Tidewater Terminal.[39]

A Sense of Humor, Helping Hands

Early Wakefern member Castroll, owner of a grocery store in North Plainfield, New Jersey, launched a small chain within the co-op with two other store owners as partners. It was incorporated as General Super Markets.

One of Castroll's early experiences included the difficulties of product selection. Sometimes, the product selection did not meet customer demand. For example, one product developer had added chlorophyll, a deodorizing agent, to toilet tissue, and Wakefern purchased around two carloads of the product. But chlorophyll-treated toilet tissue was not a best seller; customers shied away from buying it.

According to Castroll:

[When] we first started to do our advertising, when we were down in Port Elizabeth, and we didn't have much of an office at the warehouse. … We sat out on … the receiving dock, and we'd take out [the cases of toilet tissue] to sit on.

"We were stuck with lots of cases. … We used to use the boxes and sit on them, and with three-quarter plywood boards we made a table out of it, and the mice were running around, and we had a good old time," Saker said. "I'm not sure, but we may have given all the toilet tissue away."

In ways more far-reaching than cooperative buying, it was the "warm family feeling" shared by members along with the knowledge that they needed one another that drove Wakefern's success[40]—much to the astonishment of a cynical industry that believed the co-op would fail.

According to Illard, when members enlarged or opened new stores, usually by converting existing spaces, the work was mostly completed over the weekend. At the time, Illard managed a store owned by Alex Aidekman in Union, New Jersey. In the early 1950s, when Illard's brothers Chuck and Tom Infusino were first expanding

This is Steve Salkowski's store in Bayonne, New Jersey, circa 1943. Salkowski was an early member of Wakefern.

—Tom was in Nutley and Chuck was in Newark—Alex Aidekman would send Illard with a crew of "expert people" from Union to pitch in.

"In those days, money was everything. You couldn't afford to miss a day's receipts," Illard said.

Store expansions notwithstanding—and in the early years by no means could all members afford to branch out—new members were sought for both volume and capital (to cut down on overhead), and to lend clout to the co-op's long-term viability in the eyes of manufacturers. Landing new members was tough, however, due to the required financial investment—anything more than $1,000 was significant for a small-time grocer.

By 1950, the buying and warehouse management functions had expanded to where full-time managers were needed. Wakefern hired its first full-time staff, starting with a warehouse worker and an owner-operated trucking company to make deliveries. After a few challenges in filling the general manager position, Wakefern finally struck gold when it hired Herman Wechsler in 1950. Wechsler, in turn, hired 29-year-old Silverberg as his assistant. An accounting secretary, Ann Buratin, and a buyer were also hired.

"I felt that this was an extraordinarily exciting group," said Silverberg, recalling his initial reaction to the co-op members' irrepressible exuberance. "We lived the business, not just thought about it. The thing that kept us going in those early years was the members' commitment to and enthusiasm about the co-op. ... It was a very exciting time."[41]

Moving Forward

Changes in the supermarket industry were occurring at a dizzying rate, and it was tough for financially strapped grocers to keep pace.

"None of us were experts in finance, advertising, store layout, whatever it takes to put these things together," Illard said. "It was a process we had to learn."[42]

According to Tully, some 50 percent to 60 percent of co-op members attended the annual Super Market Institute meetings in Chicago to learn about the latest developments in equipment, business strategies, and ways to display grocery products. Wakefern was looking to the future, supporting its members any way it could.

For the first three years of its existence, Wakefern existed as a buying group, and word of its success spread throughout an industry that continued to be dominated by the chains. While the co-op members were frequently forced to sell retail at a loss, they were also busy building up their wholesale volume. They were no longer as intimidated by the big chains and focused on the progress made toward their own success. In 1950, Wakefern Food Corporation membership had risen to 28, and the company's annual wholesale volume had grown to $2.2 million, up from the first year's earnings of $336,114.[43]

A new retail venture that would expand the co-op's reach and provide brand-name recognition was on the horizon. The best was yet to come.

The first ShopRite ad ran on March 13, 1951, in the *Newark Evening News*. It boasted the co-op's car-load buying and consumer savings, stating "more business at less profit is good business." *(Photo taken from the* Newark Evening News, *March 13, 1951, edition. Reprinted with permission from Media General, Inc.)*

CHAPTER TWO

ONE VOICE, LOUD AND CLEAR

1951–1955

THE BIRTH OF SHOPRITE

If they think big, and they think together, nothing is better than a co-op.

—John Tully, president of the
ShopRite group, formed in 1951[1]

THE 1950S IN AMERICA WERE marked by a social and economic revolution that saw the birthrate skyrocket, with the U.S. population growing from 152 million in 1950 to more than 180 million by the end of the decade; a housing shortage that became a suburban building boom, in which 12 million houses were built between 1945 and 1960; and a new affluence that put millions more cars and drivers on the roads, including a new interstate highway system.[2] Increasing numbers of families owned television sets, and most had refrigerators. Better seeds, fertilizers, and equipment resulted in unprecedented food production capabilities. In 1951, *Collier's* magazine reported: "All over the U.S., supermarkets—the prodigious issue of a marriage between brilliant showmanship and the world's most modern distribution techniques—are springing up almost faster than they can be counted. Last year, they opened at the rate of better than three a day."[3]

As Randolph McAusland noted in his 1980 book *Supermarkets: 50 Years of Progress*, "With all these new mouths to feed, America's food distribution system was tested as never before, but the challenge was met and the demands fulfilled."[4] Stores built during the 1950s were well organized, easy to

navigate, flexible in layout, and epitomized self-service efficiencies created to meet shoppers' new, and increasingly sophisticated, expectations.

The stores were also able to offer more convenient packing of foods. The advent of "plastic film" and wrapping machines made the widespread availability of prepackaged meat possible, just as they already had done with fruits and vegetables, bringing "the last important section of the store into the realm of self-service." One of the co-op's early problems with meat purchasing was that each member went about the process differently. As Dave Fern explained, "We had some members who used prime, others [who used] only cheap cuts." For this reason, the importance of consistent quality—preferably in the form of U.S. graded choice—was hammered home at the weekly co-op meetings. "Probably what really did the trick, though," Fern said, "was

George Retig (inside truck), ShopRite's first trucker, hauled goods in the greater Newark area for the co-op until 1956. He is seen here, with Bart Twitty, backing up to the Cranford warehouse loading dock.

to charge members for buying services whether they used them or not."[5]

Price Is Not Enough

McAusland noted that with the opening of more supermarkets, shoppers were given more choice. The result was that "customer allegiance was no longer to 'the supermarket', but to a specific chain or independent operation." The more competition intensified among supermarkets, the more "price alone became a tenuous way to secure loyalty," he wrote.[6]

Despite its inexperience, the fledgling Wakefern Food Corp. did realize that buying power and price weren't the only factors necessary for successful competition—especially in its case, where prices weren't uniform among the member stores. One store might price a given product high, another low; some stores advertised, while others did not. The inconsistent pricing also made it difficult for members to earn significant advertising allowances from manufacturers. Grocery ads that did exist were radically different from one another, in both content and appearance. The result was confusion among retail shoppers, who thought they were dealing with a co-op, and it created a sense of disorganization among co-op members, who otherwise were quite unified.

In response to the frustrating dilemma, some members began tossing around the idea of shared advertising; after all, they were part of a co-op. They asked themselves: "If we can benefit from cooperative purchasing, couldn't we gain infinitely more power from joint advertising and merchandising? By pooling our financial resources and promotional talents, couldn't we undertake programs to build traffic and increase customer loyalty in a much more effective way? Wouldn't one voice shouting loud and clear be heard more readily than all of us making our own little noises?"[7]

Their interest—and confidence—was reinforced by an article published in the fall of 1950 in the trade journal *Progressive Grocer*. The article told the story of a cooperative in Cleveland, Ohio, called Foodtown Super Markets. Some months later, several Wakefern members traveled to Cleveland on a fact-finding mission. Encouraged by what they learned about Foodtown Super Markets and its shared advertising effort, the Wakefern members decided to do the same—merge their separate and disjointed promotional, advertising, and merchandising efforts under a single banner. The idea became a reality in March 1951.

After considering various names for the new "group within the group"—a subsidiary that would essentially advertise and merchandise like a chain—"Shop-Rite" was selected (the hyphen, used initially, was dropped later in the mid-1970s). The name derived from the co-op members' philosophy that it was essential for them to "buy right" from wholesalers and manufacturers to enable their retail customers to "shop right" at the stores. Their hope in creating ShopRite was that they would be one step closer to being able to offer shoppers the savings and self-service advantages of the large chains while maintaining the independence and personality of the traditional neighborhood grocer, as each store would be individually owned and operated.

No one is certain exactly who came up with the catchy moniker. Joe Saker, who joined his father's small mom-and-pop grocery store in 1946, remembered telling his father in 1947 when they joined the Wakefern co-op, "Dad, we've got to buy right to sell right, and we just cannot match the prices of the chains in paying the kinds of prices [demanded by] wholesale grocers."[8] In the book *Elephants in My Backyard*, which tells the story of Wakefern founder Alex Aidekman and his subsequent split from the co-op and founding of

Pathmark Supermarket, author Lynne Dumas states that the name "Shop-Rite" was created by a niece of one of the Wakefern founders, who "was given a $25 U.S. bond for her efforts."[9] Other names were tossed in the ring for consideration, but none of them carried the "short, snappy sound which exemplifies the hard-hitting merchandising program the group had in mind."[10] A vote was taken finally, and "Shop-Rite" won.

In the early days, ShopRite had its own board of directors, one that operated separately from the Wakefern Food Corp. board. In terms of organizational structure, the lines between Wakefern, the wholesaler, and ShopRite, the retailer, remained blurred for quite some time. In fact, a separate, ill-defined structure existed for ShopRite as late as the mid-1960s. To add to the confusion, in the mid-1950s, it was the Wakefern board, not the ShopRite board, that reviewed applications from independent grocers wishing to become ShopRite members—

With the name George's Super Mart on the front of the marquee and a ShopRite sign to the side, this photo shows the dilemma faced by many early Wakefern members: keeping the store's name or using the ShopRite name. George Szibdat, vice president and owner of the West Orange Shop-Rite, provided an easy solution: feature both.

Above: Sam Aidekman, right, poses in front of his Irvington, New Jersey, store, during the 1952 Del Monte Round Up sale.

Left: The façade of the Romano family's old store, the Daisee Quality Market, was modernized, and the store was renamed Netcong Shop-Rite, shown here in this 1955 photo.

which happened in droves once ShopRite advertising was under way.

Not All Aboard

Of course, not all the Wakefern members were quick to endorse the new "group within the group." While a majority-decision vote favored the formation of the ShopRite Super Markets subsidiary, about a quarter of Wakefern members chose not to join, citing reasons that included the necessity to make various changes regarding store operations and their unwillingness to relinquish any measure of their independence—they didn't want anyone dictating price and selection. Others were afraid of retaliation by the chains.

Large co-op members who didn't initially advertise under the ShopRite banner included Big V, Motts Super Markets, and Village Super Market,

Inc., in Springfield, New Jersey. However, within two years of ShopRite's inception, Nick Sumas, head of Village, had become an ardent ShopRite supporter and member.

For many Wakefern members, however, the advantages of the ShopRite concept immediately outweighed any perceived risks. In a nutshell, the subsidiary offered members a comprehensive merchandising service—one that supplied them with uniform store identification signs, window posters, and updated price-check information on competitors—with advertising at the core. Ten out of the 28 Wakefern co-op members quickly joined the advertising group, agreeing to use the name "Shop-Rite" alongside or as part of their own. Alex Aidekman's store in Uniondale, New Jersey, for example, which was one of the first to display the ShopRite banner, was initially called Uniondale Shop-Rite.[11]

It was the Wakefern board that decided which interested members would be granted a ShopRite license. Criteria for membership were few: use of ShopRite advertising and marketing collateral, adherence to the group's strict policy of selling advertised store items at the advertised price, the ability to pay a share of advertising costs, and a store location that wasn't within competitive distance of any other ShopRite store. Apart from joining Wakefern, the only fees for new ShopRite members were for store signs. A site approval was required for members wishing to open additional stores; however, as per the co-op's bylaws, a member was only entitled to a single vote regardless of the number of stores owned.

Bold Ads Boast of Cooperative Buying Power

John Tully was elected as the first president of ShopRite. At the time, he served as Wakefern's vice president and ran a grocery store in Arlington, New Jersey. Tully was backed by Herbert Brody, owner of Scotch Plains Superette in Scotch Plains, as vice president; Earl Jensen, owner of George's Food Market in East Orange, as treasurer; and Louis Weiss, owner of Consumer's Food Market in Bloomfield, as secretary.

Above right: Estelle Romano waits on customers at the Netcong ShopRite in the mid-1950s.

Below: These early 1950s ShopRite ads show the co-op's early growth, including sales of more than $10 million in the first year (left) and a growing list of members (right). *(Photo featured on left taken from the* Newark Evening News, *August 20, 1952, edition. Reprinted with permission from Media General, Inc.)*

The first ShopRite ad ran in March 1951 as a full page in the *Newark Evening News*, which at the time was the largest newspaper in the state. "The ad was to cost $1,000," Tully said, though the actual cost was closer to $1,500. "Each [ShopRite member] was to participate and pay their share. ... It was hard to get the 10 members."[12]

The reason ShopRite members shied away was purely financial. The motivation for the members to join, Al Aidekman said, was to share "both the expense and benefit of the advertising."[13] In the interest of fairness, it was decided that advertising costs would be divided among the store owners on a sliding scale, which took into account the size of the store and the amount of local coverage it would receive from the newspaper.

However, just as the founding Wakefern members had little to no experience running a co-op, the new group suffered a paucity of advertising experience, though some store owners had managed to run, with varying degrees of success, their own modest ads in the local North Jersey penny-saver newspapers. In the beginning, the advertising for ShopRite was handled by Sam Howard and Milton Mintz, who owned the Newark-area papers *Union Leader* and *Irvington Herald*. Howard wrote most of the ShopRite copy and worked with Phil Marter, a silk screener who created the original and distinctive ShopRite logo,

Above: Wakefern invited baseball great Jackie Robinson and his wife (center) to be the honored guests at the first annual Wakefern get-together in 1952.

Left: From the beginning, ShopRite supported the needs of its community. Many ShopRite ads featured popular entertainers and sports figures of the time, including Howdy Doody (top) and the Brooklyn Dodgers (bottom). *(Images featured on top and center reprinted with permission from the* Union Leader/Suburban Leader *on the following dates: March 18, 1954, and January 28, 1954. Photo featured on bottom taken from the* Newark Evening News, *February 23, 1956, edition. Reprinted with permission from Media General, Inc.)*

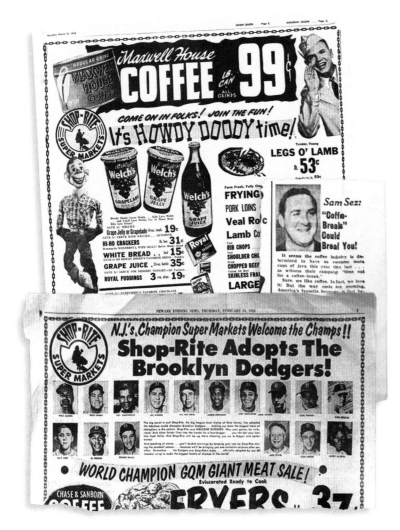

along with the first ads to run in the *Newark Evening News.*

Zal Venet, a former Kings supermarket employee and an advertising executive who specialized in supermarket advertising, came on board in 1954 after ShopRite's advertising identity had been largely established. Venet remembered that the original ShopRite logo, which depicted a woman pushing a grocery cart within a large circle, was "lifted" from the Super Market Institute logo. He recalled that with his first ShopRite ads, "increased business was almost instantaneous." As for the bright red and orange colors, "I think we kind of fell into it," Venet said. "Research proved the colors work in the store; the women relax to it."[14]

By the mid- to late-1950s, 75 percent to 80 percent of Wakefern's volume was generated by ShopRite retailers, up from a modest 25 percent in 1951, ShopRite's inaugural year. As *Supermarket*

News noted: "Wakefern's survival was no longer a burning issue. The major question was—how fast was growth going to be?"[15]

It was Sam Howard who came up with bold headlines, such as "A New Money-Saving Power Comes to New Jersey," which were accompanied by artwork depicting a roaring train—symbolizing strength—and copy promising the "Greatest Savings Possible." Other ads drove home the ShopRite philosophy through lines such as "Co-op Buying Power Saves You Money," and "We Believe That More Business at Less Profit Is Good Business." Popular radio and TV personalities were featured often, including Steve Allen, Tex and Jinx, and Howdy Doody promoting Welch's grape juice. Regardless of the content of the ads, the focus was always low price.

Surrounding each advertisement was artwork depicting a chain link, which symbolized the interconnectedness of the ShopRite stores, with the subhead "There's a Shop-Rite in Your Town," followed by the name and location of each ShopRite

Right: The first edition of ShopRite's *Ladies Home News*, November 19, 1953, highlights the company's offerings for Thanksgiving.

Below: A crowd awaits the opening of the Sitar family's new ShopRite. John Sitar, an early ShopRite member, opened the family's first ShopRite supermarket in Carteret, New Jersey, in March 1954.

store. This reinforced the concept that ShopRite was indeed a chain of stores inexorably linked together in a common purpose, which was to provide customers with everything they needed at the lowest possible price.

It wasn't long before an advertising committee was formed, composed of John Tully, Dave Fern, and Sam and Alex Aidekman, who met weekly to decide which products to feature in the ads, based upon input from members representing the var-

ious departments. "There was a lot of bickering about this," Tully remembered. "We had an unwritten law that all the stores would sell an item for the advertised price. ... The committee believed that in order to keep prices down, we needed to lower margins to cost or cost plus two to three percent. But many of the members were used to selling these items at 15 percent above cost."[16]

While the ads targeted agreed-upon specials, an individual store owner retained limited flexibility in terms of altering content to better reach his local market. The ads also were used as a means of communicating with customers and keeping them abreast of ShopRite's growth, such as store openings and new warehouse facilities. Photos and bios of new co-op members were featured in the ads when they joined.[17]

As part of its marketing effort, ShopRite began publication of a weekly newsletter, the *Shop-Rite*

Ladies Home News, which ran from 1953 until 1955. The newsletter served as a sort of shoppers' resource, imparting useful recipe and menu suggestions—"What to Serve When the Boss Comes to Dinner"—and homemaker tips on how to stretch a dollar through the fictional character "Sally Rite."[18] Additionally, the weekly newspaper ads supported consumer tips with a "Sam Sez" column providing educational tidbits. One column titled "Coffee Breaks Could Break You," instructed customers what to do in a time of escalating coffee prices with the tip of adding a little salt to the already used coffee grounds and brewing the pot again.

"Everyone was very hesitant about making changes," Tully said, noting the co-op's initial slow growth. "But in 1951, after ShopRite started to advertise, this was the key to getting new members. They saw the ads [and] what they did for the stores. They started knocking on our door, looking to become members. Advertising started the whole thing going."[19]

According to Venet, within the first six months, 18 members were participating in the ads, and by the end of the first year, ShopRite had virtually doubled its membership, totaling more than 50 store owners.

Wakefern stated in its 1953 Annual Year Book that ShopRite's "advertising impact stretches from Camden [South Jersey] to Hoboken [North Jersey]," and "Its ads appear in over 40 newspapers. Its place in the consumer mind is well established. 'Shop-Rite' is a byword recognized by thousands and thousands of housewives."[20]

Left: This ShopRite ad features new members who joined the co-op. Each new member strengthened the chain and its buying power.

Below: In this 1954 promotion for ShopRite prime meats, TV entertainer Steve Allen and John Tully, president of ShopRite and a member of its advertising committee, pose with a prize steer, "Little Stuff," that was purchased at the Chicago Livestock exposition to promote the quality of ShopRite meats.

Tully, the former delivery boy for The Great Atlantic & Pacific Tea Company in Kearney, New Jersey, was not only ShopRite's first president, he also was the first member to put up a ShopRite sign. "[It was a] wooden sign with orange and black ShopRite colors, in Kearney," he recalled. The name did well by him: By 1952, Tully's store revenue was more than $3,000 a week.[21]

Another co-op member to benefit quickly from his association with ShopRite was Danny Solomon,

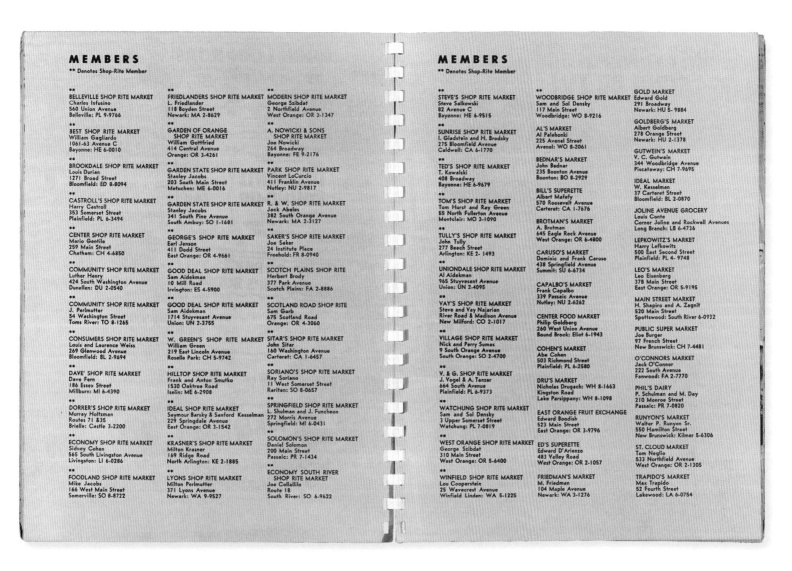

who joined Wakefern in 1951 and later served on the Produce Committee and the Membership Committee. Upon joining Wakefern, the most dramatic changes for Solomon were Wakefern's strict cash-and-carry policy, the prohibition of charge accounts and free delivery, and a general mandate of self-service in every store. Before joining ShopRite, Solomon's store in Passaic, New Jersey, had about $7,000 in sales each week. The store's sales jumped to about $14,000 per week shortly after joining the co-op.

Revenue Spurs Infrastructure Growth

The membership growth due to the initial ads and the resultant surge in revenue necessitated major changes within the co-op—despite the fact

Wakefern's 1954 Annual Year Book proudly updates the growth of the membership.

that, in 1951, when ShopRite was just under way, only 25 percent of the co-op's volume was generated through ShopRite retailers. By the mid-1950s, however, that figure would shoot up to between 75 percent and 80 percent.[22] Milestones in the early 1950s included new leadership, the hiring of buyers, the passing of important Wakefern corporate policy decisions, the launching of a private-label program, the introduction of the frozen food division, enhanced distribution channels, advances in data management technology, and the move to more substantial warehouse facilities.

In 1951, Wakefern President Abe Kesselman retired from the food business, handing the reins to Sam Aidekman. The other officers at that time were Nick Sumas, vice president; Herbert Brody, secretary; and Louis Weiss, treasurer. Irwin Sedwin was named general manager of the ShopRite group, and he quickly expanded the buying staff, streamlined what had become general meetings into committee meetings, and served as the group's coordinator to solicit new members.[23]

As for corporate policies, Wakefern's co-op members decided that keeping both the cooperative's operations

cost and product costs as low as possible would be critical to its success. Whatever was left over as profit at the end of the year would then be passed back to the membership as a rebate. Each member's rebate was based on their percentage of purchases of each product category.

Equally important, all members—regardless of the size of purchases—paid the same low cost for their products. This practice clearly leveled the playing field regardless of the size of the store and was key in attracting new co-op members. At the same time, the members also endorsed the principle of volume discounts to advertising.[24]

Private Label Lauded

There is little agreement as to when ShopRite's private-label program was launched or which product was the first to earn the ShopRite label. Most will agree that ShopRite brand doughnuts, plain or with powdered sugar, were among the first to appear on store shelves, as early as October 1951.[25] "Our doughnuts, from distributors, were packaged to compete with A&P," John Tully said.

Former Wakefern President David Silverberg noted that although the private-label program existed before 1953, prior to that time it "wasn't

While the first ShopRite private-label product—generally thought to be doughnuts (right)—appeared on shelves in late 1951, it wasn't until around 1958 that the program became truly institutionalized and was successfully under way.

pushed as a private label."[26] Others pegged the launch date as late as 1958.[27] At any rate, the doughnuts' promotion was successful. Other store-brand products followed, such as baked goods, orange juice, and frozen foods, proudly displaying the ShopRite name during a time when competitors named private-label goods after fictional people. According to a Wakefern publication, "This was a statement of their pride and commitment to the quality of the products," and it was in line with the co-op's low-price approach to doing business.

Another uncertainty is who exactly lobbied for ShopRite private labeling. Some, including Venet, believe it was the brainchild of ShopRite General Manager Irv Sedwin.

"I think one of [Sedwin's] strongest contributions was controlling the way the [ShopRite] label was used on products," Venet said.[28] Silverberg surmised that "it could have been one of the suppliers that decided, 'Listen, why don't you use it?' because we had to develop the ShopRite name."[29] Others believed that it was a collaborative effort between Alex Aidekman, Dave Fern, and Herb Brody. Brody, who served as secretary for Wakefern Food Corp. and was a member of its board of directors in 1951, worked in the grocery field until 1939 when he became a partner at a supermarket in East Orange, New Jersey; by 1948, he was the proprietor of a retail grocery business called Scotch Plains Superette.

Joel Perlmutter related an anecdote about how the new program was introduced to Shop-Rite members:

It's a regular Monday meeting and all the guys are there. … All of a sudden, they start the meeting, and a girl walks in [wearing] a Playboy bunny outfit. Everybody is looking, and as she walks around, she does her bunny dip [and] "How are you?" introduction. … Then she walks out, and everybody is looking around. Everybody is talking. … Al Aidekman says, "All right, why was she here?" Everybody is throwing ideas out … nobody guessed it. … He said, "It's because if the packaging is good, you'll notice it." And that's the way we got introduced into the private-label program. … It was a hell of an analogy.[30]

Of course, others had adopted the private-label concept in the supermarket industry. Tully, who recalled being on the committee that decided to offer private-label goods, noted that A&P already offered its Ann Page line. National Grocery and Mutual Groceries, two supermarket chains, both had their own labels, and ACME trumpeted the American Foods

Private-label ShopRite-brand products from the 1950s included hygiene products, paper goods, and cleaners.

COMMUNITY SPIRIT

OMMUNITY SUPPORT HAS BEEN CENTRAL TO Wakefern/ShopRite's business philosophy from the very beginning. Quick to embrace campaigns to raise both awareness and money, ShopRite used its high-visibility newspaper advertising to deliver the message and solicit customer support.

Throughout the 1950s, ShopRite embraced a number of community initiatives and invited customers to join its efforts via newspaper advertising. The campaigns were successful in generating support for projects large and small, from support for local Boy Scout troops and food drives to programs with a national scope. An example of this grassroots commitment is illustrated in the ad depicting the need to raise funds to find a cure for the crippling disease of polio that was sweeping the country in the early 1950s. Another example was a program founded by Pearl S. Buck, Pulitzer and Nobel Prize–

From the beginning ShopRite has been active in supporting the needs of its local community and beyond. In 1954, Alex Aidekman and Union, New Jersey Mayor Fred Edward Biertuempfel requested that customers join the campaign to raise money for the development of a cure for the feared polio disease. The same year, ShopRite joined forces with famous WRCA radio personality, Ben Grauer, to help support the effort to clothe and feed Koreans after the Korean War. *(Images reprinted with permission from the* Union Leader/Suburban Leader *on the following dates: December 19, 1954, and October 21, 1954.)*

winning author and humanitarian, to find homes for Korean children left as orphans as a result of the Korean conflict. Popular New York radio personality, Ben Grauer, is featured in the ad as he also lent his support.

brand. "The first items [at ShopRite] were put up by distributors, then canneries and manufacturers—and that's when the label started to develop very strongly," Tully said.[31]

High standards for private-label products were mandatory from the outset. A product that didn't perform would be "eliminated without hesitation."[32] Unlike many retailers, ShopRite did not use private-label products to grow profits or to substitute for national brands. "We use it for retail volume and put it side by side with the national brands," Wakefern Chairman Thomas Infusino explained. "We don't use it to knock out the national brands. We simply let the consumer make a choice."[33]

The group also reasoned that if "one can make money on national brands at relatively low gross margins, the same should be possible for one's own brands." This was considered a departure from normal food industry practices. "Shop-Rite was really offering outstanding values because the quality of their private-label products was comparable to that of the national brands. Customers soon found that out."[34]

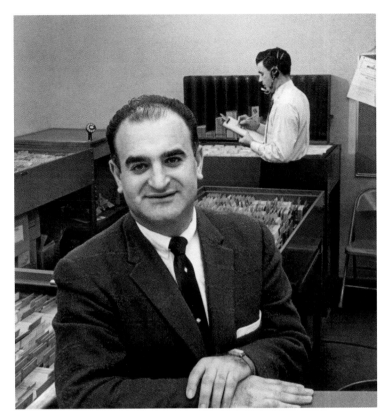

Frozen Foods—Hot New Item

Initially purchased by the carload, groceries and meat were deemed "basic" goods by the co-op members, and dairy needs were met by the large-volume, low-profit purchase of milk through central suppliers. But 1950s shoppers, with their refrigerators and freezers, demanded perishables (fruits, vegetables, meat, dairy, and delicatessen). "Dave Fern ... used to talk about perishables as being key. [He would say]

that's what brought your customers back," recalled Chuck Infusino, who joined the Wakefern co-op in the late 1940s. "He used to say that if you gave a woman a bad pot roast and they were going to use it for Sunday dinner and it was bad, the husband would say, 'Where'd you get this garbage?' [or] something like that. She'd be embarrassed and would feel she couldn't shop there any longer."[35]

Wakefern launched its frozen food division in 1951, and was led by Silverberg, who worked closely on the project with Harry Castroll, "an early ShopRite operator who made frozen foods his specialty."[36] Castroll ran

Above: This mid-1950s photo shows Wakefern founder Alex Aidekman (front) and former Wakefern President David Silverberg (back) working near the co-op's punch-card system.

Left: The growth of the frozen food category stretched the warehouse capacity as shown here in the leased frozen foods warehouse in Jersey City, New Jersey.

When Wakefern's Cranford, New Jersey, warehouse opened in November 1953, the surrounding border of all ShopRite ads still featured a chain that signified the strength of stores linked together through the sharing of resources and cooperative buying. This ad was visible proof of "The Newest Shop-Rite Power." *(Photo taken from the* Newark Evening News, *January 14, 1954, edition. Reprinted with permission from Media General, Inc.)*

Castroll's Market in North Plainfield, New Jersey, with his father, John.

In the early 1950s, not all Wakefern and Shop-Rite stores were able to stock frozen food; they couldn't afford the necessary equipment. "Those who did would have a 10-foot case—they called it a coffin case—but product was limited. Birds Eye [Foods] was one of our big suppliers," Tully remembered. "Gradually, we needed two coffin cases, especially as ice cream came in."[37] Wakefern President Sam Aidekman noted that the co-op's frozen food division, which at the time leased warehouse facilities at Union Terminal in Jersey City, "had been able to supply our stores with a very large variety of staple frozen foods, advertised brands, and specialties at a price [which was] considerably lower than the major chains."[38]

"Do Not Fold, Spindle, or Mutilate"

Data processing, however rudimentary, was vital to efficient merchandise handling and record-keeping. No one at Wakefern believed this more than former Wakefern President Silverberg. "Those business executives who will not accept and will not master the information revolution will be swept into the ash can of business history," he said.[39]

In 1952, the co-op instituted a punch-card machine system, whose warnings to not "fold, spindle, or mutilate" became household words across America. Previously, Silverberg had ordered the company's first mimeograph and a tub-card system, the precursor to punch cards. The relatively new data processing technology resulted in a better bookkeeping system at Wakefern, provid-

ing ongoing inventory control and simplifying the order-placing process.

However, the problem was that no one at Wakefern really knew how to operate the equipment—except Silverberg. "They asked me just to take it over," he said of his early involvement with technology at Wakefern, where he ran what was probably a Remington Rand (an early IBM competitor) ERA 1103 model, a general-purpose computer system. "As soon as we could, we pulled in the IBM," Silverberg said.

By the spring of 1952, all of the co-op's invoices contained useful information, such as the current chain retail price and the percentage of profit at retail for each item. "The stores were able to enter their order into our [punch card] computer, and we could take that order," Silverberg explained. "It also gave us the total amount of each particular item that all the stores were ordering, so that we could place an order with the manufacturer for whatever we needed."[40]

On the Move

Due to rapid growth in retail stores, coupled with a doubling in sales volume between 1952 and 1954, the co-op's 15,000-square-foot warehouse in Port Newark, New Jersey, was no longer adequate—despite being three times the size of the co-op's first warehouse in Newark, New Jersey, which had been a huge improvement over storing goods in members' basements. The move in November 1953 to a new 43,000-square-foot (1 million cubic feet) warehouse and office facility in Cranford, New Jersey, built by Wakefern and designed by the "nation's foremost authorities on wholesale grocery warehousing," represented the co-op's first real entry into the warehouse business.[41]

Half of the required $310,000 investment was put up by members—though some were unable or reluctant to ante up—through the purchase of stock in a real estate company Wakefern set up to construct the facility as well as through banks.[42] The Port Newark warehouse was Wakefern's largest expenditure to date.

Costs were mitigated somewhat, however, as the co-op did not have to pay for the land, which was owned by a railroad that gave it to Wakefern in return for permission to run tracks adjacent to the warehouse site. This was a mutually beneficial relationship, as Wakefern enjoyed easy rail access for shipping and the railroad received Wakefern's freight business.[43] The facility itself enabled the co-op to significantly increase the number of items it carried in addition to operating more efficiently.

Dave Fern remembered walking around the plant, thinking, "My, [what] a big place. How can we ever afford to fill it with merchandise?"[44] Despite his concerns, the warehouse would soon be run-

ning 16 hours a day. A year later, the co-op would begin to run out of space in its warehouse.

Labeling it a "modern warehouse," trade journal *Progressive Grocer* wrote that the Cranford facility "is well equipped to handle present membership and more."[45] This hardly proved the case, at least for long: Within less than two years, plans were under way for an even larger facility.[46]

By 1954, thanks in large measure to the ShopRite concept and its advertising, there were 25 active supermarkets in the ShopRite group, ordering a total of 3,500 to 4,000 cases a week.[47] Enthusiasm among co-op members was stimulated by the "crisis-excitement of new store openings" and an undiminished spirit of "lending a helping hand."[48] Joe Saker, then president of Foodarama Supermarkets, was on hand for a store opening in 1954, and found it "swarming with customers. I yelled out ... 'Get me a register,' and soon I was punching the keys. I spent most of the day there."[49]

Revenue Growth Greets New Leaders

In the fall of 1954, due to his own business expansion, Sam Aidekman requested that Wakefern

ShopRite trucks at the loading dock of the Cranford warehouse.

ShopRite ads in the 1950s had unique headlines, with topics ranging from outer-space supermarkets (top right) to buying a part of Texas (top left). The ads also announced major news, such as the move to a larger warehouse in 1954 (center right and bottom), and showcased ShopRite's trucking capacities (center left). *(Images featured top left and bottom right reprinted with permission from the* Union Leader/Suburban Leader *on the following dates: May 1954 and January 21, 1954. Other photos taken from the* Newark Evening News *July 22, 1954 (center left); September 1, 1955 (top right); and December 3, 1953 (bottom), edition. Reprinted with permission from Media General, Inc.)*

Vice President Nicholas Sumas, owner of the Village Shop-Rite Market in South Orange, New Jersey, become acting president. Shortly thereafter, Sumas was installed as Wakefern's third president, taking on the responsibility of the direction and policy of the warehouse and all of its functions.

Sam Aidekman received a noble send-off from friends and associates at Wakefern. An appreciation piece in Wakefern's 1955 Annual Year Book read: "He has personified a result-getting driving force that is reflected in both individual achievement and the continuous growth and importance of the Wakefern

and Shop-Rite operations. ... His driving business tactics have 'rubbed off' on new members. His keen competitive sense and leadership has paced many of our endeavors."[50]

The resignation of Herman Wechsler in late 1954 sparked another change in leadership, as Seth Beller assumed the position of Wakefern general manager. According to Al Aidekman, Beller was instrumental in the co-op's success: "Seth was a brilliant young man ... who helped us set up our books and institute proper control systems. ... He was invaluable to our young firm."[51]

In 1955, Al Aidekman was named vice president of Wakefern and ShopRite. Tom Infusino

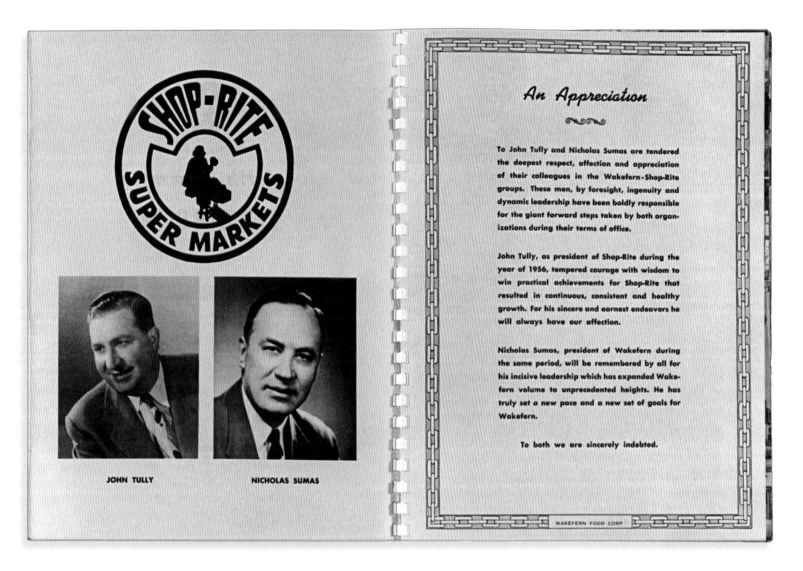

An Appreciation

To John Tully and Nicholas Sumas are tendered the deepest respect, affection and appreciation of their colleagues in the Wakefern-Shop-Rite groups. These men, by foresight, ingenuity and dynamic leadership have been boldly responsible for the giant forward steps taken by both organizations during their terms of office.

John Tully, as president of Shop-Rite during the year of 1956, tempered courage with wisdom to win practical achievements for Shop-Rite that resulted in continuous, consistent and healthy growth. For his sincere and earnest endeavors he will always have our affection.

Nicholas Sumas, president of Wakefern during the same period, will be remembered by all for his incisive leadership which has expanded Wakefern volume to unprecedented heights. He has truly set a new pace and a new set of goals for Wakefern.

To both we are sincerely indebted.

WAKEFERN FOOD CORP.

JOHN TULLY   NICHOLAS SUMAS

John Tully, of Tully ShopRite, the first president of ShopRite, and Nick Sumas, of Village Super Market, Inc., the third president of Wakefern, were honored in Wakefern's 1956 Annual Year Book.

acknowledged the type of man Al Aidekman was at that time: "Not only was Al a leader and a progressive thinker, but he knew how not to step on anybody's toes. ... Whatever he did was done quietly and seriously."[52]

By 1955, the seven remaining original Wakefern members (one retired) represented stores doing more than $13 million in annual volume. At the time, Wakefern boasted upward of 70 members (representing 90 stores), 50 of whom operated and advertised beneath the ShopRite Supermarkets banner—members of the latter group alone accounted for annual co-op sales of approximately $445 million."[53]

According to Wakefern, a 1955 survey of Shop-Rite members showed that virtually each one had "enlarged his market ... built a new one, or has plans on the drawing board since joining." Max Buck, director of advertising, sales promotion, and merchandising for Radio Corporation of America (RCA), called Wakefern/ShopRite "a real Horatio Alger story"—and their rags-to-riches tale had scarcely begun.[54]

Wakefern members gather with the governor of New Jersey in front of the co-op's new Elizabeth warehouse in 1960. Pictured from far left to right: Jerry Yaguda, Wakefern director of finance; Joe Saker, president of Foodarama Supermarkets (a Wakefern member); David Silverberg, Wakefern's director of special projects; New Jersey Governor Robert Meyner; and Wakefern board member Robert Henry.

CHAPTER THREE

LICKING PRICES, NOT STAMPS

1956–1968

*There used to be a saying among retailers in the New York market that
if you want to make money, just open a ShopRite store in New Jersey
and do everything Wakefern headquarters tells you to do.*

—*Supermarket News*, 1982[1]

BY THE MID-1950S, IT WAS CLEAR THAT being a retailer-owned wholesale cooperative not only enabled Wakefern to compete with the big chains, but also negated most of the chains' former bulk-purchasing advantages.[2] Wakefern had the further benefit of operating retail stores of its own through the ShopRite license, causing "a blurring of the distinction between wholesalers and retailers."[3] The co-op now had enough buying clout to secure quality merchandise for its growing, and soon to be highly successful, private-label program.

At the time, Wakefern was not the only supermarket bucking the large chains, which had established their own buying organizations early on. A non-cooperative group called Topco Associates, Inc., was formed in 1950 by 30 non-competing supermarket chains around the country in order to buy in quantity, and the West Coast co-op Certified Grocers of California, Ltd., was enjoying success on a par with that of Wakefern's—and for similar reasons.

As Wakefern retail stores completed the industry-driven transition from full service to self-service during the 1950s, they were remodeled and retrofitted with special meat, dairy, and frozen food cases, along with aisle gondolas and checkout lanes. Stores grew larger through expansion or new construction—the size of a typical store in the 1950s was around 3,000 square feet; by the 1960s, stores averaged 25,000 square feet. The hours of store operation also expanded and began to include evenings.

During this time, advertising was heavy, and marketing gimmicks proliferated. Promotional "giveaways," such as Hawaii vacations or a year's worth of food, emerged after World War II. By the mid-1950s, these promotions had stimulated the rebirth of "an existing but rather dormant system of promotion"—trading stamps.[4] This gambit, which made its New Jersey debut in 1956, caught on like wildfire with both supermarkets and the public.

Initially, Wakefern members were divided on the issue of whether the co-op should institute the new trend in their stores. The decision was eventually made, primarily for financial reasons, to refrain from participating in the stamp frenzy. The immediate effect was a sharp drop in business. Rather than despair, however, the members banded together. Despite some pro-stamp sentiment, not one member left the ShopRite chain.

ShopRite went public with its decision not to offer trading stamps, and to lower prices instead. Later, with this full page ad, they went on record to blame trading stamps for the predictable across-the-board increases in food prices that followed. *(Photo taken from the* Newark Evening News *August 29, 1962, edition. Reprinted with permission from Media General, Inc.)*

Back on Track

The co-op quickly initiated countermeasures to offset the stamp dilemma, including better customer service and dramatic price reductions. One member —Tom Infusino maintained it was Alex Aidekman— suggested that, in lieu of stamps, ShopRite stores give customers a 10-percent discount on all groceries. A low overall store margin of about 16 percent and a reduction of any existing high-margin products were emphasized by the group. Instead of a few big "specials," 30 to 40 of the fastest grocery movers were sharply reduced for months at a time, with others periodically added to the list.[5]

The advertising committee continued to play a major role, creating and integrating the new and effective slogan "Why Pay More?" into store advertising alongside banner headlines announcing the 10-percent storewide price cut.

As ShopRite's president, Herb Brody was at the forefront of price logistics. His challenge was determining the right "price mix"—the magic combination of low-profit, near-cost items with low-priced, higher-margin items. "While good decisions can't be made without good information," wrote *Progressive Grocer*, "the best ones, the most dramatic ones, are more likely the result of outstanding ShopRite judgment, knowledge and flair that comes from

long experience in actually owning and operating a supermarket."[6] This experience paid off in terms of increased revenue and new members (in 1957, three applications were received from stores as far away as Connecticut).

Bursting at the Seams, Again

By 1957, meat represented 25 percent of ShopRite's total store volume, necessitating the hiring of a meat executive.[7] Efforts were made to expand the co-op's meat program through additional suppliers with the hope, according to John Tully, of saving 10 percent by eliminating trucking and bringing the products to a central point for distribution.

A new non-foods division, the general merchandise division, was created as well. Alex Aidekman noted that the buyer for the division had offices in New York and 25 years of chain store experience, and the co-op members were counting on him to "get them on the right track." The seven companies using the buyer were Good Deal, Toppel, Kings Market, Martin Marcus, Mayfair, Tantleff, and, through Alex Aidekman, Wakefern. David Silverberg headed up the new division, which prompted the search for a replacement frozen food buyer.

By the mid-1950s, the co-op had outgrown its relatively new warehouse in Cranford, New Jersey. While numerous Wakefern meetings addressed this issue during the following years, there wasn't much to show for the effort initially except the consensus to build eventually in Elizabeth, New Jersey. The choice was well thought-out: The site sat on York Street in the middle of the Elizabethport Development Area, which was located near the Newark Airport in the heart of New Jersey's major transportation network.

The discussions dragged on—with the Wakefern board calculating and recalculating figures for what each store would be required to invest, and Dave Fern suggesting that those who couldn't come up with the cash be issued a note with interest—and Sam Aidekman assured the general membership, "No one is taking the matter lightly."[8]

Left to Right: Dominick V. Romano, Vincenia "Fannie" Romano, and Pasquale "Pat" Romano at a store opening in the early 1960s.

STAMP WARS

IN AN ATTEMPT TO INDUCE CUSTOMER LOYALTY to merchants, the grocery industry re-intro-duced trading stamps during the 1950s. The marketing gimmick was more popular than ever before. The Super Market Institute (SMI) proclaimed:

The battle of trading stamps was raging with more fury than any other form of promotion. Customers had books of trading stamps, frequently two, three and even more different kinds. They licked these stamps, pasted them in the books, studied the catalogues, compared values: so many stamps to get a hair dryer from this company and so many from that company and so on.[1]

When word of the impending stamp craze was received at Wakefern, about 25 co-op members were attending an SMI convention in Palm Springs, California. Recognizing the urgency of the situation, Wakefern members wondered, "Shouldn't we get on the bandwagon?"

Not all members, however, were in agreement about getting on board. Some favored the program, believing their customers expected it and that it was too strong a promotional tool to be without. Other members, especially the larger store owners, felt that stamps would cause retail prices to rise (to cover the costs of stamp vendors and products awarded)—something that was anathema to the Wakefern/ShopRite philosophy.

Upon the group's return to New Jersey, heated meetings were held long into the evening to discuss the matter. David Silverberg and Tom Infusino recalled the intense debates as "an honest disagreement," while others described the battle against stamps as "bitter."

Herb Brody, who in 1956 became president of Shop-Rite Super Markets, Inc., and Vice President Milton Perlmutter were among the more vocal anti-stamp members. They were

Members debated the use of stamps as a marketing tool to draw business to the stores. It ultimately was decided that lower prices would be more effective to attract and retain customers—and this strategy proved very successful.

convinced that stamps were a rip-off, noting that a 1.5-percent price increase for a stamp program was too high. Ultimately, they were proven right. According to SMI, the program became very expensive indeed, with costs rising from "2 percent or less to 3 and 4 percent of sales in many stores," partially due to competition. It wasn't long before the public lost interest, as did the large chains.

Several weeks after those first dramatic meetings, a majority-rule decision was made against offering stamps. Tom Infusino called the decision an "aggressive move" and a "turning point" at Wakefern, as the measure gave the co-op the "impetus to really compete against the chains, because all the chains had gone into stamps."[2]

Store sales only dropped for a few months after this milestone decision, and actually spurred new interest in membership. In fact, the number of ShopRite stores increased every year throughout the late 1950s and 1960s. *Progressive Grocer* declared, "During this period, many say Shop-Rite really came of age."[3]

The discounts and rebates would be applied to each member's specific account, just like a bank, earning interest on the money they saved. This would be a lucrative form of investment for the members, while giving Wakefern more money to work with and assist with its plans for expansion. "Considering this proposition against insurance or any other expense involved in trying to borrow money, [it became clear that] it would be cheaper," Alex Aidekman added.[11]

Breaking Ground

On June 30, 1958, the then–100-store retailer-owned cooperative awarded a contract for the construction of the first of what would total eight

By early 1957, the board was talking with Fidelity Union Bank and working a deal wherein the Baltimore and Ohio Railroad (owners of the Jersey Central Railroad, whose tracks ran through the Elizabeth property and received much of Wakefern's warehouse business) would sell Wakefern five acres at $10,000 per acre, an amount considered to be worth half the actual value, with an option to buy 10 more—an option that was exercised more than once.[9] In February 1958, the Wakefern warehouse committee, headed by John Tully, was authorized to purchase a dozen acres with an option for an additional 20 acres.

Necessary equipment for the new warehouse included pallets, racks, 18 magnesium plates, seven power jacks, seven manual jacks, 200 tow lien guards, Raymond forklifts, and air-conditioning for the main warehouse. By the time the warehouse opened in 1959, Joseph Saker, chairman of the equipment committee, reported that the total tab for new equipment was approximately $126,000, with office and lobby furniture adding almost $7,000 more.[10]

Aside from the construction of the plant, there was still the financing to consider. "An easy and painless way to get this investment up would be to have all members leave their discounts and rebates in the warehouse," Alex Aidekman noted.

COUNTING ON COMMITTEES

Jim Sumas has served as chairman of the grocery committee for more than 35 years.

THE COMMITTEE SYSTEM AT WAKEfern has been called the true "essence of entrepreneurialism" and, at times, a "tangled bureaucratic web." The system is considered a primary factor in the co-op's success. Started by the original eight Wakefern members, the committee shared all aspects of day-to-day operations and planning, including purchasing and delivery of merchandise.

As the co-op grew, a more structured method for decision-making became necessary, and committees proliferated. Wakefern committees were created originally to facilitate merchandising and pricing. The co-op's store products were eventually divided into seven groups or operating divisions—grocery, meats, produce, frozen goods and ice cream, dairy-deli, bakery, and non-foods. Each group was overseen and represented by a committee member who attended the weekly sessions with staff buyers.

Members frequently served on several committees, with six to eight members per committee. According to David Silverberg, "The members were extraordinarily active in the management of the organization [and] supervised it through the creation of committees and other activity."[1]

As Wakefern grew even bigger and the number of ShopRites increased, committee responsibilities were expanded. They focused on all aspects of the business, from merchandising, property management, labor relations, and advertising, to quality control and bylaw revisions. The exact number of committees at any given time was often kept secret, as it was considered proprietary information that could benefit competitors.[2]

Being a member of a committee was considered a sign of great respect, and committee members were extremely dedicated and passionate about the effect their decisions would have on the membership as a whole. Because of this, at times there was considerable "political jockeying" for some of the choicer committee seats. The grocery committee, for example, was considered one of the most powerful and thus the most desirable.

"Those who serve on the various committees are doing it to [ensure] the best deals, exercise greater influence on the staff and, generally, make sure they get the most for their money," *Supermarket News* wrote.[3] As with all of the co-op's decision-making, the majority ruled at the committee meetings.

Over the years, there were disagreements among various committees concerning the focus of advertising and fair use of the warehouse. These disagreements stemmed from the level of seriousness each member displayed when discussing policies—each knew that the creation of a new policy would affect all members, and it was not a responsibility that was undertaken lightly.[4]

"There isn't a system in the world that's fool proof," *Supermarket News* wrote. "But Wakefern's may be as close as any company gets. One reason, sources say, is that each committee is headed by a strong chairman, whose job is to keep things moving along."[5]

The dedicated and professional Wakefern staff combined with the entrepreneurial spirit of Wakefern members, adds up to a dynamic competitive equation.

buildings over a projected four-year period at the York Street site in Elizabeth. Wakefern hired the architectural firm Lacy, Atherton & Davis, which had designed more than 30 grocery and warehousing centers at the time.[12]

The plan for the distribution warehouse center included general offices, a grocery distribution warehouse, produce, frozen food, a dairy and general merchandise distribution warehouse, a coffee roasting plant, a bread and cake bakery, a meat processing and distribution plant, and laundry and equipment services. Although not all of the specific departments were implemented in the plan, a new division for store design and equipment procurement was established and housed in the new central offices.

The warehouse center featured a number of advanced technologies, such as closed-circuit television for controlling the loading dock and other areas, lightweight transistor radio oscillators (two-way radios) for warehouse supervisory employees, and sophisticated mechanized receiving and order assembly equipment. AT&T developed electronic order equipment for Wakefern, designed to feed order and control data from stores to central warehouse facilities. Electronic computing and memory units (called RAMAC) were ordered from IBM and installed in the new center.

The distribution center enabled Wakefern to consolidate the warehouses it had been leasing in five New Jersey cities. Harry Castroll, a member of the warehouse building committee, stated that by the end of 1962, there would be at least 200 stores in the co-op and that the warehouse would be able to service their projected needs. At the time, the warehouse center's weekly sales volume averaged $2.5 million.

On February 24, 1959, the co-op entered into an agreement to lease the Elizabeth facility and continued to expand. The term was 15 years, with a net rental of $90,000 per year. Wakefern's real estate holdings, however, did not stop there. By 1960, the co-op had bought additional acreage from the railroad. On October 18, 1964, Wakefern purchased yet more land in Elizabeth, for $237,450, and again in November and December 1965, at a cost of $153,500. In 1965, construction began on an additional warehouse in

Above: Ribbon cutting at the 1966 grand opening of the Bayonne, New Jersey, ShopRite, formerly the Bayonne Opera House. David and Linda, children of the owner Al Tarasiewicz, do the honors.

Left: Wakefern executives and members are seen working in the York Street boardroom of the Elizabeth warehouse in the early 1960s. Featured here are (from left) Irv Gladstein, Bob Henry, Tom Infusino, Steven Najarian, David Silverberg, and Julius Perlmutter.

Elizabeth—at a total cost of approximately $2.5 million—which was completed in the summer of 1966.[13]

The vast eight-building, 410,000-square-foot warehouse operation, spread across 50 acres in Elizabeth, along with the Elizabethport facility, was able to handle all of the co-op's distribution needs. By the end of 1966, more construction doubled the distribution facility space, making the Wakefern Elizabeth plant one of the largest single-food distribution complexes in the United States.[14]

In 1966, the plant employed 900 people and moved nearly $10 million worth of merchandise each week. Soon even this giant, well-equipped warehouse operation would be hard pressed to keep up with the needs of the co-op members.[15] Ann Buratin, Wakefern bookkeeper from 1948 until 1985, said of the warehouses: "Every place we moved to seemed to get smaller, even though they were bigger."[16]

Expansion, however, fostered discussion and debate when a potential new member was considered to be too close in proximity to an existing ShopRite store. Ultimately, the resolution was illustrative of the civil and equitable way in which the cooperative worked. Wakefern President Al Aidekman explained that sometimes an existing member would be worried about the decision and

In February 1963, co-owners Vince Lo Curcio, Jr., (center, without a hat) and Tom Infusino (third from left) celebrate the reopening of their ShopRite in Nutley, New Jersey, with Mayor Harry W. Chenoweth and other dignitaries.

needed to consider that "such a move is a blessing, for it enables one member to advertise with the other member in the same area and could ultimately be helpful to the growth of the entire cooperative."

Taking Care of Business

During this expansion period, an attempt was made to bring Wakefern's long-ignored corporate bylaws up to date as well as schedule additional board meetings "so that everyone will be familiar with the business that is conducted at Wakefern," Alex Aidekman explained. "There is a lot of money tied up here and lots of futures depend on what happens with Wakefern. ... The group that sits here has a responsibility to see that Wakefern is protected."[17]

The co-op also faced the pressing matter of discount houses, which re-emerged with giveaways and trading stamps during the supermarket promotional battles. They sold hard goods (consumer durable goods) at low prices, and, as bait to lure customers into their stores, they sold groceries at prices less than those charged by A&P. Eventually, these stores would be located within a close radius of co-op members, cutting into their profits. Because these discount houses were Wakefern warehouse customers, discussions ensued as to whether to stop selling to the discount houses or sell to them at higher prices than other members.[18]

Supermarkets also joined the ranks of discounters. Grand Union created Grand-Way stores, Stop & Shop created Bradlees, and Food Fair offered J.M. Fields.[19]

Another issue soon arose, when Sam Aidekman criticized the board, as well as the co-op, for not having brought in any "new men" during the past 10 years. "It has been proven that many companies fall by

ShopRite cashiers often wore buttons featuring various promotions, slogans, and helpful or friendly greetings. Seen here is an array of buttons that ShopRite owner Dominick Romano collected over the years.

the wayside because they do not train their younger men," he said. Aidekman was also disturbed by the lack of interest of some board members who were "once very active in this organization," suggesting they should step down to allow for new ones. He also proposed that those who did attend the board meetings should be paid for their efforts, while those who did not be fined.[20] Although no action was taken to address Aidekman's specific concerns, a member grievances committee was formed at his urging in November 1958. The group, composed of Wakefern officers, was tasked with making major decisions concerning member grievances of all types.[21]

While 1959 marked the beginning of a new era in terms of the warehouse's ability to serve the growing ShopRite membership, it also marked the end of one with the resignation of Sam Aidekman. He would, however, continue to play a role at the co-op, serving as executive vice president on Wakefern's board of directors. Replacing Sam Aidekman as Wakefern president was his brother, Alex Aidekman.

More expansion at Wakefern occurred in December 1961 with the purchase of the issued and outstanding capital stock of the Veri-Best Produce Company, Inc., for $10,600. Veri-Best, a produce cooperative since 1948, became a wholly owned subsidiary of Wakefern and relocated to the new warehouse distribution center in Elizabeth.[22]

During this time, ShopRite's private-label brand also continued to flourish, becoming the first to market cigarettes, which successfully competed with national brands for a while. The program started with 20 percent of the sales volume and eventually settled into about 10 percent by the year's end.

Recognizing that the success of the private-label program was due to the quality of the products, Wakefern instituted an inspection program in 1961, and expanded the line of canned goods to include more than 20 items. As a result, $17,500 was saved during the program's first six months due to quality control. Also of note was an agreement with one of the packers of private-label vegetables that resulted in savings of 8 percent to 10 percent.[23] In 1961, the private-label line, which constituted

TIMES A' CHANGING

THE EARLY 1960S WERE CHARACTERIZED BY A huge wave of change across the country—socially, politically, economically, and culturally. The children of the baby boom redefined the nation's agenda. These Boomers questioned authority, challenged conventional politics and mores, and were the catalysts for dramatic social shifts. These pressures led to protests against the Vietnam War, the elevation of the Civil Rights movement, the birth of the women's movement, and the launch of the consumer movement.

In the spring of 1962, President John F. Kennedy addressed Congress and outlined a Consumer Bill of Rights. It was a milestone, as it was the first time a consumer-oriented message was delivered by a president to the legislative chamber. He outlined the right to safety, the right to be informed, the right to choose, and the right to be heard. This message ultimately became the foundation for the consumer movement and led to major changes in the food industry.

In the fall of 1963, President Lyndon B. Johnson pledged to carry out former President Kennedy's consumer program and appointed Esther Peterson as the first special assistant to

More than 200,000 Americans gather at the National Mall during the 1963 March on Washington for Jobs and Freedom (left), where Martin Luther King, Jr., (above) delivered his historic "I Have a Dream" Speech. *(Images courtesy of the U.S. National Archives & Records Administration.)*

the president for consumer affairs. Concurrently, ad hoc consumer activists such as Ralph Nader and his so-called "Nader's Raiders" set an agenda for establishing standards that led to changes in the auto industry, the food industry, and the advertising industry. Peterson and the activists contributed greatly to the Fair Packaging and Labeling Act passed by Congress in 1966. For the first time, it mandated that labels identify product name and place of manufacturing and distribution, and net quantity of contents in terms of weight, measure, or numerical count. The legislation laid the groundwork for greater transparency in food packaging and granted that, at minimum, consumers would at least know where the products they were buying were made and the amount the package held.

Future Chairman Joe Colalillo as a young boy, cutting the ribbon at his father's ShopRite in Flemington, New Jersey, in 1966.

18 percent to 25 percent of each store's total grocery sales, included more than 20 new items, with 24 more added the following year.

New Today, Gone Tomorrow

From the start, Wakefern was considered extremely progressive—a food industry "trailblazer," according to *Supermarket News*—when it came to electronic data processing (EDP) technology.[24] *Progressive Grocer* said Wakefern's constant upgrade of technology was done at "revolving door speed ... to keep pace with [the] enormous growth of ShopRite stores' volume."[25] David Silverberg said, "We placed substantial emphasis [on technology], and this enabled Wakefern to use its limited capital very effectively."[26]

By this time, the co-op's punch-card system was upgraded with the IBM 305 RAMAC, which could store the equivalent of 64,000 punched cards. Although the 305's use was limited to grocery billing and payroll, it generated about 25,000 lines of billing per day.

Wakefern also updated its warehouse payroll system with an IBM 1401, which was capable of processing 50,000 lines of billing a day. The company continued to stay on the technological fore-

front, updating the computers as necessary, and a second 1401 was leased in 1963, which increased billing capacity further. By then, Wakefern's leased computer equipment was valued at more than $2 million.[27]

"Long before it was economically feasible, Wakefern instituted a complete teletype store-to-warehouse ordering system, thereby reducing lead times for delivery and increasing order accuracy," wrote *Supermarket News*.[28] By the mid-1960s, Wakefern enjoyed the benefits of what some called "the food industry's largest, most complete direct store-to-warehouse ordering system."

The combination of EDP and Teletypewriter Exchange Service (TWX) enabled around 12 high-volume ShopRites (those with revenue exceeding $100,000 per week) "to convert shelf stocking to the SLIM system [Store Labor and Inventory Management]," to what ShopRite retailers called the "instant groceries" system. This system sent grocery orders from trucks to store shelves with minimum leftover stock and brought about "substantial reductions in stocking time, and inventory and backroom space requirements."[29] Ultimately, the time between ordering and receiving product from the warehouse was less than 24 hours.

Finding Better Ways to Grow

The strong growth that Wakefern experienced after the 1951 launch of ShopRite continued for nearly a decade. The period was marked by a flurry of store openings, especially in the North Jersey market, although the co-op began to attract new members from neighboring states. Alex Aidekman reported in February 1960 that "30 or 40 stores" in Connecticut had expressed an interest in joining the Wakefern cooperative.[30] Unfortunately, the co-op could not accommodate them. The Elizabeth distribution center, despite expanding nearly every year, had trouble keeping pace with the current ShopRite stores' booming volume.

In 1960, Wakefern General Manager Seth Beller resigned to become a Wakefern member, opening ShopRites in Oakhurst and Middletown, New Jersey, and Reading, Bethlehem, and Allentown, Pennsylvania.[31] Beller holds the distinction of being the first of several Wakefern staff who made the transition to member status over the years.

At the time, the ShopRite chain consisted of about 100 stores, with a total annual volume of approximately $200 million.[32] Yet growth had ground to a near halt by the early 1960s. Only two new members were added between 1960 and 1966. Word in the industry was that ShopRite had closed its doors to new retailers.

At this time, in 1962, stockholders were required to advance $10,000 with each new store opening application. A year later, in May 1963, the co-op's certificate of incorporation was amended to increase the authorized capital stock to 1,000 shares of No Par Value Common A Stock; 50,000 shares of $100 Par Value Common B Stock; and 50,000 shares of $100 Par Value Common C Stock.

To spread risk and financial drain, some ShopRite owners set up corporations and pooled their money. As with the larger Wakefern cooperative entity, they shared responsibilities. By the mid-1960s, there were 27 co-op companies, or chains, that operated two or more stores each. Foodarama Supermarkets had 15 units, Big V Supermarkets had five, Village Super Market, Inc., had six, and Motts Super Markets had nine. Super Markets Operating Company (SOC) operated 33 "supers," and General Super Markets (GSM) ran 31. From 1958 until 1962, corporations and individuals added approximately 35 stores through these types of chains.[33] By 1966, five companies had gone public.[34]

These internal chains and multiunit companies proved profitable and beneficial to their members. GSM's first store opened in Bloomingdale, New Jersey, and was one of the first ShopRites to be located in a mall. "Business was so good they had to close the doors and let some customers out so others could come in," Harry Castroll said, adding that the store opened with the largest weekly volume of any store in the ShopRite chain, nearly $200,000.[35] For other store groups that took over existing properties, sales multiplied tenfold compared to that of the previous tenant.

In terms of this so-called second-hand growth, the supply of out-of-business stores had all but dried up by the end of 1962. Further expansion required new stores; however, lenders and builders weren't convinced that the still relatively unknown co-op was a sound credit risk. Following the success of several new ShopRite stores that managed to open, word spread that ShopRite was to be considered a sought-after tenant.[36]

Major sources of working capital remained unavailable for the most part, and going public remained the only viable option. ShopRite member

The Szibdat family admires a plaque honoring George Szibdat, a Wakefern member who operated two ShopRite stores in West Orange, New Jersey. Szibdat was an enthusiastic supporter of Wakefern, claiming that the co-op could "inspire you to greater things." Standing behind the Szibdat family (from left) are: Nick Sumas, Ed Gold, Sid Singer, David Silverberg, Joe Saker, John Tully, and Bob Henry.

GSM went public first, in 1961, with an initial offering that netted $800,000. Within a few months, SOC followed suit. By February 1962, SOC had seven stores operating in Long Island, New York, with one under construction and more planned. Ultimately, the Wakefern board approved SOC's nine Long Island store applications.

GSM was launched in March 1959 through the merger of Dave Fern and four other ShopRite retailers in North Jersey: Ray Green and Tom Hurst, owners of three stores; and Danny Solomon and Harry Castroll, owners of one store each. Their combined stores—relatively small at 3,500

to 4,200 square feet apiece—averaged $20,000 per week. "We wanted to expand. ... By pooling our talents and money, it would be less of a gamble," Green recalled.[37]

Prelude to a Split

Co-op founder Dave Fern would tell prospective Wakefern members: "We're a democracy, our thoughts are free. Disputes? Yes, we have them, too, but we work together. And we're all owners managing this, not just employees of a big company. We can stand up and say 'I made a big mistake' and not be afraid. And our employees must feel this way too."[38]

Despite this collaboration, on February 4, 1966, GSM and SOC announced plans to merge, a move that was met by opposition from half of the co-op's 18 directors—the other half were also

The Perlmutter family's new ShopRite in Toms River, New Jersey, opened in the early 1960s. Shown here are the well-lit and organized produce aisles adjacent to the dairy section.

officials of the two merging super-market chains (GSM had five seats on Wakefern's board; SOC had four). At the time, SOC had 32 ShopRites and 10 drugstores, with 1965 earnings of more than $2.1 million on sales of approximately $165.5 million. GSM had 30 supermarkets and a discount department store, with profits for the year totaling approximately $1.6 million on volume of more than $114 million.

According to Wakefern board member George Szibdat, who was not associated with either chain, the two chains intended to merge without the required approval from Wakefern "in regard to the transfer of any Wakefern stock to the ownership or control of the merged company." The *Wall Street Journal* stated that Szibdat was fearful that the merger was a prelude to a "power grab," as the new entity would be incorporated in Delaware and "threaten the independence of Wakefern."[39] Szibdat noted that he was not against the merger per se, but felt that approval should be sought and granted by Wakefern.

In April 1966, the Wakefern board of directors green-lighted the proposed merger between GSM and SOC. The resulting company, led by Milton Perlmutter, was called Supermarkets General Corporation (SGC).

In May 1967, Fern was elected president of Wakefern. Fern's ties to both Wakefern and SGC led many to hope that he could form an agreement between the parties. But it was not to be, and when SGC decided to withdraw from Wakefern, "[Dave Fern] ironically found himself out of the group to which he was so devoted."[40]

In June 1967, the Wakefern board received a letter from Perlmutter on behalf of SGC, outlining the reasons for its dissatisfaction with the co-op. Perlmutter read the statement to the board members himself, claiming that

651 ROUTE 17 PARAMUS, NEW JERSEY

there was a lack of trust among members, but also stating the obvious: SGC had grown and it was felt that it needed its own warehouse operation.[41]

Perlmutter added that although those at SGC "have tried hard to be faithful to the cooperative spirit of Wakefern ... satisfaction with yesterday's successes will not solve tomorrow's problems." SGC's desire to have its own warehouse as soon as possible meant a phased reduction in purchases from Wakefern. SGC went on to operate its stores under the name Pathmark.

Even though it appeared that the co-op was losing out, an inherent opportunity opened up. According to Dean Janeway, current Wakefern president who was a 24-year-old junior buyer at the time of the split:

[Wakefern] wanted SGC to leave on good terms, even though they were going to be competitors. ... SGC [had] controlled the board. They controlled all the sites. Nobody else could get any sites.

When they left, there was this big sledgehammer that said boy, we're going to lose 50 percent of the volume. In the same token ... [now] there was real estate available all over the place, and within two years, [ShopRite] opened up enough stores to make up what that volume was. That's why today you'll see many ShopRites within two blocks of Pathmarks because Pathmark had that site locked in. When

Above: This 1968 ad for Pathmark appeared after the split from Wakefern. The headline says it all: "So long, Shop-Rite. Hello, Pathmark." *(Reprinted with permission. Courtesy of North Jersey Media Group ©1968 The Morning Call.)*

Left: ShopRite also took the opportunity to remind its own customers that it was "business as usual," and they would continue their effective low price promotions.

Left: Showing support for President Kennedy's Physical Fitness Council, this full-page ShopRite ad ran in the *Newark Evening News* in February 1963. It endorsed a healthy lifestyle and exercise program and reminded customers they could help keep their family budget healthy by shopping at ShopRite. *(Photo taken from the* Newark Evening News, *February 20, 1963, edition. Reprinted with permission from Media General, Inc.)*

Right: This May 21, 1967, newspaper ad noted both the opening of ShopRite's 199th and 200th stores, located in the Washington, D.C., area, and the appointment of Betty Furness as consumer advisor to President Lyndon B. Johnson. *(©1967. The* Star-Ledger. *All rights reserved. Reprinted with permission.)*

[SGC left], boom, we opened up a ShopRite as fast as we could and fought for that volume.[42]

SGC also eventually entered the home improvement business, the drug store business, and the catalog business, expanding beyond the grocery business. Even though Wakefern initially lost 50 percent of its volume, not one person was laid off—the members were committed to moving forward and regaining their strength.[43]

In September 1967, an agreement was reached between Wakefern and SGC that provided for the ultimate payout of monies invested in, deposited with, and loaned to Wakefern by SGC, an amount totaling more than $3.7 million. It was also decided by the Wakefern board of directors that SGC personnel were no longer permitted to participate in committee meetings.

On September 28, 1967, the Wakefern board also changed the amount of investment required from $30,000 to $45,000 per store, except for stores owned by SGC. A year later, in December 1968, the Wakefern board would change the investment required for membership to $50,000 per store.

A Leader Emerges

In 1947, Wakefern recorded $300,000 in volume from a mere 5,000 square feet of warehouse space. By 1960, warehouse volume out of its Elizabeth distribution facility exceeded $100 million. Five years later, warehouse sales approached $450 million per year, making Wakefern a leading cooperative food distributor.[44] Wakefern President Alex Aidekman declared that Wakefern became "the world's largest cooperative food distributor" in the 1966 annual report.[45]

The number of ShopRite stores not only doubled during the period between 1960 and 1965, but their volume tripled, showing a 42 percent annual increase. The figures reflected both new retail stores and the growth of existing stores. "Sales per Shop-Rite average around $3.3 million per year, about twice the national average for chains in the 101–250 store bracket," reported *Progressive Grocer*. "Co-op stores' sales will exceed $1 billion

by 1970, it is estimated conservatively."[46] Having played second fiddle to the warehouse operation for many years, ShopRite now constituted the bulk of Wakefern sales.

ShopRite reached a milestone in 1966, when the 200th ShopRite opened in Washington, D.C. It was a big change from the previous decade, when operations extended about a 30-mile radius from the Wakefern warehouse facilities in Cranford, New Jersey. While 30 of the co-op's supermarkets (mostly older and smaller) chose to retain their own identity, 170 stores proudly operated under the ShopRite banner. The co-op's growth continued when, in November 1967, Wakefern Realty Company, a Wakefern Food Corporation subsidiary, was incorporated.

By the end of 1968, there were 1,703 ShopRite-label products. During this time, the dairy and general merchandise departments expanded to become full corporate divisions, with the promise of "dynamic future volume growth."[47]

The volume of the average ShopRite was now more than twice the volume of the average North American supermarket. Wakefern sales climbed for the 22nd consecutive year, reaching the highest level in Wakefern's history, at more than $5.87 million.

While the stage was set for continued growth and success, the full impact of the SGC split from Wakefern—the largest setback the co-op had ever endured—was yet to be seen.

This 1968 full-page ad ran in New Jersey newspapers following Wakefern's tumultuous split with Supermarkets General Corporation (SGC). The message is clear: ShopRite hasn't changed.

FLOURISHING DESPITE ADVERSITY

1968–1979

Wakefern typifies a survivor. Several times since its inception, its very existence has been threatened, first by outside factors and later by factions within the organization. And after each of these bouts, Wakefern and its ShopRite retailers appear to have come out even stronger than before—not merely surviving but, in fact, flourishing in the face of adversity.

—*Supermarket News*, 1982[1]

By EARLY 1968, THE FIRST OF the "Wakefern Wars"—the media's term for the co-op's internal and external battles— was under way. Wakefern President Dave Fern's efforts to reconcile the differences between the co-op and Supermarkets General Corporation (SGC) during 1967 had failed. A tentative agreement was forged with SGC regarding its intended departure from the co-op, one that would be phased out in several waves based upon volume.[2]

On April 1, 1968, the two parties reached a final agreement: a payout of $3.74 million from Wakefern to SGC.[3] On April 9, Fern stepped down as president and left Wakefern to follow SGC, which set up headquarters in Woodbridge, New Jersey.[4] Robert Henry, a former Wakefern board member and vice president under Fern, was nominated interim president of Wakefern and officially became president on May 27.

"At the time [SGC] represented 48 percent of our volume, and we were looking at a $2 million loss the first year they were gone," recalled Tom Infusino. "Very easily, it could have meant the end of our business."[5] SGC took 71 out of a total 202 Wakefern stores with them, resulting in a 42.5-percent loss in sales volume for the co-op.[6]

The leaders of the new SGC chain, whose stores operated under the trade name Pathmark, tried to recruit David Silverberg, offering him the same general manager position he held at Wakefern.

"I would have had ... significant stock in the organization, but I felt I just didn't want to do it," he said.

While some in the industry worried that the organization had lost a significant amount of "brain power" when the SGC leadership left, they didn't have to be concerned for long as the organization regrouped. One of the strong leaders to emerge from Wakefern membership was Infusino, who joined the co-op in 1954, served on the board for eight years, was active on numerous Wakefern committees, and served as a director of the Super Market Institute.

Infusino played a vital role in keeping the co-op together during the tumultuous split, thereby earning the respect and trust of the Wakefern members. "In those days, when guys were leaving or trying to take over the co-op, [Infusino] was a rock and stood in the middle," said retired Wakefern executive Robert Gal, who had joined the company in 1966.[7]

In the wake of SGC's departure, the co-op managed to stick together. Come 1968, however, Wakefern's future seemed to hang in the balance.

The grand opening of the Little Falls, New Jersey, ShopRite in 1972. Pictured with customers and cashier are (from left to right): Harry Infusino, Chuck Infusino, Jr., and Chuck Infusino, Sr.

The co-op members agreed that it was necessary to act immediately, rather than wait for the end of SGC's scheduled two-year phase-out. The co-op's bylaws stipulated that if a member or member group with 3 percent or more of the volume wished to leave the co-op, they had to give two years' notice.

The first actions taken by Wakefern were raising the investment required from $45,000 to $50,000 per store and launching a powerful store-opening campaign.[8] A fair number of the new ShopRite stores opened in areas where there were SGC/Pathmark supermarkets. "We were now in direct competition with them," Infusino said.[9]

The competition was fierce, and Wakefern kept in stride. Infusino noted that within two years, there was a ShopRite across the street from many Pathmark stores. "We got all of those sites," he said. "So it was a home run in that regard."

At Wakefern, the troops were rallied, the objectives were clear, and the co-op forged ahead.

SGC did not remain idle either. In August 1968, Venet Advertising Agency left Wakefern to work for SGC.[10] Wakefern hired the ad agency Conahay and Lyon to replace Venet in October 1968, which in turn was replaced by Keyes Martin & Company in March 1970.[11] During this time, there were several lawsuits around SGC's contractual infringements, including the premature use of the Pathmark name and using the ShopRite label alongside the SGC label, as well as coupons that referred to ShopRite in ads, all before the SGC phase-out was completed.

Forging Ahead

Amazingly, Wakefern regained its lost volume through new ShopRite stores and increased its capital through higher investment requirements between 1968 and 1970, "so that [the anticipated] $2 million loss never happened," Infusino said.[12] At the end of 1968, there were 126 ShopRite and Wakefern retail stores.[13]

While grocery volume for the co-op's first year in 1946 was 75,000 cases, more than half that

David Silverberg, an adept diplomat and strategist, was highly regarded for his visionary leadership. Silverberg is shown at his office at company headquarters in Elizabeth, New Jersey.

number was being shipped in a single day in 1968.[14] Regarding the size of the co-op's warehouse operation, *Forbes* magazine noted: "Average Shop-Rite store volume is $5 million a year vs. an industry average of over $2 million."[15]

In April 1969, Wakefern acquired the remaining stock of Food Haulers, Inc., making the trucking operation a wholly owned subsidiary.

Expansion continued into the late 1960s with the major remodeling of 11 existing stores and the opening of eight new markets and one home center in New Jersey and Connecticut.[16] At the time, ShopRite provided a livelihood for more than 20,000 employees and an additional 1,625 Wakefern employees.

Under David Silverberg's dynamic leadership, the co-op continued to grow and prosper. Silverberg began to focus intensely on the structure of the organization, identifying long-term objectives—which included decentralizing the organization—and placing younger directors in each of the major divisions. The average age of Wakefern's management was less than 40 years. In late 1966, frozen foods became the co-op's first decentralized division. Wakefern President Dean Janeway, recalls the pivotal point this organizational change represented for him and for Wakefern:

I was a 23-year-old junior accountant at the time, and I was given the opportunity to be a part of this new structure in the frozen food division. Decentralization meant each division operated separately with great autonomy. Each division had its own buying, advertising, financial, customer service, and transportation functions. As a result, I was exposed to more than just the financial opportunities for job growth, and ultimately served as a director of the frozen food division and dairy deli.

Wakefern Food Corporation Annual Report 1972

From its inception, the co-op placed a high priority on the well-being and growth of its employees. To enhance employees' "professional management education and development," new programs were added in 1970 for warehousemen, including a weekly class in conversational English and warehouse terminology, as well as a class for Wakefern warehouse supervisors in conversational Spanish.[17]

In 1970, the Corporate Retail Division was established, with its own management, as a wholly owned Wakefern subsidiary and operated three acquired ShopRite stores in Clark, Spottswood, and Passaic, New Jersey.[18] In the technology arena, an automatic two-way communication system was installed, controlled by the co-op's powerful IBM 360 computer, allowing ShopRite stores to receive pertinent information such as "out of stock," time of delivery, and general administrative messages.[19]

In 1970, the combined retail sales of ShopRite were more than $700 million, ranking ShopRite 13th among all supermarkets and 28th among all retail organizations in the United States. In April, the Wakefern board once again increased

its capital base raising the investment requirement per operating ShopRite supermarket from $60,000 to $70,000, reaching the highest point in the co-op's history with more than $9 million in working capital.[20]

"Wakefern Wars" Redux

Although Wakefern was successful in recovering the volume lost because of SGC's departure, the co-op still faced risks and divisions that could destroy it and its members. The members that remained after SGC left had irreconcilable visions about the future nature and structure of the co-op that strained relations among them, even as they were pulling together to recover ShopRite's losses. The early 1970s were marked by internal disputes over how and by whom the co-op should be governed and the constant threat of another large member leaving. These internal disputes erupted

Left: Ron Gianettino, senior vice president and account supervisor at Keyes, Martin & Company, the ShopRite ad agency, and Stan Cohen, chairman of the ShopRite advertising committee and president of Motts, review an early rotogravure mailer/newspaper insert.

Below: At the ribbon cutting for the Passaic, New Jersey, ShopRite, from left to right: Sid Singer; Tom Infusino; Ed Barneman, store manager; Ed Gold; Passaic Mayor Goldman (cutting the ribbon); Joe Zola; and Irv Gladstein.

into litigation that ultimately lasted six years in state and federal courts.

The battle that was joined with the commencement of the litigation in 1971 was a war over the future of the co-op. Both sides recognized that Wakefern was ill-equipped to deal a second time with problems like those presented by the SGC withdrawal, but they could not agree on how to restructure Wakefern to avoid such problems. Some members sought a truly democratic organization of one vote per member, while four of the older, class A stockholders believed since they had initially made greater financial investment in Wakefern than did the class C stockholders, they were entitled to greater control. The dispute had the potential of tearing the co-op apart because if these four members withdrew it would have represented an estimated 50 percent loss in volume. Their withdrawal would have had even more severe consequences than the SGC withdrawal.

Throughout the 1970s, the Wakefern members were both litigants sitting on opposite sides of the courtrooms where the legal battles were fought and, often on the same day, partners sitting around conference tables working together, creating policies and innovations and implementing the programs that enabled Wakefern and ShopRite to forge their retail successes. That period became the crucible in which the Wakefern culture and identity were forged and tested. The decisions and actions taken by all the parties during the litigation laid the foundation for the success of Wakefern today.

Even while legal battles consumed much of the members' attention, because of the commitment of both sides Wakefern and ShopRite continued to grow at a strong pace. In spite of the economic climate, the company became the largest retailer-owned cooperative in the supermarket industry in the United States in 1972, with record sales in all divisions and an all-time high of more than $745 million in total sales. In addition, a new full-line bakery division opened in a 70,000-square-foot warehouse in mid-November, with sales expected to reach $10 million a year.

"A true testament to the strength of Wakefern membership and management was their ability to move forward, together, after the lawsuits had consumed eight years of resources and attention," said Janeway. "I was working in a product division at the time and the message was clear. ... All members are to be treated the same. The legal issues will be decided in court, our job is to serve every member so they can take care of their customers.

These products show open-code dating, which allows customers to know when perishables should be used. The can of corn shows the new nutritional labeling required by the government.

And at the conclusion of the lawsuit, everyone understood that the past is the past and moved forward in unison."

The litigation finally concluded in 1977. Surprisingly, only one of the losing plaintiffs, Bob Henry, eventually left the co-op, six years later.

According to the defendants' lead attorney, Dennis Block, the co-op's "real history" began after that final court decision. Both sides had compromised.

"The ability to become a real co-op started then," Block explained. "[Both sides] … put the lawsuit behind them and decided to reunite for the good of all. [Wakefern] was really in quicksand as a result of its inability to deal with the problems presented first by SGC and then … with the lawsuit."

When those issues were resolved, Wakefern's leaders started to look at "what the organization should be," and concluded that a new set of bylaws was definitely required to set forth the rights and responsibilities of all the members and to make clear the guiding concept of the co-op: Equal treatment for all. Wakefern's new bylaws were instituted in 1979.

"It's a contract with the members, in essence, and truly provides protection and fairness," Block added.

The same year, to finance a badly needed new warehouse, all members signed a stockholders' agreement, agreeing in an uncanny echo of Wakefern's founding, that each member would guarantee a portion of the loans used to construct the new warehouse. The new bylaws and stockholders' agreement were, according to Block, "fundamental blocks in the building of the organization."

The bylaws and the current stockholders' agreement are still in force today and continue to be the cement that holds the co-op together. No other co-op in the United States has established the relationships among its members similar to those created by Wakefern's bylaws and stockholders' agreement. This explains, in part, why no other co-op is as large or as successful as Wakefern.

Solutions from Within

The 1970s were not only a time of turmoil for Wakefern, but for the country as a whole. In 1971, the United States left the gold standard, the dollar fell, and President Richard Nixon imposed a wage and price freeze in an effort to rescue a weakening economy. Initially intended for a 90-day period, the freeze continued for nearly 1,000 days, a measure unprecedented in peacetime. This helped regulate inflation, but not enough, as it would eventually soar to 12 percent in 1974.[21] In comparison, in 1947, when Wakefern was in its infancy, the average rate

Wakefern's Manager of Consumer Affairs Sylvia Nadel (left) speaks with Esther Peterson, first special assistant, who served in President Johnson's administration for consumer affairs and later served as consumer advisor for Giant Foods in Washington, D.C.

of inflation was 8.43 percent; four years later, when ShopRite launched, the rate was 7.88 percent.[22]

Increasing prices fueled the growing consumer movement, resulting in heightened consumer demands for which the supermarket industry was relatively unprepared. It became evident that several short- and long-range problems of serious dimension were facing the supermarket industry—problems in areas of demands for better values and honest merchandising.

The urgent need for the formulation of concrete policies for consumer programs, such as product date coding and unit pricing, was discussed at a board meeting in October 1970. Citing the consumer programs of competitive chains, Joe Saker felt it was imperative that funds be appropriated for the development of initiatives to provide ShopRite customers with the best value and impress upon them that "the best place in the market is ShopRite."[23]

The early 1970s ushered in a new wave of federal legislation focused on providing more detailed information to consumers about the products they were buying. Open-code dating, nutritional labeling, and more detailed product content labeling were among the most important advances in transparency for customers. The co-op formalized its increased attention to consumers by establishing a consumer affairs division and a quality assurance division in the early 1970s. Together with the product divisions, they instituted procedures to comply with federal mandates.

In a related effort, the co-op took off in a new direction with its merchandising and advertising, and by 1971, had initiated heavy use of television to promote product sales. The "Fight Inflation" campaign continued to drive home the ShopRite mantra: "Why Pay More?" The campaigns resonated with customers as they struggled to cope with the daily realities of increasing inflation and the effects on their households.

Under the relentless pressure from consumer groups—and increasing government regulations—the supermarket industry's net profits in the first half of 1972 were hit hard, reaching a new low of less than 1 percent. Independents such as Wakefern/ShopRite, however, were "doing very well indeed and in many ways [found themselves] with a competitive advantage in the retail area," reported *Progressive Grocer.*[24]

By April 1973, federal wage and price controls had largely been dismantled, but they did not curb inflation. There were also a number of consumer boycotts that year, including meat sales, which captured the attention of the meat industry as well as retailers.[25]

The co-op responded to such disruptions and an inflation-weary public with a unique—and incredibly effective—ad campaign. "In October 1973, shoppers in areas served by the ShopRite stores found an unusual advertisement in their mailboxes: a 16-page full color ShopRite circular. It changed the way supermarkets advertised," wrote the *York Dispatch*.[26]

According to Karen McAuvic, Wakefern's director of advertising, this new type of advertising took volume through the roof. At the time, newspaper ads were the most used medium for supermarket advertising. The first chainwide circular ShopRite published was prepared by Keyes, Martin & Company with the intention of combining numerous sale items in one format. This would help with the cost of using color, instead of traditional black-and-white advertising. It also used rotogravure, or four-color print technology, which was unique.

The idea of selling many items in one source was simple: "Anybody who says that price and item advertising isn't image advertising doesn't know retail," explained Ron Gianettino, senior vice president, account supervisor at Keyes, Martin. "By selling a lot of items in every ad, you're selling the whole store."[27]

It also used the concept of "a lot more for a little less," that built on ShopRite's objective of volume sales. The circular was distributed directly to 2.2 million homes, as well as an additional 280,000 that were placed in the *New York Sunday Times* in suburbs where ShopRite has stores.[28]

The consumer also won in the conversion to front-end scanning. Now customers would receive an improved and easy-to-read register receipt, specifically spelling out each product name, manufacturer, size, and price. Previously, customers received a register receipt with prices only. Now they could be sure they were charged the correct price and had a record of the transaction when they returned home.

The ShopRite toy truck, introduced in 1970, became an extension of the brand and a holiday tradition with ShopRite customers for almost 40 years.

"Can" Do

The co-op faced a challenging need to increase sales during the post-holiday doldrums in the early 1970s. Their strategy was to create a unique merchandising/advertising event to generate needed revenue. Launched in January 1971, Can Can took the market by storm and succeeded beyond anyone's expectation. January was a traditionally slow month for ShopRite retailers, "so the sale was

HIGH KICKS, LOW PRICES

WAKEFERN'S MOST SUCCESSFUL—AND POPUlar—advertising campaign kicked off in January 1971. The music created for the early Can Can event's radio and television ads became memorable, to say the least. The Can Can lyrics, just like all of ShopRite's advertising, focused on low prices:

Today it's great to save some cash,
So come to ShopRite's Can Can bash.
From can to can to can to can,
You'll save much more on every brand.
You'll save much more on every brand!
Now's the time to shop at
*   ShopRite's Can Can blast,*
Now's the time to stock up
*   while the values last!*

Karen McAuvic, who managed Gianettino & Meredith's Wakefern account for 20 years until being hired by Wakefern in 2000, recalled George Meredith telling the story of visiting an art museum, "probably in Paris." The show featured a "very Moulin Rouge–type of artwork," and the music that played in the background was the Can Can tune. This inspiration led to the most profitable and memorable ShopRite campaign.

The Can Can sale took five years to become profitable, but perseverance paid off. At first it featured only a few canned fruits, vegetables, tuna, and beverages. Products were listed alphabetically in the earliest ads—for instance from applesauce to zucchini—and were even mentioned in the jingle. At the time only ShopRite's private-label goods were included; however, today many national brands are also available.

The sale eventually turned the slowest weeks of the year, which followed the busy winter holiday season, into the busiest weeks of the year. It also allowed stores to reuse the endcaps that had featured products for use in preparation for holiday meals and treats instead of dismantling them.

No other supermarket has been able to replicate ShopRite's Can Can sale, although others have tried, including Pathmark's Can-tastic sale and Price Chopper's King Can sale. The sale, along with its catchy music, lyrics, and dancing cartoon characters, remains a well-known feature of ShopRite. McAuvic noted that when television personality Rosie O'Donnell had her daytime television show from 1996 to 2002, "she knew all the lyrics, and she sang [them]" whenever the Can Can commercial aired.[1] In 2002, a summer Can Can sale was instituted, allowing ShopRite customers to enjoy both low prices and the Can Can advertising twice a year.[2]

In 2010, many sales records were broken, including 5 million cans of Progresso soup, 5 million cans of pet food, and 5 million cans of tomatoes. ShopRite also had its biggest sale in company history that year, when 40 million cans of Coca-Cola were sold.

In 2011, the Can Can promotion will celebrate its 40th anniversary.

The festive and smiling dancing Can Can girl remains an icon for one of the biggest promotional programs in ShopRite history. The happy jingle that encouraged shoppers to buy canned goods became an instant hit—many who have heard it can remember the words even years later.

Wakefern was serious about the quality of its merchandise and the cleanliness of its stores, as evidenced by its use of this mobile quality inspection lab in the 1970s. It didn't hurt that the van doubled as advertising for the co-op.

aimed at leveling the peaks and valleys."[29] ShopRite supermarkets slashed the prices on canned foods, and customers flooded into the stores, taking advantage of the bargain opportunity to "stock up."[30] The Can Can promotion gained even more success in subsequent years, as customers enthusiastically anticipate the annual event.

In January 1974, the industry was hit hard by a shortage of canned goods, and the co-op came close to canceling the Can Can promotion. After much deliberation, Wakefern decided to proceed, reasoning that by maintaining the sale as "an established feature in the customer's mind ... we gained her appreciation, and we demonstrated again, this time very dramatically, that ShopRite produces real values for the shopper."[31]

"To this day, other supermarket retailers have struggled to compete against the Can Can promotion," stated Janeway.

Although the supply of canned goods was relatively thin industry-wide, Wakefern's high-volume buying philosophy had allowed it to maintain an extensive inventory.[32] People flocked to the sale because the savings were substantial on literally hundreds of different products, primarily ShopRite-brand and national-brand vegetables. In January 1974, cans of stewed tomatoes, for example, were four for 89 cents.

In addition to advertising success, the mid-1970s saw the formation of several new committees at Wakefern, including the automated front-end planning and information committee, chaired by Chuck Infusino, and the in-store banking committee, headed up by Harry Starn.

Even in the midst of Wakefern's protracted legal battles, the retail business was strong. By the end of fiscal 1974, Wakefern/ShopRite was the largest retailer-owned cooperative in the United States, with annual sales of more than $914 million. That year, 10 new supermarkets opened, for a year-end total of 173.[33]

During this mid-1970s period, the merchandising committee engaged in extensive discussions regarding the company's philosophy and mission. The committee aimed to reaffirm the traditional ShopRite position that "the principal desire of [ShopRite] customers was to obtain the best merchandise available at the lowest possible prices."

In 1978, Keyes, Martin & Company created an advertising program with the well-known copy lines, "No stamps, no games, no gimmicks." In February 1979, the co-op severed its longtime relationship with Keyes, Martin & Company and followed George Meredith to his new agency, Gianettino & Meredith, Inc.[34]

Meredith was responsible for creating the successful and well-remembered Can Can campaign, where a snappy jingle sung to the cancan tune was accompanied by the colorful art of a Moulin Rouge–era dancing girl. The dancing girl, wearing a traditional full skirt and performing a high kick, became the iconic figure for the sales campaign.

Leveling the Playing Field

Even though much of the decade was marked by Wakefern's legal battles, the retailers continued to grow and reinvest in their businesses. This retail growth and success meant that they once again faced the perennial problem of inadequate warehouse space. The increased volume pushed the dry-grocery warehouse facility in Elizabeth beyond its capacity. However, because of the serious nature and unknown resolution of their legal issues, banks were not willing to extend credit to Wakefern for much of the decade, resulting in a significant deficit for warehouse operations. This lack of space and overcrowding in all of the warehouses made it difficult to service the ShopRite stores effectively.

They pieced together a solution by renting additional warehouse space in a facility owned by the agricultural company Monsanto, adding footage every few years. The facility in Elizabethport, first leased in 1965, was overused as well.

Finally, in the late 1970s, with the legal battles behind them, and the new bylaws and stockholders' agreement in place, Wakefern was in a strong position to secure the credit needed to reinvest in facilities and operations.

In October 1978, the property management committee closed on a land deal in Wallkill, New York. This would be Wakefern's first fully planned facility and largest capital investment to date, with an expected price tag of more than $20 million.

In late December 1979, steel was delivered to the Wallkill site, and construction began on the

ShopRite "Fights Inflation" by helping customers lower their monthly food bills, from left to right: Nicholas Sumas, Village ShopRite: Edward Breenan, Conahay & Lyon Advertising Agency; Robert Henry, President of ShopRite; and Joseph Saker, Foodarama ShopRite.

warehouse that would serve an expansion into upstate New York, the northern tier of Pennsylvania, and parts of New England. But Wallkill wasn't the only warehouse project in which the co-op was involved. Due to congestion at the Elizabeth grocery warehouse, Robert Gal, Wakefern's director of special services, had leased some 250,000 square feet of space from a warehousing company on Raritan Center Parkway in Edison, New Jersey, primarily for bakery and grocery items.[35]

In light of "changing conditions in the trucking industry," and to better serve co-op members from the new warehouse, Wakefern formed a new trucking company, National Transport Services Company, Inc., as a wholly owned subsidiary of Wakefern Food Corp.[36]

Perhaps the most significant development—especially in regard to the co-op's philosophy of member equality—was the creation of its site development committee (SDC). The original committee, made up of Wakefern members and staff, was designed to take the guesswork out of site decisions and accurately predict the sales potential of new, enlarged, or relocated stores.

But the program did have its shortcomings. The committee, run by well-intentioned member–volunteers, was by its very nature neither impartial nor infallible. That was to change in 1978, however, with a site development group formed entirely of outsiders, thereby removing the "subjective judgment" and any motive for self-serving site determinations.

As per new bylaws, the SDC was composed of three members, with a fourth as an alternate, elected by the board. The first men hired to serve on the SDC were Paul Cifrino, Bill Nichols, and Wendell Earle, who was also chairman of the committee.[37]

"The people who approve the sites for new ShopRites ... make their decisions based on the economic viability of each

```
SHOPRITE

        STAFF PEAS      .45
        HG SKIM MILK    .79
    1   ST SL PEAR      .34
        FRENCH BREAD    .59
        FISH           1.89
        PUFFED WHEAT    .65
    1   ST SL PEAR      .33
    1   ST SL PEAR      .33
        SANDWH BREAD    .53
        GROUND ROUND   2.09
      5 DOUGHNUTS       .75
    2   ST COLD CUP     .89 T
        PRODUCE         .59
CL  3   PRODUCE         .59-
        DAIRY           .59
        GREETNG CARD    .25 T
        RED ROSE TEA   1.59
        CHEESE SHOP     .59
    4   DELI            .79 T
        CUT FLOWERS     .89 T
        TAX DUE         .20
    5   TOTAL         14.53
SC      RED ROSE CPN    .60-
MC  6   GROCERY         .15-
        TAX DUE         .20
        TOTAL         13.78
    7   CSH TEND       20.00
        CHG DUE         6.22
        TAX PAID        .20
  8 7/29/76 14:03  0024/ 1
  THANK YOU,COME AGAIN
```

Above: Wakefern members, including Jim Sumas (seated fifth from right), Dominic V. Romano (seated sixth from right), and Joel Perlmutter (seated second from right) gather in the early 1970s for a grocery committee meeting at the co-op's complex in Elizabeth, New Jersey. Two commonly addressed issues of the time were warehouse space and ShopRite advertising.

Left: Wakefern was one of the first supermarkets to test and implement the UPC system in the 1970s. Here is a sample receipt.

UNIVERSAL PRODUCT CODE

ALTHOUGH THE FIRST PATENT FOR A BAR CODE SYM-bology was issued in 1952, it took more than 20 years before the first item was scanned at checkout at Marsh's supermarket in Troy, Ohio, in 1974.[1] The Universal Product Code (UPC), or bar code, was a technological invention that revolutionized the retail industry, and the grocery industry was at the forefront of the technology.

In 1966, the National Association of Food Chains met to discuss the possibility of using an automated checkout system. RCA, the company that owned the patent to the coding technology, also attended the meeting, and the Kroger grocery store chain volunteered to test it.[2] In 1970 McKinsey & Co., a consulting firm, along with an ad hoc committee of the Uniform Grocery Product Code Council (UGPCC), a corporation formed by the grocery industry's leading trade associations, defined a numeric format for product identification. They then put out a request for a company to propose a code, a symbol that incorporated the code, and provide specifications for each. George Lauer, an IBM employee who expanded on the initial work of Norman Woodland and Bernard Silver, was given the project, and in 1973, IBM's proposal was accepted and became the basis for the UPC.

By 1972, RCA began an 18-month test of the technology at a Kroger in Cincinnati; unfortunately, the ink used on the code lines sometimes

After retailers saw how the use of bar codes and computerized scanning improved the tracking of inventory and product prices, they embraced the new technology.

smeared, making it illegible by the scanner. By 1974, this printing problem had been fixed, and the first product scanned was a 10-pack of Wrigley's Juicy Fruit gum (now on display at the Smithsonian Institution's National Museum of American History).

Using the UPC

Each UPC code acts as a product's "social security number" as the product moves through

location and the financial strength of each operator," Tom Infusino explained. "As a result, distance between member stores is not a factor—as long as it is the committee's judgment that a store will be economically viable regardless of its proximity to another ShopRite."[38]

Jerry Yaguda, Wakefern's director of finance at the time of SDC's inception, added, "There can never be too many ShopRites in an area if each is deemed economically viable."[39]

Upgrades and Earnings

Having earned a reputation as a company committed to staying on technology's cutting edge, Robert Evans, director of Wakefern's communication information systems division, oversaw the upgrade of two IBM computers, the addition of three IBM control units, and the upgrade of IBM tape drives. A pilot program was introduced in 1979 that involved the installation of in-store minicomputers

the distribution process. It contains manufacturer or vendor information (the first five digits) and product information (the last five digits), but does not contain pricing information. Besides improving the speed of checkout, it also eliminated the time-consuming task of individually marking items for price. The computer system also allowed for a more accurate and efficient inventory process that eliminated manual counts of merchandise. It became popular in grocery stores simply for its ease of use and time-saving factors. It also had an added benefit—shoplifters could no longer switch price tags, effectively buying a high-priced item for the cost of a less-expensive item.

The receipt now became a valuable consumer tool, and the change to front-end scanning also gave consumers information on the receipts that had not been available previously. Now, they could see the time and date they shopped and which checkout lane they had used. The receipts also identified the specific item purchased, taxable items, store coupons, and refunds. It would also list the number of items a customer purchased regardless of where they appeared in the order. Prior to the utilization of

All ShopRite stores were converted to electronic checkouts by 1980.

the UPC and front-end scanning, receipts only included the amount of each item with a generic description, such as produce or grocery. Once consumers gained confidence in the new system, operational gains were forthcoming as the need for individual pricing of every item in the store was eliminated.

Although the high costs of installation of the new system weren't recouped as quickly as hoped—the entire checkout counter cost $10,000 ($44,000 today) and the scanner cost $4,000 ($17,600 today)—the technology slowly began making its way through the industry. It was a lengthy process as retailers were depending on manufacturers to implement the code on their products, while manufacturers were depending on retailers to install the checkout systems to read the code. As more stores began using it, more product labels were printed with UPCs. It was a cumulative effect that eventually made its way across all retail industries, as it was proven to save money, time, and labor.

According to Board Meeting Minutes from April 19, 1973, Wakefern contributed to the establishment of the UPC program.[3] That October, there was more discussion about the use of electronic cash registers that could read the UPC symbol, and it was predicted correctly that IBM would be at the forefront of the technology.[4]

in six ShopRites. The new mini-computers ran 10 times as fast as the equipment they replaced at Wakefern, at a cost of approximately $30,000 each, which was borne by individual retailers. The test results were positive, and the following year the equipment was introduced across the board.[40] It was a technological upgrade that placed Wakefern/ShopRite ahead of its competitors.

Earnings for the co-op were a bright spot as well. The fiscal year 1977 ended with the highest vol-

ume in the history of Wakefern, totaling nearly $1.3 billion, an increase of more than 13 percent over the previous year. The strong performance maintained the company's position as the leading cooperative in the United States and the largest volume retailer in its marketing area.[41]

Management each year instituted various measures to offset various general expenses. For 1977, these measures included increasing control of labor by warehouse supervisory personnel as well as productivity innovations on the part of management. The savings were extremely significant and provided an increase in rebates to members. In 1976, these rebates totaled approximately $9 million.[42]

Ten years after the dramatic split with SGC, Wakefern's total volume sales from its 186 stores for the fiscal year 1979 totaled $2 billion. Comparatively, SGC sales were $2.1 billion for that same period, of which approximately $1.8 billion was attributable to SGC's Pathmark Supermarkets division, which were previously ShopRite stores.[43]

Competition was not limited to Pathmark. During this time, competitors began to experiment with alternative format stores focused on lower prices. A&P launched the "box" store concept called PLUS stores, and Grand Union launched a BASICS format. Wakefern members met these

challenges head-on and took credit for the inability of Grand Union to spread its new format beyond one store.

As part of the stockholders' agreement of July 2, 1979, all members were required to buy at least 85 percent of their supermarket purchases from Wakefern. Wakefern now required a report on or prior to November 30 of each year showing the dollar amount of each stockholder's total

Below: The 1979 groundbreaking for the co-op's new warehouse in Wallkill, New York.

Inset: This aerial shot is of Wakefern's warehouse at Raritan Center in Edison, New Jersey. The warehouse, which housed bakery and grocery items, was leased in 1979.

CHAPTER FOUR: FLOURISHING DESPITE ADVERSITY

Irv Gladstein's (far left) use of Japanese decor for his ShopRite was also expressed in the store's grand opening. Instead of a ribbon-cutting, the ceremony included a resounding karate chop.

supermarket purchases—from any source—for the preceding 12 months.[44]

The co-op was well positioned for the 1980s, with expanding warehouse space, strong revenue, and revised bylaws to ensure that the company remained true to its original intent. The leasing and construction of new and much-needed warehouse facilities was finally under way—computer systems were upgraded, affording the co-op in-store capabilities previously unimaginable, and the decade closed with the highest warehouse volume figures in the co-op's history.

As *Chain Store Age* wrote in December 1979: "Whether the cooperative can match its dynamic performance of the last decade in the next is hard to predict, but it's certain that Wakefern and ShopRite will continue to be the names to reckon with in northeastern food retailing."[45]

Wakefern's warehouse operations expanded throughout the 1980s as more members joined the organization and the operations became increasingly computerized for ordering, selecting, and delivery procedures.

CHAPTER FIVE

THE NORTHEASTERN POWERHOUSE

1980–1989

What makes us special is [the] dynamic of Wakefern members and staff working together. … We all realize that every time one of us fails, we all fail. It sounds so simplistic and … cliché, but it really is [true]. It's just how we operate.

—Joe Colalillo, Wakefern board member[1]

ESPITE THE LINGERING EF-fects of inflation from the 1970s, ShopRite entered the 1980s as an "undisputed northeast supermarket power-house."[2] In the shadow of in-creased competition from huge stores with diverse wares, such as the 50,000-square-foot Path-mark Super Centers that offered no-frills items as well as specialty departments to encourage one-stop shopping, and despite rising energy and labor costs, Wakefern/ShopRite prevailed.

But it took hard work and innovation. In addition to the increased competition, the coun-try was mired in a recession defined by "stag-flation"—a condition that combined increasing inflation and unemployment with a stagnant business climate. By the early 1980s, inflation had reached more than 13 percent, with interest rates peaking at more than 21 percent. Unem-ployment reached almost 11 percent, with the housing, steel, and automobile industries particularly hard hit.

The new decade also brought a major change in the demographics of family households across the United States—an increasing number of women were employed outside the home. With about 200 stores under the ShopRite banner in six states—New Jersey, New York, Pennsylvania, Mass-achusetts, Connecticut, and Del-aware—Wakefern was ready to adjust to this new dynamic.

In the hotly contested New Jersey market, ShopRite re-mained prosperous thanks to a "powerful combination of ad-vertising, merchandising, and op-erations savvy that help[ed] the majority of members roll up net-to-sales ratios considerably above the 1 percent national average [close to 3 percent]," according to *Chain Store Age*.[3] ShopRite shoppers were ringing up approximately 120 million transactions each year, and the average transaction was more than $17—about 70 percent higher than the national average.[4]

"I think supermarket execs are the smartest in the country," longtime Wakefern member and Foodarama President Joe Saker said of Wake-fern and the supermarket industry in general. "They have to work off the tightest margins and still produce profits. I'd like to see some FORTUNE 500 companies do that."[5]

In the early 1980s, ShopRite continued its suc-cess by flooding the consumer market with its "Price

An advertising flyer emphasized the freshness of ShopRite's produce.

Plus" and "Why Pay More?" advertising campaigns, which were designed to help co-op members compete against an onslaught of limited-assortment stores and warehouse supermarkets. By the mid-1980s, ShopRite sent out about 118 million circulars each year, ran some 2,500 different newspaper ads, and produced more than 6 million store signs and banners. It also coordinated television and radio spots. The annual Can Can Sale, which became tremendously popular, also contributed to the co-op's success.

In keeping with its consumer-centric approach to business, in 1980 ShopRite implemented a new consumer education initiative called HELP (Health Education Labeling Program), which featured consumer brochures, teacher lesson plans, in-store tour materials for schools, and advertorials on key consumer issues of the day. These 500-word columns were run separately from the ads and covered a variety of consumer issues, such as hunger awareness and the need to support food banks, the Farm Aid crisis of the early 1980s, and the need to take personal responsibility in an increasingly litigious society.

By the early 1980s, most of the new ShopRites were considered superstores (units with more than 30,000 square feet). This was a far cry from the typical 3,000-square-foot store of the 1950s, and up from the top-end 25,000-square-foot supermarket of the 1960s. While some ShopRite stores were on the smaller side for the early 1980s, others were increasing their size and offerings, such as Foodarama's development of its World Class store format, which emphasized perishables, food service, and a kosher department.[6]

For most ShopRite stores, private label products played a key role in their merchandising strategy, with more than 2,700 items, and sales accounting for 25 percent to 30 percent of volume. This prompted *Chain Store Age* to call the program "one of the co-op's sturdiest pillars of strength."[7] Like the co-op's advertising blitz, its

private label was a powerful weapon to wield against the price-chopping assortment and warehouse stores that had cropped up in the region.

The quality of ShopRite private-label goods—a line by then nearly 30 years old—was deemed by *Chain Store Age* as "good or better than many advertised brands."[8]

Warehouse and Distribution Growing Pains

With the northern warehouse distribution facility in Wallkill, New York, still under construction, the now-inadequate Elizabeth, New Jersey, warehouse was forced to try to keep up with demand from Wakefern members. Warehouse space was not the only issue the Elizabeth facility faced. Adhering to a single-day delivery schedule, trucks from Elizabeth traveled as far north as Glens Falls, New York—more than 200 miles away. Due to the chronic paucity of space at the Elizabeth facility, the warehouse experienced one of the highest inventory turnover rates of any warehouse operation in the United States for many years—often reaching 75 turns annually. As the company noted, "This turnover rate signals that more efficient operations and other advantages would accrue from larger facilities."[9]

ShopRite Food Encyclopedia #1

Recipe Ingredient Substitutes

when you're out of what you need!

Left and below: In 1980, ShopRite began a consumer education initiative called HELP (Health Education Labeling Program), which included consumer brochures, teacher lesson plans, and in-store tour materials for schools.

Opposite: To position the co-op as a public leader, Wakefern began publishing advertorials dubbed "Consumer Insights" in the 1980s. They were placed in newspapers and covered topics on a variety of consumer issues.

Our Health Education and Labeling Program was developed to help you with your buying decisions. We welcome your questions and comments in order to serve you better.

Please write to:
Consumer Affairs Department
ShopRite Supermarkets
600 York Street
Elizabeth, N.J. 07207

Warehouse space was so tight that, were inventory not regularly removed, the stacks would block the warehouse receiving doors. At times, inventory would not even reach storage areas of the warehouse. Trailers would back up to the receiving doors, where workers waited to unload items off the truck to be shipped immediately to the stores.[10]

In 1980, the warehouse activity at the Elizabeth facility included the following: grocery, with 300,000 square feet, shipped more than 1 million cases each week; produce, with 47,000 square feet, shipped 215,000 cases per week; meat, with 44,000 square feet, shipped 3 million to 4 million pounds per week; and frozen foods, with 34,000 square feet, shipped 150,000 cases per week.[11]

By 1980, the warehouse shortcomings had reached critical mass, despite the co-op having leased warehouse space at the Raritan Center industrial complex in Edison, New Jersey, for some of the slower-moving product lines.[12] Wakefern reluctantly initiated a system of "forced distribution" of most new and all advertised items to ShopRite stores, wherein retailers were shipped merchandise whether they had ordered any product or not. "This

The completion of the Wallkill distribution center was a milestone event and marked a new era for the company's distribution capabilities.

is a somewhat unusual method for a co-op," *Supermarket News* wrote, noting that it mirrored a system used by the large chains. "But Wakefern is an unusual animal."[13]

Automatic distribution of advertised items was a necessity for promotional events, such as the annual Can Can sale, to ensure retailers were adequately stocked. As for new items, the co-op's grocery committee was responsible for the selection. "It boils down to what the staff feels is best for the warehouse and the stores," *Supermarket News* explained.[14]

New State-of-the-Art Facility

By the spring of 1981, Wakefern's $20 million–plus grocery distribution center at the 94-acre site near the Catskill Mountains in Wallkill was fully operational, with a workforce of about 300. The plant covered a total of 522,700 square feet, with room for future expansion.[15] In order to secure financing, stockholders were required to make an additional investment in Wakefern's capital stock based upon the dollar volume of their warehouse purchases from Wakefern, as per the bylaws.

Costs notwithstanding, as *Supermarket News* put it, "Wakefern officials talk about Wallkill with the zeal of a kid on Christmas morning."[16] However, some felt the co-op might be in for a few rough years. "The problem now is to get the sales to support the

WAKEFERN'S CREDO

IN 1980, THE CO-OP'S CREDO WAS UPDATED AND presented at a meeting of the Wakefern board of directors. The credo was an important manifesto for members to abide by and take to heart. It set the tone for the company's goals and future, and served as a reminder of the struggles and successes of its past. The Credo Read:

Wakefern/ShopRite is a retailer-owned cooperative. Its membership consists of entrepreneurial families who have banded together to secure merchandise and services that they could not obtain economically or retail competitively if they acted individually.

They have accepted the creed of the cooperative movement because they recognize the value of people working together for their mutual benefit.

They assume the sacrifice of time and effort in order to achieve common goals.

They accept these burdens because they believe in the far-reaching benefits obtained through cooperative methods.

The social purpose of Wakefern Food Corp. and the ShopRite stores shall be to raise the standard of living of the consumers served by our stores by providing better merchandise at lower prices.[1]

---

additional 500,000 square feet provided by Wallkill," *Supermarket News* reported. "Companies have died trying to support a warehouse."[17] Some industry pundits criticized Wallkill's "out-of-the-way location" and sheer size, citing its potential for becoming a white elephant if volume wasn't increased enough to support the warehouse, which primarily served the needs of co-op members in North New Jersey, Big V, and Mott's.[18]

These concerns turned out to be unfounded. Wakefern officials had predicted that this market region would provide strong growth, and they were right. Big V was steadily moving upstate in New York, and Mott's had a "virtual lock" on Connecticut and southern Massachusetts.[19]

"The co-op's New York/New Jersey market, New Jersey in particular, has become an increasingly cutthroat area in the past several years," *Supermarket News* reported. "While ShopRites are well entrenched in market share, the co-op's major growth over the next few years will be in areas Wallkill is best positioned to serve. ... This, coupled with speculation that Wallkill may be Wakefern's gateway to upper New York State, puts the co-op on the verge of renewed growth."[20]

And grow it did. During the first year of operation, Wallkill received and shipped more merchandise in the first year than it had planned, which led Wakefern to believe that the warehouse could expand its area in use by 25 percent to 30 percent. The new warehouse boasted 143 truck doors for shipping and receiving (compared to approximately 70 at the Elizabeth facility) and an indoor two-track rail dock, which could accommodate 13 train cars on each track. The warehouse was fitted with 39 rows of grocery pallet racks, seven of which were drive-in racks.

Wallkill warehouse "selectors" used computer terminals installed in the supervisor's office to pick up their orders. The selector keyed in his number, which provided supervisors with a more efficient tool for measuring productivity.[21] The system highlighted the best way to utilize the workforce, what time a particular billing would be finished, and the number of items to be selected by the end of the shift. "Since each move is verified by computer, terminal operators know immediately when a particular slot can be released for receiving," *Supermarket News* explained.[22]

Capital Ideas

With Wallkill up and running, Wakefern turned its attention to planning for the future needs of the cooperative and its members. Wakefern commenced a long-term strategic planning process. Together, Wakefern staff and membership developed a five-year plan to see "what we need to serve members properly," according to Jerry Yaguda, chief financial officer at the time. The plan called for even more warehouse space, including a new frozen foods facility at an undecided location.[23]

"Wakefern is no pauper," *Supermarket News* reported. "The co-op may not have the prettiest balance sheet in existence, but its financial resources, including inventory and capital from members, put the company in a strong position." Capital traditionally was raised through member deposits, which were required for the opening of new stores. But for the first time ever in Wakefern's history, financing was handled through four large insurance companies, so as not to affect members.[24] According to Yaguda, the co-op's use of sophisticated data processing technologies, including accounting and budgeting procedures, was attractive to outside lenders.

Shoring up the co-op's support of members' need to invest in technology, Wakefern Finance Corporation, established in March 1980, helped members purchase minicomputers and other front-end equipment for their stores. The finance arm was joined in 1981 by another company, Insure-Rite Limited. The captive offshore insurance company was set up in Bermuda to handle certain Insure-Rite requirements for Wakefern and its members, enabling the co-op to reduce insurance costs and lower premiums, and ultimately driving costs out of the system.[25]

Under the direction of Wakefern President and Chairman of the Board Tom Infusino, the co-op's bylaws were finally updated in 1981. After a special review committee had been created in June 1978 to study, formulate, and recommend the adoption of a complete revision of Wakefern's bylaws, the revised bylaws were approved and adopted in April 1981. Changes were not radical but were designed to reflect the present times and needs of members.[26]

By 1982, Wakefern subsidiaries included Food Haulers, Inc.; ShopRite Supermarkets, Inc.; ShopRite Beverages, Inc.; Wakefern Realty Company; National Transport Services Company, Inc.; and T.R.R. Carriers, Inc., which was established in April 1981 as Wakefern's third common carrier.[27] In May 1982, Wakefern Realty Company was liquidated through a merger with Wakefern Food Corp.[28]

The company also implemented A Departmental Reporting System (ADRS), which operated out of Wakefern's IBM mainframe computer and assisted in investment, fixed assets, inventory control, and projected financial statements. As a planning model, ADRS was able to pose vital "what if" questions, such as "What if expenses were 5 percent and Wakefern gained or lost stores?"[29] Wakefern Finance Corporation also used the system to help with member loan data.

In 1983, the Wakefern Mutual Aid Fund was established "to minimize any adverse impact upon Wakefern's business as a result of labor disputes at its members' stores."[30] The co-op anticipated difficulty in the upcoming negotiations with Local 464 (the meat cutters' union). With the support of all co-op members, contingency preparations were made in case of a work stoppage to ensure members covered by the union were able to continue operations with Wakefern, with members outside of Local 464 territory providing backup assistance.

In January 1984, approximately 7,000 butchers and delicatessen workers represented by Local 464 in New Jersey and New York rejected a three-year contract offer and launched a 26-day strike against Grand Union, Pathmark, Foodtown, and ShopRite.[31]

The Wallkill warehouse utilized high levels of lighting and reflective or painted surfaces to reduce the risk of operator error during storage and retrieval of product.

Wakefern executives braved a snowstorm to kick off the annual Can Can sale in 1987. The quality assurance van is followed by a caravan of ShopRite trucks on their way to the stores. Pictured from left to right: Jerry Yaguda, Dean Janeway, and Bill Noto.

Wakefern's response to the strike was a great example of the company's steadfast resolve, so evident throughout its history: Wakefern supporting members, and members supporting each other. Wakefern worked around the clock to keep all the stores open with as little inconvenience to customers as possible. Associates at all levels staffed the stores, many working their regular jobs during the day, and then working the night shift packing out groceries. Dean Janeway, current president, then vice president of merchandising, remembered the *esprit de corp* so obvious throughout the entire organization. Janeway recalled:

Everyone knew the goal was to do whatever was needed to keep the stores open. ... After our "normal day," we would head out to the stores that needed an extra hand. I worked in various meat departments cutting meat. Other vice presidents organized their own pack-out teams for the night shift. Members who were not a part of the affected strike did whatever was needed to support those who were struck. Once again, it was a tribute to the cooperative spirit of teamwork and dedication to the membership.

Acting collectively, the industry joined together in the negotiations. The agreement that ended the strike was significant, as it recognized the changing shopping patterns of consumers, including the increased numbers of women in the workforce. Among other things, the new contract provided for extended evening and Sunday shopping hours, which necessitated the presence of meat personnel at these times to ensure personal service.

After the crisis of the 464 strike, Wakefern suffered another blow when longtime Wakefern member and former Wakefern President Bob Henry, the only member not to sign the stockholders' agreement, decided to sell his two large-volume stores to Supermarkets General (SGC). These stores became Pathmark stores.

In 1984, Wakefern members once again had to deal with a strike. This time it was at the Wallkill distribution center where members of Teamsters Local 445 walked out in April over demands for parity with workers at the Elizabeth facility.

It was a particularly difficult time, coming on the heels of the 464 strike and during the construction of the Wallkill perishable facility. But Wakefern members and associates rallied to keep the warehouse open, providing the necessary support throughout the protracted negotiations, until the strike ended in September of that year.

While the mutual resolve and support of Wakefern and its members to keep the stores open was a powerful example of the strength of the cooperative during the 464 and 445 crises, that same support is demonstrated on an everyday basis.

Second-generation ShopRiter Bob Clare, who is a member of Wakefern's board and operates the 80,000-square-foot ShopRite in Oakland, New

SHOPRITE SUPERMARKET CAREERS PROGRAM

Supermarket Careers was a groundbreaking program that offered training as well as work experience at local ShopRites to students enrolled in vocational programs in New Jersey.

WORKING AT WAKEFERN HAS PROVEN TIME and again that good ideas come out of the most unlikely conversations. Ken Capano, vice president of perishables, was at a Little League baseball game when he was asked about the possibility of hiring special education students.[1] This seemingly innocent comment was the beginning of a program that has become so successful it garnered national recognition.

Wakefern developed the idea of building a small ShopRite store right in the school, so students could get practical experience before they arrived on the job at the store.

In conjunction with Cornell University and Bergen County, New Jersey, vocational-technical schools, ShopRite developed a Supermarket Careers Program to train special education students to attain jobs above the entry-level cart collecting and bagging positions. Students spent half a day in their traditional education classes and half a day in their school's supermarket. In their senior year, the students earned half-a-day's salary while receiving on-the-job training.

During its first year in operation, two New Jersey high schools participated, and all 40 seniors enrolled in the program were working in the supermarkets. The schools expanded their "supermarket" training facilities by adding a stand-alone scanner and frozen food, dairy-deli, and produce cases.

The Supermarket Careers Program attracted a $250,000 grant from the U.S. Department of Education (USDE) in 1989 and was designated as one of the agency's National Demonstration Projects, ranking No. 1 out of 182 programs.[2] In 1990, Wakefern was awarded the prestigious "Secretary's Award" for outstanding vocational-technical education programs by the U.S. Secretary of Education. In 1994, the program received the "Employer of the Year Award" from the Council for Exceptional Children.[3]

It was also recognized by the Association for Retarded Citizens (ARC) of Bergen and Passaic counties, which awarded Jean Pillet, manager of retail recruitment, and Mike Reilly, former retail recruiter, its Humanitarian Award for Community Service.[4]

The program was so successful that it reached a peak of 42 schools in five states.[4] Two of the original students of the Hunterdon County program are still employees of ShopRite.

Jersey, remembered another example of Wakefern's service to members. It was around 2 A.M. at his store: "A driver pulled in late at night with a full produce trailer, and when he pulled his cab out from under that trailer, the landing gear that he had put down collapsed. The trailer rolled over and burst open, and all the produce was destroyed. ... By 6 A.M., a replacement trailer with all that product was sitting in our loading docks being unloaded. ... [Wakefern's] first instinct is to keep the store in operation. It's their very first goal."[32]

Change continued within Wakefern as well, when, in September 1985, ShopRite Supermarkets, Inc., (SRS) was established as a separate Wakefern company, elected its own board, and appointed Tom Zaricki to head up the company. The subsidiary consisted of ShopRite supermarkets in Clark, Spotswood, and Passaic, New Jersey. It would open its first new store, ShopRite of Doylestown, Pennsylvania, two years later.

Late 1985 saw the relocation of the co-op's entire frozen foods warehouse operation from Elizabeth to new quarters at the Enterprise Warehouse in Secaucus, New Jersey.

After years of managing multiple Wakefern office sites, the company began consolidating operations with a move of the Communications Information Services Division (CISD) and data processing center to Raritan Center in Edison, New Jersey, in the fall of 1984. It was followed by additional administrative offices moving there in the fall of 1985.

The year also marked ShopRite's institution of what became the popular "Kids in the Kitchen" program. The program was a hit with parents and kids, each year attracting more than 3,000 entrants from throughout the ShopRite territory. The highlight was the final competition in which contestants had a live cook-off in front of celebrity judges such as chef Jacques Pépin and Mildred Ying, food editor for *Good Housekeeping* magazine. Category winners were awarded a grand prize of an all-expenses paid trip for four to Disney World. Older contestants also had an optional prize of a culinary scholarship.

Co-op Challenges Critics

In the mid-1980s, rumors circulated throughout the food industry that Wakefern would soon become a chain like A&P, that the co-op had lost market share and given up its price-leadership position, and that its focus was on warehousing over retail.[33]

As for the co-op losing market share in northern New Jersey, Connecticut, and portions of New York, Wakefern President David Silverberg maintained this was "absolutely untrue."[34] It was true, however, that some smaller members were hurt by the 1984 meat cutters' strike and that others were set back somewhat by stiff competition, namely in sections of Connecticut previously dominated by Mott's and in Big V's stronghold in central New York. Despite this, Infusino maintained that "on a store-for-store basis, our sales are better than ever."[35]

Yet, Wakefern/ShopRite had begun expanding beyond its traditional market area in 1980, when George Zallie, a former Shop N Bag owner/operator in Philadelphia, joined. He was the first member to join after the departure of SGC. This started what became known as Zone 2 growth, when the Philadelphia/South New Jersey area became an increasingly important region. Other members who joined at this time included Steve Ravitz and Jordan Krassner in 1984, and Jeff Brown and

ShopRite's "Kids in the Kitchen" participants from various age groups proudly demonstrated their cooking skills, preparing many different types of dishes as they competed for prizes.

THE LEGACY OF DAVID SILVERBERG

During his 37-year Wakefern career, David Silverberg contributed to various departments, from frozen food to research and development, before becoming president in 1971.

IT WAS NO EXAGGERATION WHEN the media dubbed former Wakefern President David Silverberg "an industry leader"[1] or when his successor Jerry Yaguda stated at Silverberg's retirement dinner in 1987 that Silverberg influenced not only Wakefern but "the entire supermarket industry throughout his career."[2]

Silverberg, who was born in Proskurov, Russia, in 1921, immigrated with his parents to New York in 1925. After majoring in city and regional planning at Cornell University and in economics at the University of Michigan, he taught economics at Wayne State University in Detroit. Shortly after the co-op's inception, Silverberg began his career at Wakefern in 1950.

A pioneer in the frozen food field, Silverberg established Wakefern's frozen food division during his first year with the company. He held many positions at Wakefern in his career, including director of the special services and research and development divisions, assistant to the general manager, general manager, and, in 1971, became the first Wakefern staff member to be named president.

Silverberg was instrumental in introducing electronic data processing, not only to Wakefern, but also to the food industry as a whole. In addition to establishing the co-op's Communications Information Services Division, he was also the driving force behind the planning and construction of the extensive warehouse distribution center in Elizabeth, New Jersey. During his career, Silverberg helped establish the Health and Beauty Aid (HABA) and dairy divisions, and was instru-mental in "decentralizing" the organization in the wake of Supermarkets General Corporation's split with Wakefern—a measure critical to ensuring the co-op's long-term success.[3]

Considered "conceptually brilliant" and an adept political strategist, Silverberg was thought by some to be too much of an intellectual for the grocery business. Although he could have enjoyed a career in academia, he chose to follow his passion and enter the food industry instead. His academic side shone through, however, in the numerous articles he authored on management organization and electronic data processing systems and procedures. He was also a guest lecturer at various universities and institutions, including the Super Market Institute and the Gottlieb Duttweiler Institute for Economic and Social Studies in Zurich, Switzerland.[4]

Wakefern Chairman Emeritus Tom Infusino, who served alongside Silverberg for 20 years, said: "I was always confident of and grateful for David's leadership. We relied on him to lead us in new directions and knew he was always a step ahead of us in carving out a solution to the next challenge facing us. He looked beyond the supermarket industry for answers. Without a doubt, David was the right leader for the right time. He made us a better organization in more ways than we will ever know."

Rafe Lissack in 1989. ShopRite Supermarkets, Inc. (SRS) opened two stores in Philadelphia—one on Roosevelt Boulevard in 1988 and another at the Front and Olney location in 1989. With this number of stores, ShopRite had established a significant competitive presence, and had a separate advertising and merchandising strategy to fit the specific needs of the region.

Yet there were rumors that Pathmark was taking the market from ShopRite, to which Jim Sumas, vice president of Village Super Market, Inc., and head of Wakefern's Grocery Committee, responded emphatically with: "Baloney!" He added, "Without exception, we still are the price leader."[36]

Pathmark, in fact, was having troubles of its own. It was essentially forced into a leveraged buyout to avoid a takeover by Dart Group Corp. In 1987, management took SGC private in a $2.1 billion leveraged buyout, in which it only retained 10 percent of the shares (Merrill Lynch Capital Markets,

Inc. received 55 percent of the shares and the Equitable Life Assurance Society of the United States received 30 percent). The debt that incurred became problematic, and the company sold 25 of its freestanding drug stores.[37]

Coupons were another bone of contention with co-op critics. An article in *Supermarket News* cited reports that ShopRite coupons had been used "more to unload warehouse surplus than bring customers into the stores" in the past few years.[38] "We don't rely on coupons alone," Sumas noted.[39] He explained that coupons had never been used as the company's primary promotional tool; rather, the co-op's everyday low prices were what enticed customers and kept them returning. He added that ShopRite's coupons had hardly lost their punch: "They're still strong and aimed at winning the shopper."[40]

In a continual effort to prepare for the future, Wakefern members and staff underwent a strategic planning process. Not only was competition

Wakefern's board of directors in 1987, from left to right: Seated: Larry Inserra, Sr.; George Zallie; Dominick V. Romano; Dorothy Druian; Tom Infusino; John Sitar; Sid Singer; Tom Clare; and John Tully. Standing: Jim Sumas, Al Tari, Larry Laurenti, Steve Ravitz, Tony Smutko, Ron Cutler, Dave Bronstein, Irv Glass, Ned Gladstein, Joe Saker, Joel Perlmutter, Chuck Infusino, and Jerry Yaguda.

Left: Gordon Kuhn of Conrail (left) and Frank Rostan, Wakefern vice president of produce, receive Conrail's first delivery—Sunkist oranges—at the new perishables distribution center in Elizabeth, New Jersey.

Below: Former Wakefern President David Silverberg (left), who first joined the co-op in 1950, is seen here at his retirement dinner in 1987 with Wakefern Chairman Tom Infusino.

changing, so were customers' interests and needs. The question on the table was: "What will keep ShopRite customers coming back to ShopRite?" Corporate "soul searching" once again generated diverse member responses—some wanted to stay the course while others were intent on redefining the ShopRite customer offering. The resolution was greater emphasis on perishables across the board, from produce, meat, deli, and prepared foods, to expanded bakery departments. Once again, the direction proved to be the right one, with the company gaining significant momentum as a result.

A Change in Pace

A radical change took place on January 3, 1987, when Silverberg retired after 37 years with the company. Fortunately for Wakefern, Silverberg, who had been associated with the co-op in various capacities since 1950, stayed on to work as a consultant. "Silverberg played a pivotal role in working with Wakefern's staff and member-retailers in developing Wakefern's position as the nation's largest retail cooperative," Wakefern Chairman and CEO Tom Infusino noted.[41]

Wakefern's board of directors elected Jerome D. Yaguda to fill Silverberg's position as president. Yaguda, executive vice president at the time, had been with Wakefern since 1960. "Wake-

fern is fortunate to have such an outstanding executive as Mr. Yaguda to lead Wakefern on the path to continued success," Infusino said.[42]

By 1987, Wakefern was reaping the benefits of having substantial distribution facilities in three strategic locations: Elizabeth, New Jersey, home to a now 850,000-square-foot warehouse for groceries, perishables, and nonfoods; Raritan, New Jersey, where the co-op operated a 300,000-square-foot grocery warehouse and computer center and a 400,000-square-foot bakery distribution center; and the giant Wallkill, New York, distribution center.[43]

New growth in terms of retail units was existent but certainly not like it once was. "Over the past four years [1983–1987], new members are few and far between, because it's such a highly capital-intensive business today that the potential for new members is less than it was 15 years ago," Infusino explained.

Nonetheless, the expectation that many new co-op stores would likely open during 1987 and 1988 again raised the question of warehouse space. "Our existing facilities are adequate for serving all our present needs, but we'll need to expand, probably within a year or so." Yaguda said in 1987.[44]

To meet the growing need for warehouse space, a 220,000-square-foot perishables distribution center was designed and built in Elizabeth, kicked off by a gala groundbreaking ceremony in October 1988.[45] The new warehouse was more than five times the size of the old warehouse, with 53 truck shipping and receiving doors and seven railcar doors. The cost was estimated at about $26.5 million.[46] The facility opened in October 1989, a year in which Wakefern's sales volume grew by 7 percent.[47]

The perishables warehouse was the new home for the produce, floral, and seafood divisions, com-

ShopRite sponsored the celebration of the New York Giants' 1987 Super Bowl win. Standing on the field at Giants Stadium are (from left) Irv Gladstein, singer Ben E. King, Kathryn Romano, Dominick V. Romano, Dean Janeway, and Mary Ellen Gowin.

plete with a state-of-the-art seafood processing facility and ambient temperature zones, to keep all perishables at optimum quality. It also included a citrus juice processing plant that would allow Wakefern to supply stores with fresh juice on a daily basis.[48]

The fully consolidated perishables distribution operation was adjacent to Wakefern's main offices and dry grocery, meat, and dairy-deli warehouses. The new facility was less prone to congestion problems and allowed for the "prompt receiving and shipping of goods," which resulted in "a longer shelf life for product at the store level."[49]

The perishables facility also housed various horticultural products, some of which were imported daily from Europe and Latin America. The three different temperature and humidity zones helped to maintain the freshness requirements of the different types of vegetables and plants. "Basically, we're responding to the demands of the co-op members, who are responding to consumer demands for freshness," said Frank Rostan, vice president of produce and a Wakefern associate since 1969.[50]

Rostan's successor, Al Ferri, was in charge of some 2,000 perishable items when he took over produce in the early 1990s. The turnover for perishables, such as strawberries, was never more than a day and a half, Ferri explained, which led to the implementation of seven-day-a-week deliveries. "In fact, Wakefern is the only wholesaler to serve stores seven days a week with produce," Ferri noted. "Our customers recognize this ... and know with the high volume of business at ShopRite that the product is fresh. Nothing stays here [in the warehouse]. We keep it fresh. We keep it flowing."[51]

The co-op continued to set industry-wide standards during this period as well, now that this new facility also had a contemporary seafood processing facility. In 1989, Wakefern's quality assurance division was instrumental in implementing the nation's first U.S. Department of Commerce (USDC) Grade A inspection program for seafood processing plants. Implementation of the program also meant that a USDC inspector was on site to further verify the Grade A quality of the processing, working alongside Wakefern's quality assurance inspectors. This was a drastic change as now Wakefern associates would control the entire production sequence from whole fish to fillets, including cleaning, cutting, brining, weighing, and labeling. A five-ton ice machine supplied the facility with 10,000 pounds of slivered ice each day.[52]

It would now be possible for the stores to order as little or as much as they needed to suit the needs of their customers. This new processing facility made

it possible for every single fish to be screened by Wakefern, which hired experienced fish processors. Wakefern also developed its own packing containers for seafood to keep the product colder longer throughout the distribution process.

Helping the Community

During the 1980s, Wakefern became more involved with the community than ever. The co-op first worked with the Community FoodBank of New Jersey in 1982. Kathleen DiChiara, founder of the nonprofit organization, had just leased a building that had been a former slaughterhouse in October of that year. Almost immediately, her organization was offered two trailer loads of frozen food from another

Left: A newspaper ad promotes the nation's first U.S. Department of Commerce (USDC) Grade A inspection program for seafood processing plants, which began in 1989. (©1989. The Star-Ledger. *All rights reserved. Reprinted with permission.*)

Below: Chief Financial Officer Jerry Yaguda (left) and President David Silverberg (right) congratulate Ulysses "Sugar" Hayes with a plaque commemorating his 40th anniversary with Wakefern in 1988. Hayes was one of the co-op's earliest employees.

THE WAKEFERN FOOD CORP. STOCKHOLDERS' AGREEMENT

ONE QUESTION OFTEN ASKED OF WAKEFERN EXECutives is: "How does the Wakefern cooperative thrive where others seem to falter and fail?" The answer lies in the company's unique Stockholders' Agreement. Although the co-op was founded in 1946, the Stockholders' Agreement first emerged in July 1979. The agreement arose out of Wakefern's need to expand its warehouses and facilities.

As a cooperative, Wakefern would not retain any of its earnings; instead it passed its profits back to its members in the form of a patronage dividend. When Wakefern sought to build a new warehouse facility in Wallkill, New York, it needed to attract large corporate lenders, such as national banks and insurance companies, to fund its expansion. Without the ability to issue stock, the Stockholders' Agreement would be the means by which the members would financially commit to each other, ensuring the co-op's future.

On July 2, 1979, all but one of the members signed a binding promise that would guarantee Wakefern the sales volume it needed to support the new 522,000-square-foot grocery facility. With the stroke of a pen each member committed to purchasing 85 percent of their products from the cooperative. This feature of the agreement would set Wakefern apart from all other co-ops.

Just four years later, with the advent of a new perishables facility in Wallkill, the ten-year agreement was revised, on July 6, 1983. A new provision further committed members to each other. Each member agreed, in the event of the sale of a store or of their entire business to someone other than a qualified successor who would continue to operate the stores as ShopRites, to pay their proportional share of Wakefern's outstanding loan on the new facility.

This binding agreement reflected the members' personal commitment to each other and to the co-op. The 1983 Stockholders' Agreement would not be the last iteration of this document. Two subsequent Stockholders' Agreements, one signed in 1987 and the other in 1991, would deepen and strengthen the ties that bound Wakefern members and created the staying power Wakefern needed for long-term growth.

With the commitment of its members secured, Wakefern could negotiate better terms from its suppliers, secure the credit of lenders, and make the capital investments it needed for growth. With the 1991 agreement, the members set Wakefern on a course that would ensure its legacy well into the future. An "evergreen" clause would automatically renew the agreement, keeping it in effect for a period of 10 years following the members' decision to dissolve the union that bound them.

In 2000, the strength of the Wakefern Stockholders' Agreement would be tested when member Big V sought to leave the co-op. Wakefern prevailed and the strength of the co-op was confirmed.

---

donor—except the Newark building didn't have any freezers yet.

"I picked up the phone and called Tom Infusino at Wakefern," said DiChiara. "I didn't know him at all. He didn't know me. I explained that we were in this building [without freezers] and we had the opportunity to get food to people in need. Could he help us?"[53]

Amazingly, Infusino said "yes" to a woman he had never even met, and arranged the use of a refrigerated trailer for more than two weeks to store the donated food items.

"From then on, Wakefern just became a wonderful partner for us," said DiChiara.

Through the years, Infusino's immediate response confirmed the Wakefern culture of community spirit and concern. Wakefern took on the issue of hunger through a variety of methods, including utilizing ad space to deliver the message. "I'm not aware of any other supermarket that did that [at the time]," explained DiChiara. "We partner with all of the retailers in New Jersey, but our relationship with Wakefern has been the longest and the strongest."

Over the years, the co-op's involvement has grown, from increasing the amount of donations the FoodBank received, to raising awareness of the issue of hunger in the community.

The co-op became an active supporter of the Special Olympics in New Jersey in the summer of 1988. Hundreds of Wakefern associates and family members volunteer each year, serving some 10,000

meals—with food donated by Wakefern—to the athletes and their families. It has become a co-op tradition for Wakefern associates and their families to volunteer for the event each summer.

"Apples for Students," a 26-week program involving the donation of Apple computers to schools through the redemption of ShopRite cash register tapes, was introduced and overseen by William Crombie, vice president of merchandising.[54] By 1989, more than 2,800 schools had received free Apple computers and accessories as a result of this program.

"Scouting for Food," a national food collection program conducted by the Boy Scouts in which Wakefern was a participant, collected nearly 15 million cans of food, an increase of 3 million over the previous year.[55] In comparison, the 19th annual Can Can Sale of 1989 sold less than a third of what the "Scouting for Food" program raised (more than 4.2 million cases of product, up 6.5 percent over the previous year).[56]

Eclipsing Pathmark

In October 1987, a new stockholders' agreement was forged, effective through the year 2000. It was designed to meet the needs of both individual supermarket owners as well as Wakefern's public co-op members: Village Super Market, Foodarama Supermarkets, and Big V Supermarkets.[57]

The idea of a new stockholders' agreement was not taken lightly. Member discussions were heated and contentious, as it was understood that the agreement would define and solidify the strength of the co-op. Above all, the agreement, which was eventually endorsed by all members, was designed to enhance Wakefern's "long-term future growth" and set the foundation for "orderly planning and expansion into the 1990s," Infusino explained.[58]

Wakefern regularly participated in local community service programs, including the "Scouting for Food" program. In this late 1980s photo, Boy Scouts and New Jersey Governor Thomas Kean (right) hold a ShopRite bag full of donations, representing the significant contribution that Wakefern and ShopRite have made to the program's success.

STORE WARS
ShopRite now top N.J.-N.Y. food store

By Ron Stepneski
Record Business Write

THE RECORD, FRIDAY, MAY 13, 1988

ShopRite has overtaken Pathmark as the leading metropolitan food retailer, says Modern Grocer, a trade newspaper.

The Hackensack-based weekly reported that ShopRite, a Cooperative chain of independents supplied by Wakefern Food Corp., reaped 11.8 percent of the $23.3 billion spent in supermarkets in New York City, the 14 northernmost counties in New Jersey and parts of Connecticut and New York state.

Pathmark, owned by Supermarkets General Corp., of Carteret ranked second with 11.37 percent of the market, the newspaper said in its 1988 annual market report edition.

"Pathmark has been No. 1 as long as I can remember," said Howard Ackerman, Modern Grocer's 45-year-old publisher.

But the leveraged buyout of Pathmark's parent company, Supermarkets General Corp. of Carteret, left the company with a heavy debt load that slowed expan-

WHO TAKES THE BIGGEST BITE?

Market shares of competing supermarkets in the northern New Jersey-New York metropolitan area

Company	SHOP-RITE	PATH-MARK	FOOD-TOWN	WALD-BAUM'S	A&P	GRAND UNION	C-TOWN	KEY FOOD	KING KULLEN	MAY-FAIR
Percent market share	11.8%	11.37%	6.69%	5.86%	4.3%	3.96%	3.83%	2.44%	2.31%	1.74%
Rank	1	2	3	4	5	6	7	8	9	10
Sales in market area	$2.762 billion	$2.659 billion	$1.563 billion	$1.370 billion	$1.001 billion	$926 million	$897 million	$571 million	$540 million	$407 million
Number of stores in market area	122	98	186	102	200	111	178	150	54	33

Shares of $23.3 billion total metro New York food sales in 28 boroughs and counties that make up and surround New York City, including southern Connecticut and New York state and 14 northern New Jersey counties.

Source: Modern Grocer, Hackensack.

KEVIN O'NEIL / THE RECORD

He added that the company would not change its advertising

New York to New Jersey in 1984. It has a total circulation of about

average sales per store each week is considered.

Ronetco Supermarkets Inc., a Succasunna-based member of the ShopRite cooperative, leads the list of most weekly sales with $552,885 at each of its four stores and $28.7 million in average annual sales at each store.

Pathmark ranks second in that category with $521,782 average weekly sales per store and $27.1 million in average annual sales at each.

The entire ShopRite cooperative group ranked third with average weekly sales of $435,372 at each store and average annual sales of $22.6 million. Singer's ShopRite Supermarkets in North Bergen ranked fourth with $387,820 in average weekly sales at each of its six stores and $20.1 million in average annual sales at each.

Other weekly averages rankings include:

Village Supermarkets of Springfield, ranked fifth with an average of $385,628 in weekly sales at each

The 1980s was a turbulent period for the retail grocery industry, but Wakefern/ShopRite pressed forward to overtake Pathmark and become the leading grocery operation in the area. *(Reprinted with permission. Courtesy of North Jersey Media Group ©1988 The Record [Bergen Co., NJ] / NorthJersey.com.)*

Infusino's goals were realized in part by the spring of 1988, when ShopRite overtook Pathmark as the leading New York metropolitan area food retailer, according to a newspaper article carrying the banner headline "Store Wars: ShopRite now top N.J.–N.Y. food store."[59] The paper noted that ShopRite had garnered 11.8 percent of the $23.3 billion spent in supermarkets in the 14 northernmost counties in New Jersey, New York City, and parts of New York State and Connecticut. The Carteret, New

Jersey–based SGC Pathmark chain, long in the No. 1 position, ranked second with 11.37 percent of the same market. In 1987, Pathmark ranked first in *Modern Grocer's* survey of chains in the New York metropolitan area, followed by ShopRite. At the time, Pathmark had 100 stores and $2.71 billion in sales, compared to ShopRite with 118 stores and $2.66 billion in sales.

"Becoming No. 1 was a pivotal moment for us. ... We worked hard for that honor and took claim of it in all our advertising. It was a real feat of accomplishment for all of us," recalled Janeway, who was Wakefern's vice president of merchandising at the time.

Despite slowed growth in the number of new Wakefern members and stores toward the end of the 1980s, it was clear that the co-op and its ShopRite stores had claimed the northeast supermarket throne.

As part of its environmental awareness initiative, ShopRite launched its 2-cent bag reuse program in 1991. A 5-cent rebate was implemented in 2008, for each non-disposable, reusable bag such as canvas or nonwoven polypropylene. *(Photograph by Robert Pallesen.)*

CHAPTER SIX

GROWING THROUGH DIFFICULTY

1990–1996

For 50 years we've been able to adapt to all of the changes in our society and in our competition. Today we are more successful than ever—changing with the times and continuing to grow and prosper.

—Wakefern Chairman and CEO Tom Infusino[1]

Part of your family for 50 years!

WAKEFERN FOOD CORPORA-tion entered the 1990s as the largest member-owned wholesale cooperative in the United States, and it continued its success with record annual sales of $3.4 billion for the 1990 fiscal year. At the beginning of the decade, Wakefern supplied 178 stores, with the intention of opening many more stores over the next three years. Nearly all of the stores were under the ShopRite banner, and they were spread across six states: New Jersey, New York, Pennsylvania, Massachusetts, Delaware, and Connecticut.[2]

Chairman and CEO Thomas Infusino and President Jerome Yaguda had hoped for a repeat of the 7 percent volume growth that Wakefern experienced in 1989, which totaled approximately $200 million. They believed that rapid membership growth, aggressive store acquisitions for members—possibly including units from highly leveraged competitors—and the remodeling of nearly one-third of existing stores would help achieve this goal.[3] They knew they would face some obstacles, including an ever-changing industry full of new demands, and the acquisition of rival chains in the New York metropolitan area by supermarket giant A&P of Montvale, New Jersey. These unique challenges could thwart the co-op's efforts if not addressed with vision and care.

Keeping Up with Customers and Competitors

The dynamic needs of the average shopper had altered drastically during the past two decades, and was still in flux during the 1990s. The most recent changes included a shift to dual-income families, as well as increased numbers of single heads of households and working mothers. Women comprised 31.7 percent of the workforce in 1947—by the end of the 1990s, that number had risen to 60 percent. People had less time to cook, a growing desire for convenience, and increased awareness of nutrition and environmental concerns. Consumer expectations had never been higher in the supermarket industry. Infusino said:

We've got to offer quality, taste, and value, as well as menu assistance and quick meal alternatives. … We have to adapt and change with our society in order to stay competitive and remain in business.[4]

Although ShopRite's logo changed many times over the years, its trademark shopping cart was always a prominent feature. This logo was used in 1996 for the co-op's 50th anniversary.

In 1992, ShopRite became the sponsor of the LPGA (Ladies Professional Golf Association) Classic. Wakefern Chairman and CEO Tom Infusino joins the winner of the 1994 ShopRite LPGA Classic, Donna Andrews.

This served to reinforce the one-stop shopping concept, which had expanded throughout the industry to cover full-service pharmacies and enhanced food service offerings, such as party platters, catering, special-occasion cakes, and floral departments. Some stores had the capability to cater an entire wedding.

Wakefern and its membership once again embarked on an aggressive strategic planning process as it determined the best next steps to take in preparation for the changing customer climate and competitive landscape.

While the demands were great, the co-op was eager and ready to comply. "We're all trying to protect and enhance our business, and it's all a matter of evolution. No matter what the competition is, the good ones stay in business," Infusino said.[5]

Keeping up with shopper expectations was just one of the nonstop challenges. An economic slump occurred in 1991 and the retail industry hit a wall.[6]

According to *Supermarket News*, Wakefern and some of its members faced difficulties that accompanied the recession, including "food disinflation and even deflation," along with increased competition and the financial burden of building several new warehouses.[7] As a result, the co-op was forced to eliminate 177 jobs, many through an early retirement incentive. "We tried to have as few terminations as possible," Infusino explained.[8]

There were also predicted labor shortage issues that could affect the retail business. A study published in 1987 called *Workforce 2000: Work and Workers for the 21st Century* predicted a "drastic reduction in the availability of qualified young labor force entrants." The retail industry would be forced to look elsewhere for possible employment candidates.[9]

Adding to the already challenging environment, niche marketers, from pet stores to gas stations, began selling grocery products. And, for the first time, margin-threatening competitors Walmart and Costco, and drug chains such as Rite Aid, CVS, and Phar-Mor, started to appear on the retail scene, in addition to other mass merchandisers and wholesale clubs. All threatened Wakefern volume as never before; all were after a piece of the same retail dollar.

By 1992, some warehouse club stores enjoyed a significant price advantage over supermarkets. Also, ShopRite continued building nonfood inventory.[10] This was a far cry from ShopRite's inception in 1951, when executives held that nonfoods did not even belong in grocery stores, a belief that did not begin to change until a decade later.[11]

Wakefern faced more traditional competition in its regional markets as well. Some of its competitors included A&P and Pathmark, over which ShopRite continued to hold a modest lead; Foodtown cooperative, Grand Union, and Kings; the big-box format of the Carrefour's Philadelphia store; and hundreds of independents supplied by some of the largest wholesalers in the nation.

How Did the Industry Fare?

There was also the changing landscape within the retail grocery industry itself. Pathmark, after going through a leveraged buyout in the late 1980s, was reinventing itself with huge supercenter stores, some as large as 64,000 square feet. By 1997, there were 53 of these stores, which offered an expanded line of perishables, video rentals, and even UPS services, as well as an expanded private-label brand.[12] In 1996, Ahold bought Stop & Shop for $2.9 billion, and expanded the chain in the Northeast. By the end of 1996, there were more than 200 stores, making Stop & Shop the largest supermarket chain in New England.[13]

Grand Union was not faring so well. After multiple buyouts in the late 1980s and early 1990s, the chain was buried in debt. It declared Chapter 11 bankruptcy in 1995, and in 1997, the chief financial officer, president and chief operations officer, and vice president of operations all resigned, which sparked a complete restructuring of the foundering company. In 1998, it again declared Chapter 11 bankruptcy, and its debt load stood at more than $1 billion.[14]

A&P also struggled with its identity during the 1990s, from reinvesting in its small stores, entering markets in the South, to, later in the decade, shuttering the small stores in favor of opening 50,000- to 60,000-square-foot format. It also revamped and streamlined its private-label offerings. A&P both entered and exited the decade posting millions of dollars in losses.[15]

Kings Super Markets was bought by Marks & Spencer, a retailing company based in Great Britain, in the late 1980s. In 1999, the group announced plans to sell Kings, as it no longer fit the company's plans going forward. When Marks & Spencer purchased the chain, Kings had 16 locations; when it announced that it was placing the retail chain on the chopping block, the chain had expanded to 29 locations.[16]

Foodtown rounded out the list of grocers having difficulties during this time. Twin County cooperative supplied the chain, and in 1995, two members with a total of 45 stores sold their chains to Ahold (these became Edwards Super Food Stores), resulting in a loss of more than half of its volume. Two years later, Jon Greenfield left Twin County to join Wakefern/ShopRite, bringing with him two Long Island, New York, stores. In 1998, Twin County co-op declared bankruptcy, and embezzlement charges were filed against its former CEO. Some Foodtown members were able to survive the turmoil through a relationship with White Rose Food, an independent wholesale food distributor.[17]

In addition to the struggles and changes on the retail side, the environment was ripe for changes

Executive Vice President Dean Janeway illustrates to associates the detailed cost of operations at a company forum held in 1992.

in warehousing. Improved and evolving technology tracking systems proved too costly for retailers to implement on their own. Some, like Pathmark, A&P, Grand Union, Edwards, Stop & Shop, and even Walmart (for its stores that carried groceries) began outsourcing to take advantage of cheaper and more efficient services, closing their own warehouses. C&S Wholesale Grocers was the largest wholesaler in the Northeast, and began working with each of these retailers. From 1995 to 1996, the wholesaler saw an incredible 40 percent increase in sales,

allowing retailers to keep prices lower. One business journal claimed that C&S would have to find markets outside the Northeast as it had nowhere else to expand.[18]

Stepping Up to the Plate

Once again Wakefern embarked on a strategic planning process to examine how to best compete with the ever-changing retail landscape. It required detailed examination of the business, from the entire customer offerings to the warehousing operations. The ultimate decision was made to concentrate on the core basics, and the co-op decided to meet customers' growing preferences for fresh, perishable items by upgrading the produce, meat, seafood, dairy/deli, and bakery departments.

The co-op marketed its message through a heavy advertising campaign utilizing print ads,

Above: ShopRite tractors and trailers are shown in 1996 at the rear of the grocery warehouse at the distribution complex in Elizabeth, New Jersey.

Right: As part of an aggressive campaign, ShopRite reintroduced a successful strategy from the 1980s, locking in reduced prices for 60 days, as shown in this Locked-In Savings circular.

Right: In 1990, Wakefern purchased Durling Farms dairy, located in Readington Township, New Jersey. It became Readington Farms, Inc., and helped serve ShopRite's dairy needs.

Below: ShopRite debuted its Price Plus Club card in the early 1990s. It saved the consumer money while allowing the co-op to better track customer shopping segments.

billboards, and radio and TV advertising. The contents of the circulars and other marketing materials were, as always, decided upon by committee, not corporate dictate, and the focus was on price and perishables.[19] Slogans throughout this period included: "We Save You (more) Money! ShopRite Does It Right"; "ShopRite and Always Save"; and "ShopRite Has the Answer."[20]

True to form, Wakefern reacted to new challenges with an aggressive advertising program called "Locked-In Savings." ShopRite would offer certain products at a reduced rate for 60 days, thus "locking in" prices.

"ShopRite was made for those times," stated Joe Sheridan, current executive vice president. "In the face of adversity, Wakefern is at its creative best. While there's no denying it was a tough time for both wholesale and retail, it stretched us beyond our comfort zone and consequently we developed programs that were competitive and attractive to our customer base."

To attract customers—and especially to hold onto them—the company introduced its Price Plus Club card, driven by the "We Save You (more) Money!" theme. The Price Plus program was one of the first of its kind within the supermarket

industry. Armed with the card, for which registration was free, a customer would present it upon checkout and receive instant discounts and savings on hundreds of Price Plus Club items featured in-store, along with special offers and promotions.

As for the benefits to ShopRite, it enabled the co-op "to track every purchase and break down consumer purchasing habits based on a variety of variables, even what time of day the consumer prefers to shop."[21] The card was also important in terms of conveying the message of savings, and while "it may not bring in new customers," it was considered a "powerful customer loyalty weapon."[22]

The early part of the decade also saw a number of critical new warehouse initiatives—part of an aggressive capital improvement program implemented during the battle for market share—totaling more than $100 million. As Wakefern President Jerry Yaguda explained at the time, the development of new warehouse space "is of paramount importance to the co-op's membership … and will give us the facilities we need to adequately service our members for many years when it's complete."[23]

In May 1990, Wakefern began construction on a 735,000-square-foot distribution center, that would service all ShopRite stores. The new warehouse was located on 56 acres in South Brunswick, New Jersey—about 25 miles from Wakefern headquarters in Elizabeth, New Jersey, where the co-op already operated 358,000 square feet of warehouse space to service its stores in New Jersey, Pennsylvania, and Delaware.

The new facility, which became operational in the spring of 1992, had 45,000 square feet of office space; employed about 400 staff members; and featured a state-of-the-art computer inventory system, 1.3 miles of computer-controlled conveyors to allow for maximum storage and distribution control, and a custom system for tracking product movement.[24] The center housed three Wakefern operations that previously were located in Elizabeth: non-foods, HABA, and pharmacy.[25]

Stores located throughout New Jersey, New York, Connecticut, Massachusetts, Delaware, and Pennsylvania benefited from the new central location.[26]

Another Wakefern initiative in the early 1990s involved dairy. In August 1990, Durling Farms, originally a creamery founded in 1888 that grew into a substantial dairy business located in Readington

Township, New Jersey, was purchased by Wakefern and became a wholly owned subsidiary under the new name Readington Farms, Inc. The acquisition allowed ShopRite to produce ShopRite milk and milk by-products, enabling them to stay competitive within those categories as well as enhancing Wakefern's effectiveness in servicing its stores.

In 1991, Wakefern further focused on consumers by implementing its own corporate consumer advisory board and local consumer advisory boards to assist local ShopRites in meeting customer needs. To provide a 360-degree look at customer feedback, Wakefern implemented an annual customer satisfaction process in 1994 that conducted surveys of customers from each Shoprite store. The 20,000 customer satisfaction surveys provided an in-depth evaluation of how satisfied customers were with each department. Armed with this information, store owners and managers could institute necessary improvements and track changes over time. It also provided an across-the-board snapshot that proved useful in decision-making at the Wakefern committee level.

Jim and Perry Sumas, owners of Village Super Market, Inc., opened a new store in English Creek, New Jersey, under the Starn's ShopRite banner. Shown here is the interior of the store, decorated for the grand opening.

JERRY YAGUDA RETIRES

WHEN JEROME "JERRY" D. Yaguda succeeded David Silverberg as Wakefern's president, Yaguda had already been at the co-op for 27 years.

Yaguda first joined the co-op in 1960 as an assistant controller and later served as Wakefern's chief financial officer for years before becoming president and chief operating officer in 1987.[1]

Throughout his career, Yaguda was credited with building two warehouse distribution complexes, the perishables building in Elizabeth, New Jersey, and the general merchandising facility in South Brunswick, New Jersey. He also was responsible for improving the co-op's computerized ordering system and "expanding programs and technologies to improve the service level to the Wakefern membership."[2]

"Jerry's strength was working with people—developing and training them and giving them more authority and responsibility," said Dean Janeway.[3]

In 1995, Yaguda retired, and Janeway became president and chief operating officer. Yaguda continued his ties with Wakefern, acting as a business advisor.

Tom Infusino summed up Yaguda's contributions to the co-op, both professionally and personally, at Wakefern's 50th Anniversary Gala:

For more than 35 years, you have touched the lives of many as a friend, mentor, counselor, and confidant. As a leader, diplomat, and skilled negotiator you have consistently managed to facilitate the critical process of consensus among membership. Your guidance and vigilance has laid the foundation of our financial stability. The scope of your care goes beyond position. Your compassion and humility are authentic. Your unquestionable ethics and morals are a standard against which all should be measured. And your dignity and courage shown through the years continues to serve Wakefern.

Yaguda passed away on December 22, 2009. He was 84 years old.

This process was unique among food retailers in that it could track satisfaction by individual store, and it has been so valuable that it continues to this day.

Further focusing on the customer, Wakefern staff and members went through a rigorous examination of how they could better meet customer needs. They developed a company-wide "Hassle-Free" retail policy, which the Wakefern board adopted at their June 1993 meeting. It included: hassle-free refunds, hassle-free coupons, 100 percent accuracy of price information in scanners, and consistent availability of advertised items. In addition, all advertised sales would clearly state whether an item's quantity had to be limited, or if the sale price applied to only selected varieties or flavors. Further priorities in providing exceptional customer service were also identified, and associates were trained accordingly.

Wakefern benchmarked the ShopRite customer service experience with that of the Disney organization, and held a series of training sessions, culminating with a Wakefern member getaway at Disney World.

Acknowledging the challenges faced by Wakefern, and its response in the form of substantial—and ongoing—capital expenditures, *Progressive Grocer* said of ShopRite: "They are doing fine. They have made substantial strides. They are literally determining what is going on in the [New Jersey] market, their heartland."[27]

Growing from Without and Within

Enhanced warehouse capacity and efficiency weren't Wakefern's only strategies for growth. After a relatively long hiatus, the co-op began actively recruiting new members as a result of a strategic planning initiative in the early 1990s. This initiative was taken not only to expand business but to get back to the founding philosophy of the cooperative. Wakefern added 10 new members at this time, including the Cingari family, in Stamford, Connecticut, in 1991, and Tom Harte in Philadelphia in 1993. In 1995, eight more members joined, including the Collins, Glazier, and Rich McMenamin families in Philadelphia; Mike Larkin in Bethlehem, Pennsylvania; the Miller family in West Chester, Pennsylvania; the Bernie Kenny family in Newark, Delaware; and Charles Shakoor in Old Bridge, New Jersey. These additions would "help fuel the square-footage growth," *Supermarket News* wrote.[28]

Left: Dennis Snow (left) of Walt Disney World's Disney University and Dean Janeway in front of a picture of Walt Disney. Snow was the featured speaker at Wakefern's 1997 annual shareholders' meeting that focused on customer service.

Below: The Cingari family in one of their Connecticut ShopRite stores. From left: Chip, Sam, Joe, Karen, Tom, and Rocky.

The Cingari family of Stamford, Connecticut, exemplify the value of the Wakefern organization to independent operators. As part of the expansion, the co-op had welcomed the Cingaris as members in 1991. The family owned a small chain called Grade A Markets, and opened a new ShopRite store in Grade A ShopRite Plaza, a 120,000-square-foot mall in Norwalk, Connecticut.

Like some of the co-op's founders, the Cingaris were immigrants and became multigenerational store owners. Present-day Wakefern members Sam and Rocco Cingari were introduced to the business through their father, who started in the 1920s by peddling groceries in a small truck outside of Stamford. Brothers Sam and Rocco run the business, with Rocco serving on Wakefern's board of directors.

"We're building a store and getting a permit. One day, a good friend of mine, a real estate man, says ShopRite would like to talk to you about becoming a member," recalled Rocco. "They looked at our operation in the Shippan Avenue store and you might say it was a gift from heaven when they came down."

"We're still in business because we're with Wakefern," Rocco added. "We probably would not

THE SPECIAL OLYMPICS

Wakefern volunteers serve lunch at the 1993 Special Olympics in New Jersey. *(Photograph by Robert Pallesen.)*

WAKEFERN/SHOPRITE HAS BEEN A KEY SUPporter of the New Jersey Special Olympics Summer Games since 1987, and it didn't take long for it to become a welcome tradition for associates and their families. The support of and participation in Special Olympics combines the desire of associates to volunteer and the ability of the organization to meet the needs of the coaches, athletes, and their families during the three-day annual summer event. From Wakefern's inaugural year of support to today, there is great enthusiasm to do whatever is necessary to make the event better for the athletes.

Over the years, Wakefern/ShopRite involvement has grown, with about 600 employees, associates, and members pitching in and volunteering. A small group of associates volunteer to manage the complex logistics for the weekend. Wakefern volunteers staff activity tents and serve the more than 10,000 meals the company donates for the athletes, their families, and coaches.

Athletes continually show their appreciation for the food and other services Wakefern provides. "Thank you, ShopRite" and "ShopRite's the best!" are often heard. A letter from a parent who attended the 1992 event with her daughter says it best:

Our family has ... participated in many functions for many, many years and never have I seen anything like what you did.

You will never know the feelings that both my daughter and I felt when we left the Olympics. I know that many other people felt the same way.

I just wanted to let you know that you all are the BEST![1]

As Wakefern/ShopRite expanded its business into Connecticut, it also supported that state's Special Olympics. Its first year was 1991, and by the next year the co-op donated enough food and drink to provide lunch for 10,000 athletes and volunteers at Southern Connecticut State University and Yale University.[2]

In 2009, Dean Janeway was named one of the honorees at the Special Olympics New Jersey 4th Annual Inspire Greatness Gala.

"Special Olympics New Jersey not only brings great joy to these athletes and their families, but participation in the games provides our associates with an opportunity for camaraderie and generosity that makes me proud to be part of the Wakefern team," said Janeway.[3]

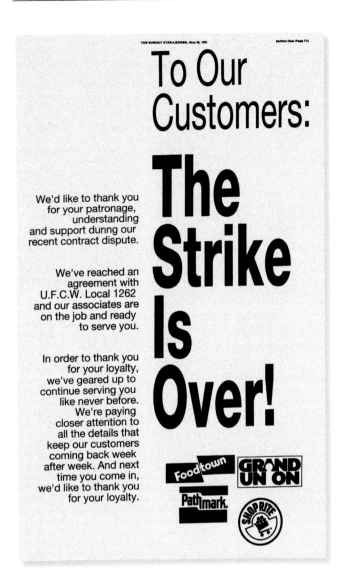

This newspaper ad announced the end of the UFCW strike against New Jersey–area grocers in May 1993 and thanked customers for their understanding and support. *(©1993. The Star-Ledger. All rights reserved. Reprinted with permission.)*

chased 16 of the Hartford, Connecticut–based chain's ShopRites for $30 million.[32] According to *Food Institute Report*, the action was taken in order to avoid the loss of the co-op's wholesale business in that market area.[33]

Continuing its growth, the co-op added more than 700,000 square feet of supermarket space during the two-year period from 1993 to 1995.[34]

The co-op didn't accept just anyone as a new member, however, and never had in the past. "We're willing to talk to anybody [who] expresses an interest in the food business [who has] a good background [and] a good reputation, knows how to run stores, and has a proven record in being successful in running stores," Infusino said, adding that the "door is always open" for potential new members.[35]

Staying at the Forefront of Technology

Keeping up with the latest in technology was something Wakefern did very well, from the implementation in the early 1950s of the rudimentary punch-card machine data-processing system to the sophisticated IBM-based inventory tracking systems of the 1990s.

Wakefern partnered with Valley National Bank to offer ShopRite customers the co-branded ShopRite MasterCard in 1996. Said to be the first supermarket card of its type, it enabled cardholders to obtain rebates of up to 2 percent at ShopRite supermarkets and 1 percent on all other purchases. The rebates were issued as certificates that were redeemable for free merchandise and food at ShopRite supermarkets and pharmacies.[36] During the 1990s, Wakefern adopted the use of computer-generated ordering (CGO), which served to fully automate the stock-replenishing process at most ShopRites throughout the chain.

"[CGO was part of] the first real technology strategic planning," explained Ned Gladstein, chairman of the communications committee, "and that resulted in the implementation of computer-gen-

be able to be in business today, if not for [Wakefern/ShopRite's] buying power, their variety, their credit, and so on. ... Anybody who belonged to Wakefern under the ShopRite label was just doing a tremendous, tremendous business."

With expanded warehouse facilities in Elizabeth; Wallkill, New York; and South Brunswick, the co-op now was able to take on the demands of added distribution.[29] "Wakefern today is in a position where we're looking for membership," Infusino said at the time, noting that for a period of time the co-op did not have the warehouse space needed to support new members.[30]

"It is a possibility that we may acquire other stores from our members, as we did in the case of Mott's Supermarkets if it becomes necessary," Infusino explained.[31] In 1987, Wakefern had pur-

erated ordering, and the implementation of centralized time and attendance."[37]

Wakefern members and the Communications Information Services Division (CISD) were instrumental in getting all the hardware and software in place at each ShopRite store for CGO, working at both corporate and retail levels to ensure a smooth transition. Wakefern associates also provided training at the store level to ensure that ShopRite employees understood how to use the new programs.

The company also introduced electronic data interchange (EDI) and launched extensive computer-based training for its employees.

In 1996, ShopRite stores debuted a powerful new inventory tracking system. *Business Wire* noted that the new system provided ShopRite stores "with a critical extension to their existing wide-area network, consisting of IBM RS/6000 systems, which run the back office systems at each store location."[38]

Another technological effort was the creation of ShopRite Financial Services (SFS). Up to this point, each ShopRite had its own separate accounting, billing, and payroll systems. Because of this there was extensive duplication of efforts as none of the ShopRites could access the Wakefern systems.

"The effective use of technological advances has been a driving force for us," Wakefern President Dean Janeway said, "and it is changing the way we do business."[39]

Unexpected Slowdown Brings Members Together

On May 7, 1993, some 26,000 members of Local 1262 of the UFCW went on strike protesting a change in health benefits, affecting the New Jersey–area grocery businesses, including ShopRite, Grand Union, Foodtown, and Pathmark. The strike lasted 22 days.[40]

The grocery retailers stood together, taking an "all for one" stance, while the union selected certain stores to strike, trying to break the retailers coalition.

"It became known as the 'M&M' strike as it lasted from Mother's Day to Memorial Day," remembered Dewey Cannella, vice president of industrial relations, Wakefern. "The union was adamantly opposed to a change in the status quo. The

[final] contract was a milestone in the history of the industry here in New Jersey. Nonunion was on the precipice of major expansion into the marketplace. The change in health plan benefits enabled ShopRite to continue its leadership as the low-cost leader in our trading area in spite of the onslaught of nonunion stores."[41]

Once again, membership came together to ensure that the stores were stocked and staffed during the worker shortage.[42]

PriceRite Debuts

When Janeway assumed the title of Wakefern president and chief operating officer upon the retirement of 36-year co-op veteran Yaguda on March 1, 1995, he stressed that his goal was not to "shake up the company, but rather to adapt to new challenges without drastically changing course."[43] Janeway, who over a 30-year period worked his way up through the co-op's product divisions, served in procurement and then marketing before becoming an executive vice president.

The new challenges Janeway referred to included the onslaught of warehouse clubs that began to enter the market at the start of the decade. "If you look at mass merchandisers, if you look at drug stores, what are their lead items? Traditionally, grocery items. We've got all of those new people that are trying to take a portion of our dollar and then you've got your traditional competition," Janeway explained.[44]

In addition, the co-op would soon face a wave of supercenters, such as those being opened by Walmart, Target, and Kmart. The Kmart supercenters, for example, were combination full-ser-

The reincarnation of PriceRite as a limited-assortment, deep-discount store in 1995 proved successful. Its mission statement was "Impossibly, Incredibly, Inconceivably Low Prices ... Every Day."

NOT ALL MASTERPIECES CAN BE RECREATED.

With modern technology, most works of art can be reproduced with incredible precision. Amazing as that may be, there's one work that can never be duplicated. The breathtaking beauty of our planet. That's why at ShopRite, being a responsible business, we've been dedicated to preserving our environment for many years and in many ways.

- Created an award-winning "2¢ back" shopping bag reuse program, which has saved, to date, over 60 million bags.

- Recycled over 75,000 tons of cardboard, plus tons of paper, plastic and stretch wrap in the past year.

- Diverted over 7,000 tons of organic waste for composting or for animal feed in 1998. Our efforts were highlighted in an EPA publication.

Our efforts have also been community focused.

- Provided the funding for 500 students to take the Hackensack Riverkeeper's Eco-tour.

- Donated over 800,000 paper handled bags for the Carry In/Out Trash Program at Island Beach, Barnegat Light State Park and Sandy Hook National Recreation Area.

- Donated over 10,000 dune grass plants to restore our beaches.

- Sponsored Clean Ocean Action's Beach Sweeps, which cleaned the beaches along the New Jersey coast.

- Sponsored New Jersey Audubon's World Series of Birding, which is the largest one-day, environmental fund-raiser in the country.

- Partnered with the Conserve Wildlife Foundation of NJ to help make citizens aware of our state's endangered species.

- Proudly supported The Nature Conservancy in their efforts to preserve New Jersey's open space.

Join us in taking the ShopRite Earth Day Challenge. You can help by maintaining your own neighborhood, beach, park, river, playground or school. All you need is the help of your community or organization and we'll provide the supplies (bags, gloves and seeds).

So this Earth Day, accept the ShopRite Earth Day Challenge. Call **1-800-ShopRite** or visit our website at **WWW.SHOPRITE.COM** for more information. Because we all share the responsibility of keeping our planet a masterpiece.

TOGETHER WE CAN MAKE A DIFFERENCE

ShopRite

vice grocery and general merchandise stores ranging in size from 140,000 to 190,000 square feet, carrying between 100,000 and 150,000 stock-keeping units (SKUs).[45] One retailing trade publication explained:

> The supercenter today, clearly, is the format around which the food retailing business turns. ... Supercenters, particularly Wal-Mart's supercenters, are acknowledged as changing the face of food retailing, even by supermarket operators.[46]

Wakefern tried a new tactic in 1995. The co-op opened its first limited-assortment, deep-discount concept store in West Springfield, Massachusetts, previously a Mott's supermarket, and called it—once again—PriceRite.[47] This new format was designed to take on the successful "no-frills operators" that were creeping across North America, such as Aldi, one of the world's largest discount merchandise chains, based in Germany; Food Basics, a no-frills supermarket chain originally created by A&P Canada; and Save-a-Lot, the sixth-largest retail grocery chain under a single banner with more than 1,000 stores in the United States. According to James Sumas, a longtime Wakefern board member whose family owns Village Super Market located in Springfield, New Jersey, PriceRite was based upon the successful Aldi model, but unlike Aldi, included an emphasis on produce.[48]

This new PriceRite was highly successful and built a reputation on its low prices and the freshness of its perishables compared to its competitors, according to Howard Fruchterman, the Wakefern executive heading up the PriceRite operation at the time. Its business model was a money

saver, at least in terms of advertising, which was limited or nonexistent, Fruchterman said. "We do not advertise every week for PriceRite. We do grand opening events, and we'll typically run maybe two or three weeks of circulars."[49]

In subsequent years, four ShopRite locations in Massachusetts and Connecticut that had been closed due to their small size were converted to what became flourishing PriceRites. Additional growth came from former stores of competitors, such as Stop N Shop, Pathmark, A&P, Shaw's, Wegmans, Acme, Tops, Price Chopper, and Latinas. Other ShopRites were converted in market areas where the PriceRite model showed more promise. The stores were located in Pennsylvania, Connecticut, Massachusetts, and Rhode Island.[50]

A major technological shift occurred in 1995 when the board of directors agreed upon the utilization of a single-source front-end computer system. Prior to this new system, Wakefern had to design software to support four entirely different computer applications—necessary to handle the diverse IT demands of various departments—from vendors such as NCR, IBM, Sweda, and others. They operated differently, communicated differently, and had different abilities. This caused considerable duplication of effort,

---

Opposite: As conserving energy and preserving the environment became more important to consumers, Wakefern/ShopRite began taking part by increasing awareness of these issues.

Right: One of Wakefern's Consumer Insight advertorials for 1991 focused on energy conservation. This call for action urged consumers to express their support of a comprehensive energy policy to government officials. (©1991. The Star-Ledger. All rights reserved. Reprinted with permission.)

A Call for Action!
Now's the Time for a Comprehensive Energy Policy

President Bush has called for a comprehensive energy policy focusing on conservation and efficiency, and the increased development, and greater use of alternative fuels. However, the U.S. is still lacking updated measurable national energy goals with specific action plans and time frames for their achievement.

Mandatory fuel efficiency standards set in 1975 have been attained. Now, these standards need to be dramatically increased. Bills have recently been introduced before Congress that are taking important steps in this direction. If enacted, these mean:

- We would save millions of barrels of oil each day.
- Auto makers would develop engines with higher fuel efficiencies to save consumers billions of dollars in fuel costs.
- Earth-warming carbon emissions would dramatically decrease.

The United States uses 60% of its total oil consumption for transportation. Over 50% is oil from foreign countries.

Alternatives such as natural gas, grain fuel, solar and wind power, can lessen our dependence on foreign oil, improve our economy and reduce negative environmental impact as well. For instance, increased use of grain fuel would be a major economic boost to our domestic farming community and the fuel's cleaner emissions will help meet the new, more stringent Federal Clean Air Standards.

Individually, we can show support of a federal energy policy by taking responsibility for our own personal actions and encouraging the cooperation of the federal government as well.
At ShopRite, for example, we saved over 430,000 gallons of fuel in one year by increasing the efficiency of our tractor trailer engines by just 1½ miles per gallon (MPG).

Celebrate Earth Day 1991 by writing the President and your Representatives to support a serious commitment to the research and development of alternative fuels and increasing the mandatory MPG standards for automobiles. Let's show the President and our Representatives that we all support a strong energy policy. Use the forms below to let your voice be heard.

Wakefern was the first private company in New Jersey to experiment with—and use—natural gas as an alternative fuel for its yard switcher and three company vans. Wakefern President Jerry Yaguda (right) and Elizabethtown Gas Company President Robert Kenney are fueling a vehicle at the press event that announced the partnership in 1992.

resulting in lost time and money. According to Gladstein, chairman of the communications committee and president of the West Caldwell and Parsippany, New Jersey, ShopRites:

> *[Because of the different systems], it was impossible for us to have any kind of a customer loyalty card. It was almost impossible, from a practical standpoint, to do any kind of points accumulation programs. Giving out free turkeys and things like that the way we do now just couldn't be done.*
>
> *It was a huge investment on the part of the members to do this, but ultimately, the membership understood the competitive advantage that we would have as a whole. We were able to make it financially possible for members to change out their systems.*

By using a single-source front-end computer, a better system was created that supported the IT needs of everyone at Wakefern. The milestone conversion not only created greater operational efficiencies but also generated competitive advantages especially against the retail chains, and continues today to provide a competitive advantage.

Other improvements at Wakefern occurred in the pharmacy department. While the function of securing and delivering product for the co-op's in-store pharmacies had always been handled in-house, the co-op's supermarket-pharmacy business grew exponentially during the

1990s, and it became more efficient and cost-effective for Wakefern to outsource pharmaceutical warehouse and distribution functions.[51]

Drug Store News explained that supermarkets were becoming "a strong competitor. They may not look like a traditional drugstore, but they certainly operate like one and compete for the same business." A survey for the year showed that out of the nation's top 50 supermarket pharmacy operators, Wakefern ranked 14th, with pharmacy sales of $138 million.[52]

A Greener Co-op

Reacting to concerns in the early 1990s about the deteriorating state of the global environment—and the awareness of corporate environmental responsibility at the co-op—Wakefern formulated a mission statement to guide its actions in the years to come:

> *Wakefern/ShopRite believes in and is committed to assume corporate responsibility for helping solve the problems of the environment that affect our customers, associates, the communities in which we trade, and the nation as a whole.*[53]

The co-op met with national environmental groups such as the National Audubon Society and the National Resources Defense Council, as well as with local organizations such as Clean Ocean Action, Hackensack Riverkeeper, and (Hudson) Riverkeeper. Wakefern was considered an environmental leader in the food industry in the early 1990s. Wakefern also worked with the Food Marketing Institute (FMI), the national trade group for retailers and manufacturers, to raise awareness within the industry that "green initiatives" were going to be an integral part of the industry for years to come. The co-op took a proactive approach, challenging the entire food industry to examine ways to minimize all resources used along the entire food chain.

Starting with the basics, the co-op launched a program in 1991 that encouraged shoppers to reuse their bags—rewarding them with a 2-cent credit. The response was "extraordinary,"[54] with approximately 5.2 million paper bags reused the first year, followed by 6.6 million the following year, and 8 million in 1993. In 1995, a record 8.4 million bags were returned to ShopRite stores for reuse.[55] By 2009, the "bring your bag back" message was thoroughly ingrained with ShopRite customers as an unbelievable 45 million bags were reused.

Plastic shopping bags were collected at Shop-Rites for recycling during this time as well. In response to the nation's overflowing landfills—of which half were projected to close by the end of 1995—Wakefern/ShopRite funded a Municipal Compost Management Course for public officials and company managers responsible for solid waste disposal; supported state solid waste management programs; and made strides in determining how better to dispose of organic waste from ShopRite stores.[56]

In terms of nonorganic solid waste, the company recycled more than 50,000 tons of materials in 1992. This included nearly 50,000 tons of cardboard, 27 tons of computer paper, 235 tons of general files, 425 tons of newspaper, 438 tons of plastic, and 64 tons of metal. In subsequent years, these figures were substantially higher.[57]

Wakefern has garnered recognition from national to local levels for its comprehensive environmental programs and was honored by President George Herbert Walker Bush at the White House during the Thousand Points of Light celebration for the co-op's efforts in cleaning up the New Jersey shoreline.

A believer in the importance of environmental education, Wakefern/ShopRite sponsored various programs for students, as well as the production of a series of videos. The first was a video titled "A Teenager's Guide to Protecting the Planet," which was shown at the Earth Summit in 1992 in Rio de Janeiro. Wakefern also established environmental scholarships at four prestigious universities, including Rutgers and the Massachusetts Institute of Technology.

Wakefern's efforts at environmental education were directed toward company staff, shoppers, and the grocery industry as well. One initiative, created in partnership with Cornell University, was the Waste Reduction through Consumer Education project, which studied product packaging in terms of environmental impact. Another initiative was a home study course for Wakefern/ShopRite staff called "Managers' Guide to Safety and the Retail Environment."

Wakefern was the first private company in New Jersey to experiment with and use natural gas as an

In 1995, as part of Wakefern's environmental initiative, the co-op donated grasses to plant in the dunes at Island Beach State Park. Pictured here are Tim Vogel, environmental affairs administrator, Wakefern (right), and Bill Vibbert, superintendent of Island Beach State Park.

alternative fuel for its yard switcher and three company vans. Electronically controlled engines, allowing for operation at lower revolutions per minute (RPMs), were installed in 12 tractors, along with onboard computers to monitor various aspects of engine performance. In 1993, these measures resulted in a savings of more than 430,000 gallons of diesel fuel.

While use of chlorofluorocarbons (CFCs) in air-conditioning was prohibited in the United States by 1996, Wakefern had already initiated a recycling program in 1993, that prevented the release of CFCs into the air.[58]

"All of these efforts—in stores, offices, and distribution centers—represented the foundation of Wakefern's total commitment to environmental responsibility, which continues today."[59]

The Co-op Turns 50

In 1996, Wakefern celebrated its 50th anniversary. The co-op had come a long way from its humble beginnings in Newark, New Jersey, and so had the many family businesses who had joined throughout those 50 years. In 1946, eight North Jersey men shared a vision of small and independent grocers like themselves successfully competing against large corporate supermarket chains.

"These neighborhood grocers believed that the most effective solution to their common problems was in cooperative

action—in the form of cooperative buying—the pooling of individual efforts for the benefit of all," according to a special "Community Report" commemorating Wakefern's anniversary.[60] Since Wakefern's founding, that concept has proved itself in an extraordinary fashion.

By 1996, there were 36 independent members, many representing second and third generations of Wakefern's early members. They combined to total 185 ShopRite supermarkets in more than 600 communities in New Jersey, New York, Pennsylvania, Connecticut, and Delaware. At the time, Wakefern, together with ShopRite stores, employed more than 35,000 people. Wakefern associates in New Jersey represented the state's second-largest workforce.[61]

Families Serving Families

Infusino believes an important part of the co-op is its connection with the community, which was an invaluable—and inseparable—part of the co-op's first half-century of history. He explained:

We have put our roots down in the communities where we operate. The family operators of ShopRite stores have a special relationship to their neighbors, who are also their customers. It was that way in the beginning. And it will continue that way in the generations to come.[62]

In 1996, Wakefern celebrated its 50th anniversary with a gala event in the Great Hall at the Ellis Island Immigration Museum. The venue was chosen as a tribute to the co-op's members, many of whom came from Europe, or whose families came from Europe, who entered the United States through Ellis Island with the hope of achieving the American Dream. The invitations depicted official paperwork needed to successfully navigate the immigration process.

Wakefern took community support a step further by establishing a business philosophy in 1997 that stated:

We are partners in caring for our neighbors' families, homes, and communities.

The official statement was an outgrowth of the strategic planning process that recognized that throughout Wakefern's history, from raising funds to helping fight polio in the early 1950s, to raising money after the Korean War to help war orphans, to supporting local organizations today, community was always fundamental to the co-op's belief system. Wakefern's commitment to

Above left: Tom Infusino and his wife Estelle at the 50th Anniversary Gala. In addition to Wakefern's 50th anniversary, it was also Infusino's 25th year as CEO of Wakefern, and his 75th birthday.

Above right: Under the gaze of two huge American flags, a testament to the immigrant spirit present in Wakefern/ShopRite, guests at Wakefern's lavish 50th Anniversary Gala were treated to a banquet held in the historical Great Hall at the Ellis Island Immigration Museum.

Right: Wakefern's business philosophy firmly declares their steadfast commitment to community support: "We are partners in caring for our neighbors, families, homes, and communities."

Our Business Philosophy
We are partners in caring for our neighbors' families, homes and communities.

Our Service Priorities
These service priorities are always in action, but following them in priority order helps you make the customer-focused decision every time.

1. Safety – Safe products and practices are always our first concern.
2. Friendliness – Treat your customers and co-workers with courtesy and respect.
3. Presentation – Our product, our people and our place of business must shine all of the time.
4. Efficiency – Do the job the right way the first time. Work smart, but not at the expense of the other three priorities.

the quality of life in each community is stronger than ever, demonstrated by each ShopRite store, member company, and Wakefern.

"Our commitment stems from a philosophy of saying 'yes' when local police, fire, and safety organizations need support," explained Mary Ellen Gowin, who served as vice president of Wakefern's consumer and corporate affairs division. "Partnering with the community, especially to help the hungry through local food banks, was at the heart of our giving."

In 1991, Wakefern piloted a groundbreaking program with the Community FoodBank of New Jersey to raise funds at the store level. By using a front-end, bar-coded coupon, customers could donate directly to the food bank. The program, Check-Out Hunger, was such a success it quickly became a major fundraising tool for food banks across America.

"We had a great relationship with Wakefern, and the co-op led the charge into 'Check-Out Hunger,' a front-end promotion to raise money for the Food-Bank," explained Kitty Schaller, former associate director of the Community FoodBank of New Jersey, now executive director of MANNA Food-Bank in Asheville, North Carolina.

"It eventually involved a total of 14 Second Harvest [now Feeding America] food banks from Delaware to Massachusetts. In its first year alone, it raised more than $200,000, which was then distributed to regional food banks."

The following year, Wakefern became the title sponsor of the ShopRite LPGA (Ladies Professional Golf Association) Classic (formerly known as the Atlantic City Classic). It was the first time that Wakefern/ShopRite had sponsored such an event, and it quickly grew into one of the top LPGA tournaments

over the years. The event was a clear winner for the co-op in that it connected with ShopRite's main customer base, women, and directly benefitted the local philanthropic community.

A Work in Progress

At the time of Wakefern's 50th anniversary, the co-op was serving more than 3 million customers per week in five states. The co-op ranked 14th in the nation among supermarket chains in sales, with

WORDS FROM THE CHAIRMAN

AT WAKEFERN'S 50TH ANNIVERSARY GALA, CHAIRMAN Tom Infusino addressed an audience of more than 1,000, composed of Wakefern members and their families, associates, and the vendor and trade community, as well as one of the co-op's founders, Sam Aidekman.

Here is an excerpt of his speech, given in Ellis Island's Great Hall on May 10, 1996:

We could never have been successful without the help of many people and companies. First among these are our families. many of our operators today grew up going to the store with their fathers—not only to learn about the business or earn extra money, but also to spend time together.

And the wives and mothers often had two or three jobs—raising the children, making a home, and managing the company's finances. Over the years, our families had to make a lot of sacrifices in order for us to grow.

Our vendors have been supportive, even instrumental, in our growth. It was a salesman

from Del Monte who introduced a couple of our founders to each other, and it was Campbell's who first extended us credit.

Our history is filled with stories like this—of others who understood our vision and were willing to take a chance on us. The food industry itself used to be all about chances … wondering if bad weather would destroy certain crops and relying on the seasons to dictate our selection. Today, the food production and distribution system is so advanced that virtually every product is available all year-round. That is an incredible change, and one which we could not have imagined when we were first starting out.

It takes all of these people—the growers, the truckers, the vendors, our associates and families—for us to be able to open our doors each morning, ready to give our customers what they want.

So while we mark our 50th anniversary, we are congratulating each of you as well. Our first 50 years together have been remarkable, and the future holds even more promise.

$4.1 billion in wholesale sales and $5.1 billion in retail sales.

Five distribution centers, totaling more than 2.5 million square feet of warehouse space, stocked more than 36,000 products and were operational around the clock.[63] In 1995, the 185 ShopRite stores (including corporate-owned units) boasted more than 6.1 million square feet of retail space. The co-op's trucking fleet consisted of 400 tractors and 2,000 trailers, which had already logged 21.6 million service miles for the ShopRite network by 1993.[64]

As for products available to shoppers, the co-op had come a long way. The typical produce department in 1952, for example, offered about 50 items— by 1996, this number had more than quadrupled.[65]

Despite the past successes, Wakefern executives and co-op members were well aware of the challenges that lay ahead.

Wakefern President Janeway expanded on this theme: "Across the country today, independent grocers are struggling to survive against the giants of the industry. We offer a dynamic combination—the strength of the ShopRite name, the support of a full line of services, and our buying power. Add to that the business acumen of the independent grocer, an entrepreneur, and you have a format that can compete with anyone."[66]

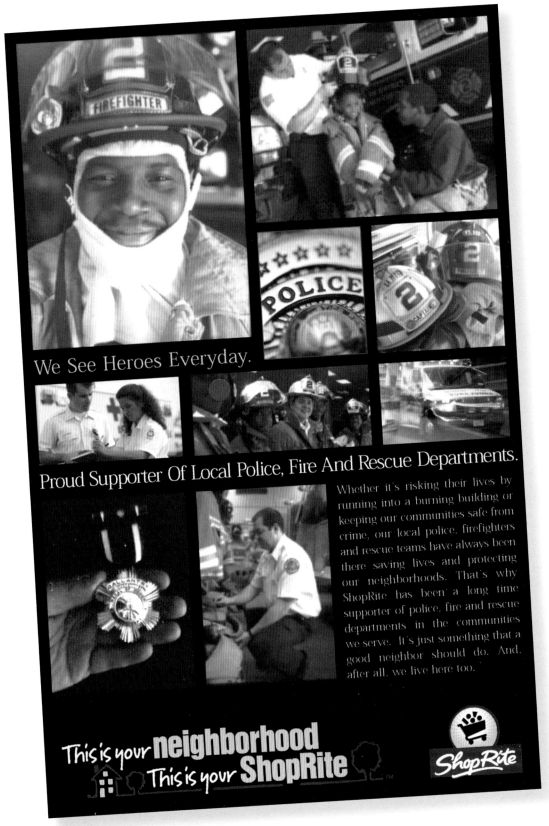

ShopRite continued its traditional philosophy of support for its local communities with its slogan: "This is your neighborhood, This is your ShopRite."

CHAPTER SEVEN

NAVIGATING A NEW ENVIRONMENT

1997–2004

We're about to go through a whole re-rationalization of the marketplace. There's a collapse of traditional supermarket chains. There's an emergence of national global powers ... at a time when the American consumer is probably under more pressure. ... The most principled and sound organizations are going to be the ones that survive this. ... I think that model called Wakefern delivers this.

—Joe Sheridan, Wakefern executive vice president[1]

THE SUPERMARKET INDUSTRY IS ever-evolving. In the mid-to-late 1990s, the demand grew for supermarkets that offered an impressive array of services to allow customers a true one-stop shopping experience. As a South Jersey newspaper observed, "Opening a new supermarket these days is a lot more than slapping brick to mortar and ordering the food."[2]

In-store offerings now covered everything from banking stations, full-service butcher counters, and bakeries, to fresh fish departments, dry cleaning services, and ready-to-eat hot meals. Of course, competitive grocery prices were expected as well. "Having the right mix of products to meet the changing tastes and traditions of our customer base will be key to our future success," Wakefern Chairman and CEO Tom Infusino declared.[3]

Having the right type of stores proved critical as well.

"In a battle for the hearts and wallets of shoppers in one of the nation's most competitive markets, North Jersey supermarket chains are opening cutting-edge stores across the region at a brisk

pace," North Jersey–based newspaper the *Record* reported.[4] From mid-1995 through late 1997, more than a dozen service-oriented, one-stop stores appeared, each offering services to claim the loyalty of time-conscious consumers in the New Jersey counties of Bergen, Passaic, Morris, and Hudson.[5]

To accommodate all the new products and services, the average size of new, one-stop-shopping supermarkets had grown from 40,288 square feet in 1990 to 57,064 square feet in 1998, with some as large as 70,000 square feet.[6] By 2000, some of these stores in Central Jersey—an area whose population had risen approximately 13 percent during the 1990s—had reached the 60,000 to 70,000, and even 100,000-square-foot range.[7]

Some ShopRite store owners opted for expansion over new construction. The advantage of the expansion of existing stores allowed for offering

This ShopRite in Lodi, New Jersey, is owned and operated by Inserra Supermarkets, Inc.

Pennsylvania State Representative Dwight Evans (left) helps Governor Ed Rendell select apples at the opening of the new Parkside ShopRite in West Philadelphia, the first to receive funding under Pennsylvania's Fresh Food Financing Initiative (FFFI) to expand the number of grocery stores in underserved areas. Jeff Brown, Wakefern member and owner of the store, developed the partnership with the state. *(Reprinted here by permission of The Philadelphia Tribune Company, Inc., which reserves all other rights.)*

expanded services to the established customer base without the lengthy, costly zoning processes.

"Sometimes it makes sense to take a good location and make it a much better location [instead of finding a brand-new location]," explained William Sumas, Wakefern member and executive vice president of real estate for Village Supermarkets. "By expanding it, you can offer products you didn't have before. The aisles are wider. Generally, you may get 10 percent to 12 percent more customers. And you're getting that same customer to buy more because now, for example, you have Roquefort cheese five times over."[8]

Both new construction and extensive renovation were aimed at gaining market share in an increasingly competitive region.

With hundreds of items on sale each week, stores needed the expanded selling space to support the ShopRite advertising program.

According to Jim Tracy, vice president of wholesaling, Wakefern provides the stores with three different templates as to what items should be merchandised and when, and it is up to the stores' discretion as to how much of a particular item to place on the shelf.

"For example, if we carry 1,500 different items in frozen food, and this is a smaller store, department managers have to be selective because they physically do not have the room for 1,500," explained Tracy. "A good merchandiser understands how to manage the product mix in order

to meet the complexity of customer needs. It's a challenge."[9]

"Members come in, and sit in on different committees and share best practices," explained Ken Capano, president of Five Star Supermarkets, Inc., and former Wakefern executive. "They talk about how we can improve."[10]

Diverse Communities

While Wakefern's members always had the flexibility of merchandising and advertising toward each community's needs, unlike a chain environment, they took that focus further in the late 1990s when they established a more formal way of identifying the needs of specific ethnicities. Wakefern members marketed toward the changing demographics in their communities, including growing numbers in African-American, Hispanic, Russian, Asian, and Polish communities. The overall results have been successful, creating yet another point of competitive difference for Wakefern.

Jeff Brown, a fourth-generation grocer and owner of ShopRite stores, is an excellent example of providing products to serve his customers' immediate needs. One community he serves comprises a population predominately from Western Africa at his Cheltenham, Pennsylvania, store, where something as basic as the size of the chickens that are sold makes a huge difference in keeping customers satisfied.

Brown added:

We have associates in our company who are tasked with the responsibility to investigate and

Right: The "This is your neighborhood, This is your ShopRite" initiative was another reminder to customers of ShopRite's commitment to the community.

Below: In an effort to develop relationships with ethnic consumers and their communities, ShopRite became an annual sponsor of Unity Day in Philadelphia, beginning in 2001.

understand the uniqueness of the communities we serve. We go to the churches, the synagogues. We talk to community leaders to find out the background of the people that live there, where they are from. We learn about the different cultures. Every [food] item has a story, and until you understand those stories, you can't serve your customers.[11]

According to Irv Glass, the diversity of the member experience just added to the success. Members on the grocery committee represent stores with "different ethnic neighborhoods, different income areas, and different degrees of customer sophistication."[12] By using that knowledge as a resource, all ShopRite customers benefit.

This is Your Neighborhood ...

To continue to nurture a sense of community at each location, and in recognition of each store's support of its community, in 2002 ShopRite launched its "This is your neighborhood, This is your ShopRite" initiative.

"We were looking for a way to communicate ShopRite's long-standing commitment to the community," stated Mary Ellen Gowin, former vice president for consumer and corporate communications. "This concept gave us the platform to accomplish that."

Since many loyal ShopRite shoppers referred to "their ShopRite," the message supported an established customer sentiment. ShopRite's long history of supporting local athletic teams, and organizations such as the Girl Scouts, the Boy Scouts, and the local police, fire, and rescue departments, demonstrated ShopRite's commitment to giving back to its community.

The tagline would appear on trailers, on in-store message boards, and in community-related advertising.

That commitment to its neighbors was demonstrated once again in the wake of the September 11, 2001, attacks. ShopRite immediately lent its support to first responders and volunteers at Ground Zero by delivering a trailer filled with much-needed supplies. Longtime Wakefern associate, Sagaaf Al Sagaaf, drove the truck to the site just a few miles from Wakefern's distribution center. "As I drove closer to the site, I could see the

Remember when neighborhoods were defined by boundaries? On September 11, 2001 all of that changed. Because, suddenly, we realized that we're all members of the same neighborhood. As a nation, we all share the same dreams, and we share the same pain. We all came together as neighbors. We hope the spirit of neighborhood didn't end with a memorial service, but continues to live on in our homes, on our streets and in our hearts.

road was lined with people ... waving flags and signs, many shouting, 'God Bless ShopRite, God Bless America.' People were just unbelievable, grateful and hospitable. I was so proud to be the one to deliver that trailer, I was so proud of Wakefern and will never forget the experience."

Wakefern/ShopRite and its customers raised more than $1 million and established a relief fund to meet both the short- and long-term needs of the disaster. Throughout the many months of work at the site, Wakefern's policy of saying "yes" to all police, fire, and rescue department requests and associate volunteerism was in full force.

New Ventures, New Customers

Wakefern's venture into new territory, literally, with the establishment of retail grocery stores under the PriceRite banner, was becoming a success. These smaller stores offered low prices on limited

---

Opposite, top: The Woodbridge, New Jersey, ShopRite, owned by Wakefern member Saker Supermarkets, Inc., proudly displays the American flag. *(Image courtesy of Insight Photography/Steven Berg.)*

Opposite, bottom left and right: In the aftermath of the September 11, 2001, terrorist attacks, ShopRite showed support for the country via newspaper advertising, billboards, and in-store displays.

Right: In the late 1990s, PriceRite introduced an extensive line of private-label products.

Below: ShopRite from Home, an online shopping program, was introduced in 2002. Customers could submit grocery orders through the Internet and pick them up at a local store.

grocery products and a large selection of produce as their main draw.

PriceRites were located in communities that did not directly compete with ShopRite, and targeted sites beyond the co-op's traditional market area.

PriceRite customers were encouraged to bring their own bags to carry out their groceries. PriceRite also did minimal advertising, in order to maintain its low-cost model. Consumers liked the concept, and by 2004, there were 19 stores with retail sales of more than $300 million.[13]

Another innovation geared toward customer satisfaction was "ShopRite from Home," which launched in 2002 and is still going strong. The online grocery-ordering service allows customers at home to choose from more than 25,000 unique items (compared to the 9,000 to 10,000 items offered by competitors with similar programs) at the same prices it features in its "brick and mortar" stores.

After selecting the items online, shoppers then drive to the ShopRite store, park in a designated spot, and await the arrival of a "personal shopper" who collects the groceries to bring out to their cars.[14]

Turmoil in the New Millennium

The year 2000 marked the beginning of more turmoil for the industry, for reasons unrelated to the panoply of services that elevated the one-stop

GIVING BACK

THROUGH THE YEARS, SHOPRITE HAS been extensively involved in philanthropic events to support its local communities. In 1998, ShopRite was named "New Jersey Corporate Philanthropist of the Year" by the Community Foundation of New Jersey.

Wakefern CEO Tom Infusino and Kathleen DiChiara, executive director of the Community FoodBank of New Jersey, hold a check indicating that more than $1 million has been donated to Partners In Caring, a year-round, community organization founded by ShopRite that fights hunger issues in local communities.

ShopRite Partners In Caring

In 1999, the co-op launched an ambitious community-based, hunger-fighting initiative called ShopRite Partners In Caring. According to America's Second Harvest Network (today known as Feeding America), a nationwide network of food banks, some 25 million low-income Americans face hunger each year.[1] A model for social corporate responsibility, ShopRite Partners In Caring was the co-op's response to this alarming number of Americans who do not get enough to eat.[2]

Although ShopRite had supported the hunger-fighting community for nearly three decades, it decided to create ShopRite Partners In Caring as a means to draw attention to the plight of the hungry not just during the fall holiday season, but all year long. ShopRite Partners In Caring enlisted dozens of food manufacturers (more than 70 by 2009) to promote its role in fighting hunger through advertising, on product shelf labels, in-store signage, and in ShopRite literature.

The first year, the program reached out to more than 500 organizations with more than $1 million in donations. Charities included soup kitchens, homeless shelters, emergency food pantries, childcare centers and after-school programs, battered women's shelters, senior citizen programs, drug rehabilitation centers, and programs for the mentally and physically disabled.[3]

Each ShopRite store selects its own local organizations to support. These food charities use their funds to acquire supplies from food banks.

According to Kathleen DiChiara, executive director of the Community FoodBank of New Jersey, one of the organizations that participates in ShopRite Partners In Caring, "The FoodBank purchases food in bulk, in tractor trailer loads that, because we buy in large quantity, we're able to get at discount, which translates into a significant savings for the charities. The Partners In Caring dollars allow many of the charities to participate in a sort of co-op buying."

Success of the Program

In 1999, America's Second Harvest recognized ShopRite as the "Grocery Distributor of the Year" for its work in the fight against hunger,[4] through the chain's ShopRite Partners In Caring program.

Each year ShopRite Partners in Caring donates thousands of pounds of Thanksgiving turkeys to the food banks in ShopRite operating areas. Wakefern associates volunteering to assist in the distribution at the Community FoodBank of New Jersey are, left to right: Marvis Jackson, Melissa Parascando, Juana DeLaHoz, Kyle Ledford, and Madge McMillan.

By the second year, ShopRite doubled its donation to $2 million—reaching a total of $20 million by 2009—to more than 1,400 charities. Each time a customer purchased products marked with the "ShopRite Partners in Caring" shelf tag, they demonstrated their support for the brands that supported the program. Each ShopRite store had $10,000 earmarked to support its local hunger-fighting charities throughout ShopRite's trading area.

Spreading Awareness

In support of the hunger community, ShopRite created a short documentary titled "Hunger Next Door," which depicted ordinary people and their struggle to feed themselves and their families. The film received awards from the New York Film Festival and was also recognized by the International Association of Business Communicators, receiving the Iris Award of Excelence in 2001.

In 2002, Partners In Caring launched a website, www.shopritepartnersincaring.org, to bring a greater awareness to the issues and provide information to those who wish to help.

For the Future

By 2010, ShopRite Partners In Caring had donated more than $22 million. On its 10th anniversary in 2009, governors in six states declared September 23, 2009, "ShopRite Partners In Caring Day," indicating the scope and reach of the program over the years.

shopping experience. North Jersey's more than $4.3 billion supermarket business was threatened with major changes—including consolidation (considered the wave of the future), as well as increased competition from non-supermarket outlets such as drug stores, warehouse clubs, and natural and organic stores. Five long-established chains—ShopRite, Pathmark, A&P, Grand Union, and Kings—had dominated the North Jersey landscape at the end of 1999. They, along with a relative newcomer, Edwards, accounted for more than 76 percent of supermarket sales in New Jersey's six northernmost counties.[15] By mid-April 2000, there were 204 ShopRite stores (187 ShopRites and 17 alternate formats[16]), and with 34,700 workers, ShopRite was the state's largest private employer. Pathmark and A&P ranked among the Top 10 in the New Jersey Business and Industry Association's annual survey. ShopRite's technology, merchandising, and marketing strategies had defined its position in the industry.

"They have a very clearly defined market position, which is price. ... They are brutal, brutal price competitors. ... ShopRite is relentless; it's not going to lose market share," reported the *Record.*[17]

However, this was no longer so certain.

A Defining Event

On November 22, 2000, the co-op's largest member, representing 14 percent of its volume, Big V Supermarkets, Inc., voluntarily filed for

reorganization under Chapter 11 of the U.S. Bankruptcy Code. Headquartered in Florida, New York, Big V had been acquired by Boston-based private equity firm Thomas H. Lee Partners in 1991 from First Boston. William Rosenberg founded Big V in 1942 and sold the family-owned company to First Boston in 1987.

Big V claimed its bankruptcy filing was needed to reduce costs for the 27-store chain, enhance liquidity, and build a foundation for future growth. The reorganization plan did not end there.

"But the big news," *Business Wire* reported, "is its intention to break ranks with Wakefern/ShopRite," of which Big V had been a member for 40 years.[18] Big V's plan would include closing seven stores and exiting the co-op, reopening its stores under its own name, and using C&S Wholesale Grocers, Inc. as its distributor.[19]

According to Big V, its departure from Wakefern was expected to result in "substantial annual cost savings [for the retailer], while providing Big V additional flexibility."[20]

The decision to declare bankruptcy followed Big V's unsuccessful attempt in 1999 to sell to Royal Ahold NV, a Dutch supermarket conglomerate that operated Stop & Shop stores in the United States. That deal had fallen through because of stipulations in the Wakefern stockholders' agreement that would have required Big V to make a withdrawal payment to the cooperative. Big V's Chapter 11 filing was a calculated move to avoid the stipulations of Wakefern's bylaws.

"This provision was put in place for exactly this reason—to protect the interests of the membership at large," said Wakefern President Dean Janeway.

The agreement would require Big V to pay the equivalent of 10 years of profits that Wakefern would have otherwise realized had Big V's volume remained in the co-op. Key to Big V's successful reorganization was the belief that its Wakefern stockholders' agreement, particularly this provision, would be waived in bankruptcy.

It was clear that Big V's departure would be a severe blow to the co-op. Wakefern Chairman and CEO Tom Infusino pinpointed the heart of the matter, explaining: "What we are defending here is our cooperative structure."[21]

On November 30, 2000, Wakefern sued Big V and sought an injunction and damages against C&S Wholesale Grocers, Inc., which had signed a supply agreement with Big V.[22] The lawsuit dragged on for 19 months.

Wakefern Wins Lawsuit

On August 9, 2001, after a two-week trial, a U.S. Bankruptcy Court judge in Trenton, New Jersey, ruled in favor of Wakefern. The court also ruled against Big V's attempt to seek a declaratory judgment, that would permit Big V to leave Wakefern "without compensating the cooperative for volume that would be lost because of its withdrawal." The judge ruled that Big V's move to leave the co-op for a new supplier, C&S Wholesale Grocers, was "one step in a series of transactions" leading to Big V's sale, and that under the Wakefern stockholders' agreement, Big V would incur "withdrawal liability in the event of a sale in a single transaction or a series of transactions."[23] Judge Raymond T. Lyons noted in his decision:

Big V has known from day one that its departure, coupled with its nonpayment of the fee, would jeopardize the economic stability of the cooperative. It would breach the implied covenant of good faith and fair dealings if Big V were to depart Wakefern as proposed without the withdrawal payment.

Accordingly, the judge required Big V to pay Wakefern a multimillion-dollar withdrawal payment, which Wakefern estimated at more than $280 million.[24]

This high figure, according to Jim Watson, general counsel for Wakefern, made it impossible for Big V to accomplish its goals via the bankruptcy.

"Delighted" with the court's ruling, Wakefern Chairman Tom Infusino maintained that "Big V sought to leave the cooperative and avoid making the withdrawal payment despite the benefits of membership in Wakefern that enabled Big V to grow from a single store to a 32-store chain."[25] Wakefern President Dean Janeway noted that the co-op's success depended upon "continued high volume purchases from a committed membership base," adding that the judge's ruling "upholds our way of doing business, and we look forward to the continued growth and success of our members under the ShopRite banner."[26]

Big V Saga Concludes

On May 3, 2002, Wakefern entered into an agreement with Big V Supermarkets to purchase the chain. On June 27, 2002, the U.S. Bankruptcy Court for the District of Delaware approved the reorganization plan, which called for the acquisition of virtually all of Big V's assets, including the 27 stores, by Wakefern subsidiary ShopRite Supermarkets, Inc. (SRS).[27]

On July 12, 2002, Wakefern closed on the purchase for approximately $185 million in cash and assumed liabilities.[28] According to Infusino, the

Wakefern continued to expand its warehouse space to ensure it could support its growing membership.

acquisition would "ensure the future of our cooperative and will strengthen our position as the leading supermarket retailer in the region."[29] The resolution of the Big V lawsuit and the acquisition of the 27 stores, now under the SRS umbrella, made SRS one of the largest chains in the Wakefern cooperative, with 35 stores in total. The Big V struggle represented something more for the co-op. "That was the last defining lawsuit," Wakefern Executive Vice President Joe Sheridan said. The Wakefern stockholders' agreement had withstood the challenge, ensuring its validity into the future.

A Change in the Landscape

While the legal battle was being waged with Big V, the co-op continued to track its primary competitors. By 2001, Pathmark had gone in and out of U.S. Bankruptcy Court, and its long-term fate remained uncertain. A deal forged in 1999 with Royal Ahold NV, in which the Dutch supermarket giant planned to purchase Pathmark for $1.75 billion, fell apart. Reportedly, the Federal Trade Commission felt the buyout would weaken competitors because many Pathmark stores were close to Ahold-owned Edwards Super Foods Stores. "Even so, Pathmark is seen as a prime candidate for acquisition by a large national chain," according to the *Record*.[30]

Then there was Grand Union, which had entered into bankruptcy and disappeared; Kings, which for the second time was on the selling block; A&P, which was busy redefining itself; and Stop & Shop, which had grown dramatically.[31]

JOE SHERIDAN: A DIVERSE CAREER

JOE SHERIDAN BEGAN HIS CAREER AT WAKEFERN IN 1976, when he worked as a selector in the nonfood warehouse, pulling product from pick slots and building pallets to fill orders shipped to retail stores.

Just a year later, Sheridan joined the inventory control staff as an inventory clerk. Although Sheridan's pay dropped from $300 a week to $145 a week, he took the job thinking that it was an investment in his future. It was also a time of great change in the industry. "We were moving from a paper-based card system into a computer-based system," he explained.

Having earned his B.S. in management science from Kean University in Union, New Jersey, he moved into the accounting department as a junior accountant, where aside from working in payables, he was also exposed to the buying side of the business by matching up invoices to purchase orders. If there was a discrepancy between the documents, Sheridan would have to speak with the buyer directly to rectify the error. He took part in the "Leaders-in-Training Program"—known then as the "Management Training Program"—during its 1979–1980 cycle, and when a buyer in the nonfoods division left for a job in another division, Sheridan applied for the opening. He was given the position, and in 1980, moved into the grocery division.

Wakefern's tradition of allowing employees to grow and develop was apparent when Sheridan was fortunate enough to work with Jimmy Sumas in grocery. He explained Sumas' ability to guide others by allowing them to learn by making mistakes:

I had a deal with Lucky Leaf Apple Sauce, 25 ounces at 58 cents, and [at the committee meeting] I said, "The deal cost is 32 cents." Jimmy Sumas looked up and asked, "Are you sure, kid?" I said "Yes." He said, "Then buy 25,000 cases." Now I'm thinking, great, I'm a

A survey by *Modern Grocer* named ShopRite as the leader in the Northeast market area, but it came with several caveats, according to the *Record*.[32] The survey did not take into account Braintree, Massachusetts–based Stop & Shop's entry into the North Jersey market. Composed of former Edwards stores and the majority of former Grand Union stores—and backed by powerful Royal Ahold NV of the Netherlands, which had nearly bought Pathmark—this new chain promised to soon make its presence known in ShopRite's market.

Foodtown, based in Avenel, New Jersey (a cooperative similar to Wakefern/ShopRite in that it is independently owned and operated by members) was also affected during this time.[33] Two major owners (Melmarkets, Inc. and Mayfair Supermarkets, Inc.) in the Foodtown chain, a northeastern super-

market chain founded in 1955 by Twin County Grocers, Inc., sold their units in the mid-1990s to Edwards Super Food Stores. This quickly set up Edwards with some 60 stores in the New Jersey and Long Island markets, and weakened Foodtown—until its comeback in the late 1990s. C&S Wholesale Grocers, Inc., had become the de facto supplier to almost all the chains. Even the wholesaling industry had been affected.

"We've seen the number of distribution centers really diminishing, consolidating over time. Some very major companies are going out of business," said Tom Zaucha, president and CEO of the National Grocers Association.[34]

During the late 1990s and early 2000s, the major growth the co-op experienced brought the total number of members in 2004 to 42. A few of

---

player, they'll know my name. I go downstairs, look at the deal sheet, and realize I had used a different packing sheet. It was really 42 cents.

The following week, I go back up and say, "I'd like to represent this with the correct cost this time." Jimmy looked at me and said, "I knew it, kid. It's two for a dollar." He moved on, didn't drill me, which I thought was pretty cool. But he allowed it to play out, knowing that I had to come back. … Our best members and our best managers are really teachers.

Over the years, Sheridan held many positions at Wakefern, including advertising manager, procurement manager of grocery, president of direct store delivery and commercial bakery, and senior vice president of marketing. The real turning point in his career was the turnaround of the South Brunswick warehouse. Sheridan launched the Health And Beauty Aid (HABA) program and supported a total changeover in staff. He walked the floor every day to talk with the employees and build a sense of respect among them.

"You go out and talk to people and treat them with dignity, then they respond to you with dignity," said Sheridan.

In 1991 he was promoted to vice president of direct store delivery and the following year to vice president of general merchandise. He was named senior vice president of marketing in 1994.

In 1996, Sheridan was elected executive vice president of Wakefern Food Corp. and became responsible for all 28 operating divisions of the co-op. In this role, Sheridan is responsible for and oversees the marketing, corporate merchandising and advertising, quality assurance, consumer and corporate communications, warehousing and transportation divisions, as well as all of Wakefern's product divisions.

Sheridan serves on the board of governors for the National Grocers Association and the Food Marketing Institute's wholesale advisory board and executive committee. He was also named the 2009 Marketer of the Year by *Supermarket News* and serves as a member of the Embrace Kids Foundation board of directors.

the new members were former executives in Wakefern's headquarters, others were from competing supermarket chains, and one came from the manufacturing side of the industry. Family businesses that joined included:

- 1997—Donald Drust, Sr., Karl Eickhoff, Jon Greenfield, Gary Hoos, Harry Janson, and Robert Kinsley.
- 1998—Sam Chapman and Mark Laurenti.
- 1999—Tony Smutko and Rich Cohen.
- 2000—Larry Ammons and Jim Colligas.
- 2003—Susan Buonadonna.
- 2004—Rafael Cuellar and Harry Garafalo.

In 1997 two longtime Wakefern board members —Dorothy Druian and Larry Inserra—retired. Druian is the only woman to have served on Wakefern's board. She and her husband Louis opened their first market in 1948 in Bloomfield, New Jersey, and joined Wakefern in 1952. Inserra joined Wakefern in 1954 and served on the board as an officer for many years. Today his company has grown to include 17 ShopRites in northern New Jersey and New York.

By 2001, the membership owned 192 stores operating under the ShopRite banner,[35] and by 2004, there were more than 200.

"The way the co-op continues to do business is attractive to existing and new members," according to the *Star-Ledger*.[36]

The newspaper noted some of the more salient benefits that had made membership in the co-op

Dorothy Druian (left) and Larry Inserra (right) retired at Wakefern's 1997 annual meeting.

so valuable since the company was established. Wakefern co-op's founding principle, set forth in 1946, was still upheld: the combined purchasing power of members gave them the buying clout to successfully compete against much larger chains and grow their own store or chain of stores under the ShopRite banner.

Logo and Branding

Because the numerous members used the ShopRite logo in different ways, it became increasingly important for the retailer to create a consistent, standardized look. In 1999, the Wakefern board of directors approved a motion that all exterior and building use of the logo and trade name had to be approved. They also noted that all signage containing the logo and trade name, as well as all informational signs, needed to comply with a set of graphics standards. If ShopRite owners chose to use individual advertising for their stores—either print or electronic— all materials would also have to adhere to a set standard that would reflect positively on all member stores.

The new standard also extended to the word usage permitted in the advertising materials of individual stores. For example, member stores could no longer claim that a product or service was offered "exclusively at" or "available only" at a specific store or group of stores.

This streamlining of the use of the logo and trademark name was just the beginning of a concerted effort to bring together the growing number of retail stores. Wakefern used two kinds of advertising: event and brand-building. Event advertising was used to create a sense of urgency, such as for an upcoming Can Can sale: "It's happening now ... come and get it!" Brand-building advertising promoted the ShopRite brand image. "We knew we had a strong price image, but you want to stand for something beyond price," said William Crombie, vice president of merchandising.

In 2002, the ShopRite logo was redesigned and updated—the last time the logo had been changed was in 1974. The company also rolled out a new brand marketing plan for its 3,000 ShopRite private-label items. These were crucial elements needed to compete in what had become

a cluttered and chaotic environment, and a new look was long overdue.

"Our new logo is more contemporary and a reflection of the changes in our customers' tastes and preferences," said Infusino.[37]

The rebranding would also reinvigorate the connection that customers had to ShopRite private-label products, reinforcing brand loyalty, which ultimately would result in increased sales. At the time, ShopRite private-label products accounted for close to 17 percent of total sales. After the majority of the new items were stocked in the stores, ShopRite launched a tremendous ad campaign to introduce its new look.

More Improvements

In addition to continuing to attract and retain new members throughout the late 1990s and early 2000s, Wakefern kept pace with technological advances and consumer-centric programs. In 1998, after a successful pilot program in Zone 2, ShopRite implemented a 1-800-ShopRite customer service phone line. The line was dedicated to answering consumer questions and concerns, such as whether there were any additives in specific products, and the nutritional breakdown of certain foods, as well as reporting complaints and answering questions about specific store operations.

In 2005, Wakefern brought 1-800-ShopRite in-house, establishing an on-site Customer Care Center to respond more quickly to customer concerns. They set an industry standard for customer service by establishing a protocol to call customers alerting them to a Class I safety recall of a product they purchased using their Price Plus card. Due to technological advances, Price Plus data could be mined to identify customers who had purchased products on recall, alerting them to the potential hazard. The first time the practice was utilized was in the recall of baby pacifiers that represented a choking hazard. "Customers who had purchased this product were so grateful we took the time to alert them to this potentially dangerous problem," reported Cheryl Macik, Wakefern's director of Consumer Affairs. Today, additional services of the Customer Care Center, 1-800-ShopRite, include access to the corporate dietitian, identifying lost keys and returning

Above: In 2002, ShopRite's logo was revamped to remain relevant in a competitive industry, but always kept to the tradition of providing customers what they need. The logo to the left is from 1974, the last year it had been modified.

Left: The 1-800-ShopRite customer service phone line was introduced in the late 1990s to help answer customer questions and concerns about products, ingredients, and nutrition, as well as store-level operations.

them to their owners; and "Chefs on Call," a seasonal customer hotline staffed by ShopRite Culinary Workshop chefs to answer food preparation questions at Thanksgiving. Over 250,000 customers utilize the service each year.

A major technological shift and organizational change came with the development of ShopRite Financial Services (SFS). While the Wakefern Board had approved the formation of the ShopRite Financial Services division in the mid-1990s, it took several years to convert all members to new procedures that would revolutionize their back office operations. Up to this point, each ShopRite had its own separate accounting, billing, and payroll systems. Because of this, there was extensive duplication of efforts as none of the ShopRites could access the Wakefern financial systems.

Now there was an effort throughout the co-op to focus on gaining greater accounting efficiencies between retail stores and Wakefern. The systems were streamlined, with a number of functions consolidated. While the advantages of such a move were obvious, it represented a major change in the autonomy of management of this vital function.

Some embraced the move enthusiastically; others were extremely hesitant.

It took several years to implement, and members eventually came to see that the "freedom" they were relinquishing was in fact simply an extension of the Wakefern philosophy, as they were all contributing to the greater good of the organization. The new technology enabled them to save time and create a single system that could achieve economies of scale.

"SFS provides an invaluable service: ... quality and timely financial information, and a top-notch professional accounting staff, at a reasonable cost," explained Wakefern member Harry Garafalo. "Overall it is cost-effective—it allows us to save by limiting the outside services needed to run the business."

"The philosophy of Wakefern [from a technological standpoint] is that they are cutting edge. They have never been followers. They've never been 'me toos.' They've always looked at what is out there that could put them in front of the curve. Others may catch up. Others may duplicate. But Wakefern will always strive to be ahead of the curve," said Tom

WAKEFERN'S "TRAINING" OFFERINGS SUCCESSFUL

WHEN WAKEFERN TEAMED UP IN 2000 WITH New Community Corporation (NCC), a Newark-based social services agency, to provide job training, life skills, and job placement skills to Newark residents on public assistance, the result was the "Partners In Training."

The partnership between Wakefern and NCC—the largest community development organization in the United States—is designed as a training, education, and employment program. The objective of the four-week course is to move individuals off welfare and into jobs in ShopRite supermarkets.

Wakefern transformed a training facility in Newark, New Jersey, into a classroom, simulating a ShopRite supermarket, complete with non-perishable groceries. In 2009, Wakefern refurbished the training facility, where program participants receive cashiering, customer service, and job readiness training. Students must master the hands-on aspects of training as well as 14 computer work modules.

Monsignor William J. Linder, NCC founder and CEO, said: "Our partnership with Wakefern enables New Community Corporation to continue its important work in the commu-

Zaucha, president and CEO of the National Grocers Association (NGA).[38]

Looming Challenges

But there was always competition in an industry driven by change, consolidation, and the rapid emergence of non-supermarket outlets in the North Jersey market.[39] In addition, the retailer faced yet another strike.

Members of United Food and Commercial Workers (UFCW) Local 1360 began striking on September 6, 2001, after union leadership had recommended its members reject ShopRite's wage and benefit proposal, deeming it "inadequate."

Ten ShopRites in the New Jersey counties of Burlington, Camden, and Gloucester were affected. Wakefern/ShopRite members and associates once again showed determination, dedication, and loyalty in helping the struck stores survive the ordeal and worked to make sure they were back in business as soon as possible after the strike.[40] The strike ended October 21, 2001, after seven weeks.

Competitors were also fighting hard to overtake Wakefern/ShopRite's success. Following a tour of Wakefern's 45-acre Elizabeth, New Jersey, warehouse complex, one newspaper reported that although these were challenging times at Wakefern, "you'd never know it by talking to its executives."[41]

Wakefern remained steadfast in its resolve and continued to bolster its ranks with enthusiasm and determination. The confidence that Wakefern executives exuded was supported by comments from ShopRite members about their own businesses.

"We were born and raised in central New Jersey. ... We know this market inside and out," said fourth-generation co-op member Richard Saker, president, CEO, and chairman of the board of Saker ShopRites (formerly Foodarama Supermarkets). "We know our customer inside and out because we've been servicing [them] for years and years. That level of focus, combined with the economics that being part of a co-op can afford you, makes you a very, very tough competitor."[42]

The co-op's formula for success lay in what became known as "The Wakefern Dynamic Equation": a $7 billion cooperative (in 2001) plus

nity, empowering individuals to work toward a brighter future."

The program expanded beyond New Jersey, as Wakefern/ShopRite partnered with Goodwill Industries in Delaware and then with ABO Haven in Philadelphia.

By 2010, more than 1,475 men and women were on their way to becoming more financially independent, having been hired as cashiers in 17 ShopRites in New Jersey and Delaware, and 157 students were hired by Philadelphia area ShopRites. The effort was deemed so effective that the Food Marketing Institute awarded Partners in Training its 2006 "Maximizing People Potential Award."

Leaders-in-Training: Building Talent from Within

While Partners in Training focused on supporting the retail needs of the co-op, the Leaders-in-Training Program addressed the need to train and ready leaders in the Wakefern wholesale organization.

Now more than 30 years in existence, Leaders-in-Training is a comprehensive 12-month program that, according to a co-op publication, "provides a way for Wakefern to bring in talented individuals with an interest in business and prepare them to become future leaders in the company." Trainees can choose a marketing, logistics, or support services career track to learn how the company works.

Ernie Bell, former vice president of Human Resources and Corporate Planning, explained that the program places talented individuals in "learning assignments that increase their business knowledge while providing real benefits to the company in terms of productivity and creativity." The program provides an open environment, in retail and corporate, which allows trainees to learn from supervisors and each other.

the professionalism of Wakefern's staff plus the entrepreneurial spirit of its members equals the ability to compete, grow, and prosper.[43]

More good news came in December 2002, when the editors of *Chain Store Age* and other trade publications conducted a survey to find out how shoppers ranked the "human values and business practices" of retailers, including which chains best satisfied their standards and why.[44] Wakefern took top honors. The reason? According to the *Record*, "... members of the co-op are entrepreneurs who push their respective enterprises toward operational excellence."

That meant continuing to hone their competitive edge. In November 1999, growth in the perishables division through the year 2004 indicated that the present perishables warehouse operation in Elizabeth, New Jersey, would be unable to service all the perishable needs of the co-op's stores. A recommendation was made to construct a single facility to house dairy-deli, food service, meats, and in-store bakery, and to increase transportation needs to support the volume.[45] By April 2000, the cost of the new facility, to be located in Keasbey, New Jersey, had been projected at $65.8 million.[46]

Consumer Improvements

In 1998, working with the National Center for Missing & Exploited Children, ShopRite implemented "Code Adam," a protocol to help find children who become lost or separated from their parents in all ShopRite stores. Wakefern/ShopRite was the first supermarket in the northeast to implement the protocol and offered its own training videos free of charge to any company that wanted to train its own employees.

Wakefern/ShopRite also was named in the joint resolution statement of June 25, 1999, in which the New Jersey State Senate and General Assembly recognized the importance of the program and commended those stores who participated. ShopRite was the only grocery retailer named.[47] New Jersey was the first state to legislate the use of this protocol in retail establishments.[48]

In 2003, another major step was taken to increase the safety of both customers and Wakefern associates when the company began installing automated external defibrillators (AEDs) in ShopRite supermarkets. In 2000, Wakefern began using AEDs in its warehouses. ShopRite employees were able to save the lives of five people with the use of

Above left: ShopRite began using a program called "Code Adam" in 1998 to locate lost children in its stores. The program, developed by the National Center for Missing & Exploited Children, is named for six-year-old Adam Walsh, who was kidnapped from a shopping mall and murdered in 1981.

Right: Russ Lefkus, supervisor, and John McHugh, senior supervisor, loss prevention, are shown here with a variety of safety and security equipment that is kept on hand at all Wakefern locations.

AEDs during the first two years. A total of 2,200 retail employees and 260 warehouse employees were certified to operate the AEDs.

Wakefern's initiative was significant, according to the U.S. Occupational Health and Safety Administration (OSHA), which stated that in 2002 only 6 percent of workplaces in the United States were equipped with AEDs, and only 16 percent of un-equipped sites had plans to acquire them.[49] "We realized early on that proximity to the machines is very important," said David Sylvester, vice president of loss prevention. "The national average is 40 percent saved, and we're batting a thousand," he added, referring to ShopRite's perfect success rate with the new machines.[50]

Moving Forward

By the end of 2004, ShopRite's 200 stores posted sales of more than $8 billion, and PriceRite was becoming successful in its own market, with sales of more than $300 million.[51]

Despite the initial turbulence that the turn of the century brought, Wakefern prevailed—as it had in the past—remaining the dominant force supporting the Northeastern U.S. supermarket industry.

Wakefern truck drivers are dedicated to providing safe and on-time delivery to co-op member stores.

CHAPTER EIGHT

CONTINUING SUCCESS

2005 AND BEYOND

We help small businesses succeed in a big business world.

—Wakefern Food Corporation Mission Statement[1]

B Y THE MID-2000S, WAKEFERN virtually defined co-op supermarket retailing. Record retail sales of $9.2 billion were reported for fiscal year 2005, by which time the company was composed of 43 member-owners, all under the ShopRite banner. The territory spanned parts of New Jersey, New York, Connecticut, Pennsylvania, and Delaware. The nearly 200 ShopRite stores employed 40,0000 associates among them.[2]

"With their roots in mom-and-pop stores, most of ShopRite's locations remain family-owned, with many run by second, third, and fourth generations," wrote *Progressive Grocer*. "Together with a few dozen corporate-run units, the co-op is known for legendarily high per-square-foot sales ratios."[3]

Market Forecast

The forecast for supermarkets in 2005 was daunting. The grocery business had become more volatile than ever, and more mergers were expected.[4] One trade journal divided the nation's top supermarkets into three categories: achievers, strivers, and architects. The achievers were described as "food retailers that wield power in their corners of the industry, that broke new ground in 2004, and that are likely to make news again in 2005," and included Albertsons, Inc., Price Chopper, and Safeway, Inc.[5]

The strivers were companies facing "acute challenges." This year could decide the fate of these companies, including Ahold, A&P (both of which were seen as on the road to recovery after suffering setbacks), and ShopRite's adversary Pathmark Stores, Inc.[6] Pathmark, based in Carteret, New Jersey, had been enduring difficulties during the previous two decades.

Then there were the architects, the "big guns" who "… set the standards for retailing and whose moves will have rippled effects across the field."[7] Included in this group were Aldi, Costco Wholesale Corp., Fiesta Mart, Inc., Kroger Company, IGA, Publix Super Markets, Wal-Mart Stores, Wegmans Food Markets, Whole Foods Market, and ShopRite, among others.[8]

Co-op's Largest Grocery Warehouse

To prepare the company for future growth and to address the needs of co-op members in southern New Jersey, Pennsylvania, and Delaware, Wakefern

---

The contemporary ShopRite brand is a powerful competitive tool. Sponsoring the Food Network New York City Wine & Food Festival's Grand Tasting aligns the brand with a high-profile event in a major market.

built a new distribution center. Begun in March 2005, the more than 1 million–square-foot facility in Breinigsville, Pennsylvania, was scheduled to open in late summer.[9]

Dubbed "Grocery West," the facility opened on August 24, 2005. It was able to stock in excess of 4 million cases of inventory, had 240 shipping and receiving doors, and was equal in size to 17 football fields. Grocery West was the co-op's largest grocery warehouse and replaced the Wallkill, New York facil-

ity, which had shut down after 20 years of operation.[10] Grocery West served ShopRites in Pennsylvania, Delaware, New York, and southern New Jersey, as well as four PriceRite stores. Grocery Elizabeth of New Jersey continued to serve ShopRite stores in central and northern New Jersey as well as New York and Connecticut.

"[Grocery West made it possible] to have the full line of grocery products housed under one roof," said Pete Rolandelli, vice president of logistics, Wakefern. "Our ability to stock, ship, and receive products more timely and accurately and the proximity to some of our major vendors will greatly enhance our service to the stores and ultimately our customers."

The facility operated under a "no locks, no clocks" schedule, running three shifts, seven days a week, 24 hours a day.[11]

Infusino Retires

On May 19, 2005, at the company's annual shareholders' meeting, Thomas P. Infusino officially retired from his position as chairman. He was Wakefern Food Corp.'s chairman and CEO for almost 35 years, and a co-op member for more than 50. He remained on the 22-member board of directors and active in the running of his own company, the ShopRite of Nutley Park. "I plan to continue doing what I'm doing," Infusino said, "until they throw me out."[12]

"After much consideration, I have decided that it's time for me to pass the leadership of Wakefern to the next generation," Infusino said.[13] He handed the reins to Joseph Colalillo, who had served as Wakefern's vice chairman for six years. A board member since 1989, Colalillo owned three ShopRite stores in Hunterdon County, New Jersey. Colalillo, whose late father joined the co-op in 1954, served as vice chairman of the Food Marketing Institute, an advocacy resource for its 1,500 food retailer and wholesaler members worldwide.[14] He also chaired the Food Marketing Institute's Independent Operator Advisory Board and served on the finance and long-range planning committees.[15]

Infusino had begun his career in the 1940s working for two of Wakefern's founding members, Al and Ben Aidekman, and was the first member to serve under the title of "chairman and CEO."[16] For many years the position held the title of "president" but Infusino recognized that would need to change. In order to get things done, he needed the clout of the title "chairman and CEO."

As Dean Janeway, Wakefern president and chief operating officer, noted at Wakefern's May 18, 2006, annual meeting, attended by more than 600 Wakefern executives, members, and store managers, "[Tom's] passion for growing and strengthening Wakefern has never wavered."[17] During Infusino's leadership, ShopRite retail sales grew from about $747 million, in 1971, to more than $8 billion in 2004.[18]

The Co-op Turns 60

Soon after Colalillo was elected chairman, he posed a provocative question to the Wakefern board: "Do you want to perpetuate this co-op?" The answer

Former U.S. Senator and Senate Majority Leader Bob Dole was the featured speaker at Wakefern CEO and Chairman Tom Infusino's recognition dinner in 2005 marking his retirement as chairman and CEO.

of course, was a resounding "yes," with a proviso that issues commensurate with the company turning 60 needed to be addressed.

"ShopRite is celebrating 60 proud years of families serving families," said Janeway. "Anniversaries are a great time to take stock of who we are, what we have accomplished, and what lies ahead."[19]

Colalillo spoke to the crowd assembled in Whippany, New Jersey: "Let's agree to be an exceptional steward of the legacy we have been given; to preserve and expand this co-op for the next generation; to make the next 60 years of ShopRite as successful as the first."[20]

At the 2006 annual meeting, Dominick V. Romano, a 36-year company veteran, retired from the board of directors.

"Through the years, Dominick has always been a mentor to me, and I know I can speak on behalf of the entire Wakefern membership when I say that we will forever be indebted to Dominick's contribution to our great cooperative," commented Chairman Colalillo.[21] Romano, who continued to serve on several of Wakefern's committees, was replaced on the Wakefern board of directors by his son, Dominick J. Romano.[22]

Dominick V. served as chairman of Readington Farms, the co-op's dairy operation, and various committees, including labor, which he chaired. He

THOMAS INFUSINO: STEADY HAND, DRIVING FORCE

No one of us is as powerful as all of us.

—Wakefern Chairman and CEO Thomas P. Infusino

W AKEFERN'S POSITION WAS ASSURED BY THE foresight and dedicated leadership of Thomas Infusino, who retired in May 2005 after serving 34 years as chairman and CEO. During his leadership, ShopRite retail and warehouse sales grew from about $969 million and $645 million, respectively, in 1971, to more than $9.1 billion and $5.6 billion, respectively, by 2005.[1]

As a teenager in the 1930s, Infusino worked part-time at a roadside stand owned by Wakefern founder, Sam Aidekman. The stand was in front of a dairy in Irvington, New Jersey.

"The clerks would empty a case and just throw it out the back door in a big pile. I had to come in and clean up the mess they made," Infusino recalled.[2]

After serving in North Africa during World War II, he returned in 1945 to work with Sam and his brother Al Aidekman. About six months later, Infusino and his brother Chuck opened their own grocery in Newark, on Sanford Avenue.[3] He later joined forces with partner Vincent Lo Curcio II (whose family had a produce store in Nutley, New Jersey, which opened in the early 1930s), as owner/operator of Nutley Park ShopRite, Inc.,

which became a Wakefern member in 1954.[4] In 1967, Tom Infusino was elected to Wakefern's board of directors.[5]

Infusino was a unifying force after the 1968 departure from the co-op of Supermarkets General Corp., and helped keep the co-op together during the lengthy legal battle over stock shares that followed.

"He was the one ... to lead Wakefern/ShopRite out of the darkness," said Burt Flickinger III,

Joe Colalillo, Wakefern chairman, shaking hands with Tom Infusino at a recognition dinner honoring Infusino.

Wakefern presented Tom Infusino, at right, with a portrait honoring his 34 years as chairman and CEO of the co-op. Joe Colalillo, left, was named as Infusino's successor.

an industry consultant whose family also operated a co-op business and worked with Wakefern across several generations. "He's got tremendous humility, coupled with phenomenal ability."[6]

"There have been many challenges in our history," said Wakefern President Dean Janeway. "Some of those challenges would have torn another company apart, but Tom kept us together. Tom has taught us to be honest, truthful, and ethical."[7]

Tom's Bundle of Twigs

Anyone who knew Infusino knew about his "bundle of twigs," and how it was representative of his philosophy of the co-op in terms of what kept it together and made it such a success. Inscribed on one side of the small glass paperweights that Infusino gave out at the annual board meeting in 1999 is the "Legend of the Twigs":

There is a very ancient legend about a wise old man who had seven sons. One day, he called his sons together and commanded that a bundle of sticks be brought in to him. Each son was given one stick and told to break it. This each did with ease. Then he took seven more sticks. And he bound them together. To each son in turn he gave the bound sticks but none could break them. "Individually," said the father, "you are easy prey for your enemies. Together, you are invincible."

On the other side of the paperweight are the words: "No One Of Us Is As Powerful As All Of Us," followed by the signature, "Tom Infusino, Chairman of the Board and CEO."

Demanding Excellence

Infusino served on the board of governors of the National Conference for Community

and Justice, was a member of the Food Council Committee for Good Government, and was chairman of the board for the New Jersey Food Council (NJFC). He has been recognized by many organizations:

- 1974: Received the Prime Minister's Medal for humanitarianism, the highest award given from the State of Israel
- Received the Lifeline Award from the Cooley's Anemia Foundation
- 1992: The annual Thomas P. Infusino Prize and Lectureship in Cancer Causation and Epidemiology was established by the Lautenberg Center for General and Tumor Immunology
- 2001: Received the first Lifetime Achievement Award from the NJFC
- 2002: Named one of "50 Visionaries Who Transformed Food Retailing" by *Supermarket News*
- 2005: Received the "Great American" award from the National Grocers Association

Infusino also was awarded an honorary degree of Doctor of Humane Letters by Seton Hall University for his commitment to professional standards and business ethics. A chair has been endowed in his honor at the New Jersey Medical School at the University of Medicine and Dentistry of New Jersey (UMDNJ), the largest health sciences institution in the nation.

From left to right: Dominick J. Romano, Dominick V. Romano, and David P. Romano are part of a multigenerational family of grocers.

called the co-op's committee structure "the essence of how Wakefern and its members grew."

Retail sales grew to the reported figure of $9.5 billion for the year ending September 30, 2006.[23] By now the nation's largest retailer-owned cooperative had 43 members, 200 ShopRites, and more than 30 PriceRite stores in Connecticut, Massachusetts, New York, Pennsylvania, and Rhode Island.[24] The co-op maintained 2.5 million square feet of warehouse space, and Wakefern/ShopRite employed 47,000 workers (35,000 in New Jersey).

Wakefern commenced planning their next strategic steps. Colalillo and Janeway personally visited each member, to better understand their needs and to offer tools for leadership succession in their companies, a practice that continues. A co-op wide discussion was held to further define member concerns and issues. Strategies were mapped out.

Estate planning, membership succession, wholesale growth, capital, associates, cooperative culture, alternate format, new stores/new markets, and existing store growth were identified as key areas of focus. Action plans were implemented by member/staff work groups.

JOE COLALILLO: A NEW LEADER

JOE COLALILLO WAS BORN INTO THE grocery business. His father became a member of Wakefern in 1954, and some of his earliest memories include shopping with his mom in the family's store.

"My earliest memory is really just going to our stores with my dad," said Colalillo. "I would spend the day and come home at four o'clock. It was just fun."[1]

When he was 10 years old, Colalillo worked in his dad's store packing out, unloading trucks, getting carts, and bagging. He continued through his senior year in high school, and after he graduated, he worked construction for two summers.

"Senior year, I talked to my dad about maybe just going to work and not going to college," said Colalillo. "He said, 'You have to go to college. If you feel the same way in four years, you can come into the business.' But I knew—I had never changed my mind whether I wanted to come into our business or not."

After he graduated from Villanova University in 1983 with a bachelor's degree in marketing, he immediately started working in the business.

IMAGE COURTESY OF INSIGHT PHOTOGRAPHY/STEVEN BERG.

Wholesale Business Expands

Wholesaling was one of the key strategic areas that yielded early results. Wakefern decided to expand the services of its wholesale distribution business to other supermarkets and institutional customers both in and out of the co-op's Northeast market.

It had begun this practice in the late 1970s on an extremely limited basis and it now looked to expand the operation dramatically.[25] Wakefern also sold wholesale internationally to countries that included Bermuda, Panama, Ecuador, and Israel. The wholesale division was established in May 2007.[26] The first new customer added was the

Novello Extra Virgin Olive Oil was one of the first imported specialty brand items introduced under the ShopRite label.

"That summer, I went through an orientation program at Wakefern," explained Colalillo. "I spent a week in every division, going to visit other members' stores, going up to the different committees, seeing the whole dynamic of what was happening. At the end of the summer, I went to work in our stores."

In 1990, Joe and his sister, Nancy, opened their second store, the ShopRite of Clinton. In 1997, he opened his third store in Phillipsburg, New Jersey. Together, the three stores employ more than 1,100 associates.

"I thought what was really impressive about Wakefern were the committees where groups of members would get together with the staff, and they would just talk about all the different aspects of what was happening at Wakefern," explained Colalillo. "But I think what impressed me the most growing up in the business early on, was that we participated in these member getaways, where the membership would go away one weekend a year with other ShopRite owners and other ShopRite members. ... This is where I developed an understanding that Wakefern is different than most large corporations. It really is a family of family businesses."

Colalillo has been a member of Wakefern's board of directors since 1989 and was appointed to the position of chairman and CEO of Wakefern in May 2005 after having served as the company's vice chairman for more than six years.

"I was instrumental in seeing that Mr. Colalillo became the chairman of Wakefern," said Infusino. "Because when I was chairman and I wanted to step aside, I asked myself, 'Who is going to sit in this chair?' Because it's not easy to be chairman of this co-op."[2]

In addition to his role at Wakefern, Colalillo serves as vice chairman and board member of the Washington-based Food Marketing Institute (FMI). He also sits on the FMI food safety task force, member services committee, independent operator committee, and strategic planning committee. Colalillo is a member of the New Jersey Food Council, and in 2005, he received its Lifetime Achievement Award for his contribution to the food industry and service to the community. In 2006, 2007, 2008, and 2009, he was named one of *Supermarket News'* "Power Fifty."

In a symbolic effort to recommit to being the best, attendees at the 2006 Wakefern annual meeting signed their names to a board categorizing the ways they would work to keep the co-op vibrant.

17-store, Ohio-based chain Heinen's Fine Foods, to which Wakefern initially sold more than 300 Shop-Rite-brand grocery and nonfood items.

Wholesale services were soon offered to other supermarkets, providing additional outlets for the 3,000-item, private-label brand. In early January 2008, Wakefern began servicing New York City–based Gristedes Markets, a 40-store chain throughout New York City, Westchester County, and Long Island, New York.[27] The co-op supplied Gristedes with ShopRite private-label products and branded nonfood products.[28] Joe Gozzi, director of specialty grocery for Wakefern, noted that the co-op enjoyed a "unique relationship" with small producers in Spain, Italy, and Greece who "created home-grown, traditional foods and recipes."

"This provides us with a line of authentic foods that are exclusive to Wakefern and its customers, further expanding our brand" he added.[29]

"After trying the ShopRite brand, I believe they are just as good if not better than national brand products," said Charles Criscuolo, senior executive vice president of Gristedes. "By bringing the ShopRite brand into my stores, I'm offering more variety and added value to my customers seeking high-quality products at an affordable price."[30]

In 2007, the co-op posted sales of $28 million from its wholesale activities alone, and only two years later, Wakefern was supplying 29 customers for a total of $108 million in sales from its wholesaling initiative. This was a tremendous leap from 2007.[31]

Across the board, service to both new wholesaling customers and Wakefern members was improved as a result of the efforts of the Operations Excellence Committee established during this time. Focused on retail and wholesale operations, they re-wrote the computer-generated ordering system (CGO) and made it an integral part of Wakefern's procurement, logistics, and finance system. The new system vastly improved the retail ordering process and served as a better tool for managing inventory company-wide.

Further co-op focus on service was directed at monitoring improvement for on-time deliveries to stores.

"We have a logistics fleet of more than 2,000 trailers. We're delivering to stores in many cases, especially in produce, seven times a day, seven days a week," explained Natan Tabak, senior vice president in charge of government, logistics, insurance, and technology. "The produce department of a store can put an order in, and because everything is connected to our mainframe, as soon as I get it, I can collect it. Years before, it took time; technology was slow. If a store put in an order at eight o'clock, we couldn't select until four o'clock in the afternoon. Today, we get that order at eight, and by noon begin selection of produce. The delivery can be eight, 10 hours later. I can inventory any store at any time."[32]

Wakefern also used its Operations Excellence Committee to find areas of continued improvement.

"We try to find ways to do things better, more efficiently, to make us more profitable, provide better service to the customer, and better service to the membership," explained Larri Wolfson, a third-generation grocer and president of ShopRite of Lincoln Park.

Wakefern was clearly on a roll. By June 2007, ShopRite was busy serving more than 5 million customers weekly.

Ten Stop & Shops Become ShopRites

In July 2007, Wakefern moved to acquire 10 Stop & Shop stores—nine in South Jersey and one in New York. Eight of the nine New Jersey stores would be owned and operated by six co-op member companies.[33] The ninth store would be a replacement store for ShopRite Supermarkets, Inc., a Wakefern subsidiary, in Middletown, New York, and the 10th store would remain closed.

Stop & Shop Supermarket Company, based in Quincy, Massachusetts, was a division of Ahold. It employed more than 59,000 associates and operated 389 stores throughout Massachusetts, Rhode Island, Connecticut, New Hampshire, Maine, New York, and New Jersey.[34] While Stop & Shop enjoyed a strong reputation in the Northeast market (having

entered New Jersey around 1997),[35] the South Jersey Stop & Shops were said to be "struggling."

The co-op proceeded to retrofit the stores, many of which were fairly new, and reopened them as ShopRites.[36]

Readying the stores for opening was a monumental task, and, true to form, Wakefern succeeded against the impossible timeline set for turning the stores into ShopRites. Nine of the pharmacy departments were converted overnight (the 10th was merged with another store), and they had an astounding 85 percent employee retention rate. Six of the stores were open 29 days after the acquisition, and three more were open within 71 days. The entire Wakefern computer network and system had to be installed in each store, requiring the expertise of a support and installation team of 34 people, who were on site for 728 hours.[37]

Stocking the stores required 28 miles of nonperishable shelving and 1.7 million unit price

WAKEFERN TODAY

- Wakefern operates 3.3 million square feet of warehouse space.
- Each Wakefern warehouse holds more than 35,000 items.
- Wakefern delivers 175,000 loads yearly to 238 stores in eight states.
- Wakefern has a 98 percent on-time delivery rate to stores.
- Wakefern drivers travel more than 38 million miles each year.
- Wakefern delivers more than 305 million cases per year.
- Wakefern drivers, each year, travel the equivalent of 1,520 times around the globe.

labels, 1.1 million pounds of meat, and 1 million cases of product.

Colalillo called the acquisition of the 10 South Jersey stores "an unprecedented growth opportunity for Wakefern and its members."[38]

Shifts in the Competitive Landscape

While Wakefern was involved with the Stop & Shop acquisition, there was movement within the industry—and the possibility of a merger between A&P and Pathmark. For A&P to make a merger economically feasible, it would have to increase its volume, and a bigger A&P network would make it tougher for co-op members.[39]

On March 5, 2007, The Great Atlantic & Pacific Tea Company, owner of A&P, agreed to buy Pathmark Stores, Inc. for $1.4 billion. The result was a 550-store operation, the largest in the Northeast.[40] Most stores were located in New York, New Jersey, and Philadelphia. Both Pathmark and A&P believed the merger would "reduce costs and help fend off competition from Wal-Mart and Costco." Industry analyst Gary Giblen, with Brean Murray, Carret & Company in New York, explained more bluntly: "This is A&P trying to keep themselves alive."[41]

It seemed likely that "the new entity should pose a stronger competitive threat to perennial Northeast power Wakefern Food Corp."[42]

Not according to Matt Casey, founder of site selection firm Matthew P. Casey & Associates, located in Clark, New Jersey. "The gap between ShopRite and A&P-Pathmark is still so wide. A&P has a lot of strong initiatives planned, but that's not going to overcome ShopRite's low-price reputation and perception in the customer's mind," he said.[43]

Honing its Competitive Edge

After almost 50 years in Elizabeth, in September 2007, the co-op moved its corporate offices from Elizabeth to Keasbey, in Woodbridge Township, New

DEAN JANEWAY: LEADING THE WAY

DEAN JANEWAY JOINED THE co-op in 1966 as a junior accountant in the frozen food division.

"I was working at Western Electric in Kearny [New Jersey], and going to night school," explained Janeway. "I saw an ad for Wakefern Food Corporation. … I went down for the interview, as I had just taken some credits in accounting."[1]

He progressed through numerous procurement and management positions, including vice president of the frozen food and dairy-deli divisions. He eventually was offered the position of vice president of advertising in 1981, at the same time the use of circulars took off.

"I was put in charge of merchandising, and I had to bring together all the divisions," Janeway remembered. "I had to try to get them to agree to gross profit margins and percentages, and try to project what our gross profit was going to be as well as sales, so we could manage the bottom line."

Janeway would meet with the committee and then meet with the ad agency to create the circu-

Jersey. In addition to expanding its wholesale operation, Wakefern/ShopRite was growing its retail store base, and opened seven new stores between October 2007 and July 2008.[44]

Wakefern initiated a program to encourage the younger generation's involvement in the business. During the next year, more than two dozen younger-generation members joined committees—some in leadership positions, according to Colalillo.[45]

With a growing concern for health and wellness, the company also expanded its focus on healthy lifestyle products and services. Now, whether in-store, online, or in advertising, ShopRite customers could find products and information to fit their specific health interests, from organic, to low sodium, low cholesterol diets, and more.

The LiveRite program was launched to identify products to meet specific dietary needs. The Culinary Workshop program taught customers in-store how to make healthy alternative meals as well as gourmet fare. And the ShopRite ads featured tips from both Wakefern's dietitian and Consumer Affairs director.

The first HealthRite center, an affiliate of southeastern New Jersey AtlantiCare Regional Medical Center, was opened in 2006 at ShopRite of Somers Point. By the end of 2007, two more in-store health centers were opened by ExpressCare Retail Health Care Centers, one each in the ShopRite of Neptune (in Neptune, New Jersey), and ShopRite of Oxford & Levick in Philadelphia.

Wakefern hired its first corporate dietitian in 2005 as part of its Leaders-in-Training Program. After a retail assignment with the ShopRite of Parsippany, New Jersey, Natalie Menza, RD, joined Wakefern's Corporate and Consumers Affairs department as its staff dietitian.

In 2007, Ned Gladstein, president of the West Caldwell, New Jersey, ShopRite and the Parsippany ShopRite; officer and member of the Wakefern Board; and longtime chairman of the commu-

---

lars. It was during this time that the co-op began shifting its philosophy from just huge volume to push sales, to examining what motivated customers to buy products and shop at stores. This was a huge change in how the co-op operated, and Janeway saw firsthand the growing pains the group experienced by how heated the conversations were at some of the committee meetings.

Yet, as he built his career, these experiences allowed him to see how the co-op worked from every level and provided insight into how members viewed the co-op and how essential it was that they all work together.

He continued to gain experience, and in 1987 he was promoted to group vice president. Just three years later, he was named executive vice president.

In 1995, Janeway was appointed president and chief operating officer after Jerry Yaguda, a longtime Wakefern leader, retired after serving the co-op for 35 years.

"Dean's style of leadership is a perfect match for Wakefern," said Joe Colalillo, Wakefern's chairman and CEO. "He has an excellent relationship with the members as he understands both their family and business dynamics. His empathic and caring attitude has created an atmosphere in which the members feel comfortable in discussing their issues openly and honestly with him, a critical need in this cooperative structure. And he also has the courage to face problems head-on and hold the difficult discussions so necessary in this type of environment. He truly cares about people, both members and staff have great respect for him."

Janeway, a graduate of Rutgers University who in 1989 completed the Wharton Advanced Management Program, has served on the board of directors and has been past president of both the Eastern Frosted Foods Association and the Eastern Dairy-Deli Association, two trade organizations that serve the New York metropolitan area. He also served as chairman of the National Grocers Association, was a member of the board of directors of the National Co-op Bank, and, since 2009, has served as a trustee of the University of Medicine and Dentistry of New Jersey (UMDNJ) foundation board.

Left: A sampling of the private brand specialty labels introduced in ShopRite Supermarkets.

Below: A company newsletter offers a coupon for any of ShopRite's seven varieties of "steam in bag" frozen vegetables and a recipe for customers seeking healthy meal ideas.

In 2007, Wakefern met the challenge when the Bracey family, with two stores located in Pennsylvania's Pocono Mountains area, joined the cooperative.

nications committee, decided to initiate a full-time, retail dietitian program for his customers.

Developed in conjunction with educational information provided by Wakefern, a number of members also began offering retail dietitians to assist customers with nutritional counseling. Programs were also developed to reach students in local schools and to help customers who needed to follow special diets due to diabetes, hypertension, or allergies to certain foods.

"It goes along with the way we approach our business, which is really understanding that the food business is about sustenance," Ned explained. "It's not just putting groceries on the shelf. It's really understanding what our customers do with that product once they get it home."[46]

Quality was addressed as well. In late summer 2008, the co-op adopted the Safe Quality Food (SQF) certification program to reemphasize food safety. SQF would "help ensure that we are working with suppliers who are maintaining and adhering to the highest standards for food safety," Colalillo said.[47]

Territory Expands

The success that the co-op and members had achieved with ShopRite banner stores was making opportunities for new ShopRite locations in its traditional geographic territory very scarce.

"We're pretty saturated up in the Northeast with ShopRites. It's becoming difficult to find a viable site that is going to bring us the volume we need and still be far enough away from every other ShopRite to not have a negative impact," explained Terry Glass. "In order for us to grow, we're going to have to go outside the core area."[48]

In October, 2008, Wakefern expanded well beyond traditional borders into Maryland by welcoming Klein's Family Markets to fly the ShopRite banner. Based in Forest Hill, Maryland, the seven-unit chain became the co-op's 45th member.[49] The transition was completed during the first quarter of 2009.

"Like our own family, many of the Wakefern members are third- and fourth-generation grocers. Joining with other independent retailers will allow us to remain competitive with larger chains while remaining true to what has made Klein's Family Markets successful," said Michael J. Klein, vice president and purchasing director for Klein's.[50]

"Harford County residents will now have access to more than 3,000 ShopRite-branded items, including imported specialty foods, that we believe will bring a new level of quality and value to our customers," said Marshall J. Klein, perishables director for Klein's.[51]

Klein's also would have the support of a cooperative with more than $10 billion in retail sales.[52]

In the spring of 2010, once again, ShopRite increased its presence in key markets with the purchase of 10 Connecticut Shaw's Supermarkets

from SUPERVALU. Nine of the stores were then purchased by individual Wakefern members to become ShopRites. One store would be operated as a PriceRite. With this acquisition, came the opportunity for two new Wakefern members. Ray Miller, a Wakefern executive, purchased the location that became the ShopRite of Enfield, Connecticut, and Chuck Joseph, an industry veteran and Colalillo associate, purchased the stores that became the ShopRite of Canton and ShopRite of West Hartford, Connecticut.

Responding to Recession

As the weakening of the economy became more apparent, Wakefern offered opportunities to strengthen its relationship with consumers.[53]

While the trend translated to a healthy increase in business for supermarkets, Wakefern/ShopRite's reaction was driven by a strong sense of civic duty in a time of crisis. A number of money-saving measures were quickly launched. On May 2, 2008, ShopRite customers who purchased ShopRite Gift Cards using a government-issued economic stimulus or tax refund check at any ShopRite supermarket received a 10 percent bonus. The ShopRite Gift Cards, with no expiration date or service fees, allowed customers to reserve funds specifically for grocery shopping.

"Consumers are really starting to feel the impact of rising food and energy prices," said Colalillo. "This is another way we can help our loyal shoppers stretch their grocery budget and hold onto their money as long as possible."[54]

Not long after the recession was under way, gasoline prices spiked. The co-op responded with a "free gas" incentive that ran from June 22, 2008, through July 5, 2008. During this period, ShopRite customers who used the Price Plus Club card and bought $75 worth of any combination of Kraft, General Mills, or Proctor & Gamble products in a single purchase received a free $25 Shell or BP Gas Card.[55]

Technology for the Customer

As customers became more computer and cell phone savvy, so did ShopRite. The retailer's website, www.ShopRite.com, distributed more than 13 mil-

Klein's Family Markets joined Wakefern in 2008 as the co-op expanded into Maryland. This store is in Cardiff, Maryland.

lion e-mails to its registered users. The retailer also used a number of customer acquisition programs to gain more shoppers to increase sales and spread awareness about the ShopRite brand.

ShopRite also integrated the use of text messaging, mobile coupons (sent directly to consumers' cell phones) digital coupons, printable coupons, and an online program that allows customers to add coupons to their Price Plus cards.[56]

In 2008, a ShopRite weekly circular was launched as a desktop widget, a software application that allows users to create a shopping list from ShopRite's weekly circular, and was downloaded by more than 600,000 customers. It could also be accessed on Facebook, a popular social networking site. Another widget, "LiveRight with ShopRite," allowed consumers to compare foods directly by nutrient, allergen, and ingredients.

Left: This PriceRite was built in Bethlehem, Pennsylvania, and opened in June 2009 as Wakefern continued to add to the number of retail grocery stores.

Below: In 2008, ShopRite launched a campaign to showcase its locally grown produce program. Some 211 stores participated and sold locally grown fruits and vegetables.

Wakefern Support

The commitment of the co-op to its members continues to this day, upholding the spirit of the organization started in 1946. In the summer of 2008, Nutley, New Jersey, was hit with a series of fierce tornadoes, taking down trees and leaving the area without power for days. Vincent Lo Curcio III remembered:

The power went out on a Tuesday night and we didn't get 100 percent power back until Friday. In the meantime, Wakefern set up trailers; we got an emergency generator, but we're constantly reevaluating: How long are we going to be out of power? Should we get dry ice? But at 1:00 PM the next day, we have the generator running, and I want to open tomorrow, but I've got to get the empty shelves filled.

Wakefern started deliveries and had about 40 to 50 people come to the store. And these are people that work in the offices—secretaries and computer analysts, not experienced packers. They came at 4:00 PM, 5:00 PM, and were working till 11:00 PM. That's just amazing. ... The members of Wakefern said, 'Nutley is in trouble. Let's go give him a hand.' And they did.[57]

The commitment Wakefern extends to its members is also extended to its own staff of Wakefern associates. While the co-op is focused on the longevity and success of its retail owners, it has a vested interest in its own staff members' job satisfaction and success as well.

Wakefern takes great pride in the longevity of its associates, as exemplified by its Quarter Century Club. Long-term associates are inducted into the group when they reach their 25th year of Wakefern employment. In the "Class of 2010," 51 associates joined the ranks of the club, bringing the total to 471 who had reached this milestone.

Next Generation: Succession Planning

As Wakefern/ShopRite has its roots firmly in the support and continuation of family businesses, it has become important to include the younger generations in the organization to ensure its ongoing success. Over the years, it has become crucial to address succession planning.

Joe Sheridan has been instrumental in creating environments where the younger generation—sons and daughters—can learn and become active participants in the Wakefern organization. The challenge is twofold: balancing the relationships between parent

Grown *Fresh.*
Grown *Locally.*
Grown *for...*

Wakefern's next generation of leaders are gathered above. Back row, left to right: Joseph Colalillo; Christopher S. Kinsley, Sr.; Jim Mandanci; Kathy Miller-Mandanci; Theresa Miller-Sheeler; Geoff Eickhoff; Don Drust, Jr.; Kristen Eickhoff Dixon; Marshall Klein; Stephanie Sumas-Tsiavos; Jennifer (Colligas) Bond; Harry J. Janson II; Melissa Buonadonna-Hernandez; Chris Kenny; Michael Zallie; George J. Zallie, Jr.; Melissa Kenny Huff; Peter Ammons; Jennifer Collins Iaccio; Rick Drust. Middle row, left to right: Jonathan Tokar; Nico Sumas; Brett Ravitz; Dominick Cingari; Tom Cingari, Jr.; Ken Capano, Jr.; Scott Capano; William S. Janson; Sarah Klein; Bob Singer; Shawn Ravitz; Larry Collins, Jr.; Larry Iaccio, Jr. Front row, left to right: Rick Saker; Karen (Glass) Holbrook; Rafael Cuellar; Alex Cohen; Christian Infusino; Jordan (Cohen) Coe; Seth Greenfield; Dara Gladstein; Bria McMenamin; Dave Bullard; Melissa Ammons-Bullard; Ben Ammons; Jason Ravitz. Not pictured: Megan Ammons; Perry Blatt; William J. Bracey II; Joe Cingari; Jeanne Clark; James DeStefano; Enza Drust; Kristine Drust; Marybeth (Miller) Duffy; Joseph Eickhoff; Richard Eickhoff; Joseph Frusteri; Cara Graci; Neil Greenstein; Julio Hernandez; Carl Inserra, Jr.; Lawrence Inserra III; Lyndsey Inserra; Amy Janson; Charles "Chuck" Joseph III; Stephen Klein; Sean McMenamin; Charles Miller; Scott Perlmutter; Ryan Smutko; Tony Smutko, Jr.; Ali Sumas; John J. Sumas; Laura Sumas.

and child and instilling in them the history and passion for the co-op that the longtime members have. As entrepreneurs, the members have a tremendous connection with the co-op and the stores that has been borne over the years out of struggle, success, and experience.

According to Colalillo, there are about 120 of the next generation, generally between the ages of 21 and 36, who are the second or third generation to enter into the co-op.

"We said, 'We've got to get succession going,'" explained Colalillo. "'We've got to get these people integrated into our co-op.' We have a next generation group that Joe [Sheridan], our executive vice president, who is the successor to Dean, heads up. [They] meet three or four times a year, and it's that next generation getting to know each other that is critical to our continued success. My parents and a lot of the longtime members you talk about, they needed each other for survival. Most of these next generations are stepping into very established businesses."[58]

"[The next generation of leaders] are several levels removed from survival mode," added Sheridan. "For example, the parents lived above the produce

Left: The Cingari family enjoys the beach at the 2009 Wakefern Member Getaway in St. John, U.S. Virgin Islands. From Left: Tom, Sr.; Tom, Jr.; John; Sue; and Matt.

Below: As part of ShopRite's Partners In Caring program, it partnered with General Mills to highlight hunger-fighting initiatives in the community. This box features 51 ShopRite associates, honored for their efforts to raise awareness and funds to combat hunger. (*CHEERIOS® is a registered trademark of General Mills, Inc. and is used with permission.*)

department. These kids are graduating from Georgetown. They're smart, and they're articulate. ... They need a historical connection to our defining moments. It's like we all remember the 'wars' [trying times within the industry] of our time. You want them to understand why our 'wars' come together to tell the [Wakefern] story."[59]

Sean McMenamin, son of members Rich and Rene McMenamin, reinforced the message:

While the co-operative has changed dramatically since its earnest beginnings in 1946, the entrepreneurial spirit that led to its inception remains at the core of Wakefern. I am hopeful and confident that the next generation of leaders will draw upon the experience and wisdom of those that have come before us in order to continue this storied tradition of excellence.

Wakefern leadership recognized from the very beginning the driving force of the co-op's success is dependent on the bond each member has to the co-operative and to each other.

It has been important to provide ways for members to maintain these vital personal connections. In the early days, they held dinner-dances and weekend retreats to the Poconos or Catskills. The concept was revived again in the early 1980s when Wakefern Getaway weekends offered family trips to Florida or island destinations. Family participation in business seminars combined with social activity helps to keep the cooperative strong.

"Over the years the member getaways always provided us great educational opportunities to help us run our companies. But more importantly, the members get to know each other's families on a personal basis, strengthening the bond between us," Colalillo reflected.

Recent getaways have been held at the Disney Institute in Florida; Washington, D.C.; and the Virgin Islands.

A Tradition of Charitable Endeavors

In 2001, ShopRite's Partners In Caring also partnered with General Mills to offer a first-ever, limited-edition Cheerios box, to focus attention on

Wakefern's annual meeting has grown over the years, and now attracts an audience of more than 650 Wakefern associates, members, and store management teams. Each year the meeting highlights the past year's accomplishments and initiatives for the coming year, and provides a noted educational/inspirational speaker. Shown above (left), is Space Shuttle Astronaut Colonel Mike Mullane, who spoke at the 2009 meeting. Past presenters include former New York Governor Mario Cuomo, Conductor Ben Zander, Astronaut Jerry Linenger, and Dr. Fareed Zakaria of *Newsweek* and CNN.

ShopRite's hunger-fighting efforts. It would be the beginning of a tradition that would continue for almost a decade. Unlike other cereal box promotions, the special-edition Cheerios boxes do not feature celebrities or athletes. Instead, continuing the Wakefern/ShopRite philosophy of community giving, they feature local ShopRite associates, workers from the community food banks, or other community volunteers who worked to raise funds and awareness for the hunger cause.

The stores held fundraising events, such as car washes and carnivals, and ask the community to donate through the purchase of $1 checkout cards at the register. They also held in-store events to educate the community about the issue. In addition to the annual $2 million in corporate contributions, in 2009, the ShopRite stores raised almost $500,000 for the ShopRite Partners In Caring Fund, a component fund of the Community Foundation of New Jersey.

"The commitment demonstrated by our members and store associates was astounding," noted Karen Meleta, Wakefern's vice president of Consu-

mer and Corporate Communications. "Whenever we called upon them to raise funds or awareness for fighting hunger, they answered the call."

Beyond the traditional support of food banks, Wakefern responded to the huge need created when Hurricane Katrina hit the Gulf Coast in 2005, affecting Texas, Louisiana, Mississippi, and Alabama. The ShopRite Disaster Relief program raised more than $1.4 million in cash and in-kind contributions to support the relief efforts, which included a donation of $50,000 to the Houston Food Bank for the purchase of a tractor trailer.

In 2008, the co-op became a major sponsor of the Food Network New York City Wine & Food Festival, which benefited the community-based hunger relief programs Food Bank for New York City and Share Our Strength.[60]

Wakefern's charitable tradition extends well beyond its core support of hunger. In recent years the co-op endowed a chair at the University of Medicine and Dentistry of New Jersey (UMDNJ) and raised $1 million for the Deborah Heart and Lung Center in Browns Mills, New Jersey. More than

$22 million has been donated to local charities through the ShopRite LPGA Classic alone.

Continued Success

By 2009, retail sales grew to $11.6 billion, and warehouse sales reached $8.6 billion.

As of June 2010, there were 46 Wakefern members and 229 ShopRite Supermarkets operating in seven states, and 45 PriceRites for a total of 274 stores. The ShopRite brand is as strong as ever and represents 14.5 percent of total sales.

While this growth has directly contributed to the combined success of Wakefern/ShopRite, the main reason for its success lies in the fact that it has a purpose beyond the simple expansion of business. Adding to the number of stores has never been the primary goal. Instead, securing longtime loyalty within its membership is a key factor and is always at the forefront of business decisions.

ShopRite has come to define cooperative grocery retailing. From a struggling cooperative with just seven members—all owners of their own stores—it has grown into the largest retailer-owned co-op in the United States.[61] Its continued focus on community and its relentless pursuit of offering services unique to each neighborhood ensures customer loyalty and embodies the small-town feel so many people seek while competing on a high level with the big chain groceries.

This sentiment is succinctly stated in Wakefern's mission statement, and ensures both Wakefern and ShopRite a successful presence within the industry: "We help small businesses succeed in a big business world."

"If you were to ask me what was the one thing [Wakefern] did that made them as successful as they were, I would say they are consistent. Price was their god. They would try to deliver food at the lowest possible cost to customers. They never varied from it no matter what the opportunity was," said Allen Bildner, former owner of Kings Super Markets.[62]

"Wakefern became a logistics expert in food distribution from a central facility and pioneered the information management used at the distribution center level," Bildner added. "But what made them really unique was their willingness to invite other wholesalers throughout the country into their facilities to benefit from Wakefern's experience."[63]

Even the competition respected the work ethic and philosophy that has served Wakefern/ShopRite through the years. The very basis of the co-op's foundation—the desire to give customers a low price—is still the means for its success today.

Chairman Joe Colalillo described Wakefern's future this way:

The future of Wakefern couldn't be brighter. First and foremost, there is a large number of next generation family members actively involved in almost all of our member companies. We have put together leadership and education forums to ensure they have the skills needed to lead their companies and the cooperative.

Second, we have established a formal succession process at the Wakefern staff level to ensure smooth transitions at every level. This is critical to the success of our cooperative.

Finally, our strategic direction for growth through multiple avenues in addition to the continued

The ShopRite in Cherry Hill, New Jersey, is owned by the Ravitz family, who joined Wakefern in 1984.

The Wakefern 2009 Board of Directors. Front row, left to right: Bernie Kenny, Rocco Cingari, Len Sitar, Dean Janeway, Joe Colalillo, Tom Infusino, Joel Perlmutter, Robert Clare, Joe Sheridan. Second row, left to right: Ken Capano, Richard Tully, Steve Ravitz, Irv Glass, Dominick J. Romano, Richard Saker, Ned Gladstein, Jim Sumas. Third row, left to right: Larry Inserra, Jeff Brown, Larry Collins, Richard McMenamin, Larri Wolfson. Back row, left to right: Chuck Infusino, Jon Greenfield.

growth of our ShopRite and PriceRite stores will allow us to remain a significant company in the food industry.

Added Wakefern President Dean Janeway:

There is no doubt that at the heart of Wakefern's future success is the entrepreneurial spirit and drive of the independent retailer in our cooperative combined with the dedication and commitment of our professional staff. Our competitive edge comes from the insights we gain from our members' frontline presence at retail. When you add the support our stores receive from our Wakefern associates—whether it is logistics, advertising, marketing, procurement, or customer care—you have an unbeatable formula for success. This has been the foundation of our success for the last 64 years, and I am confident it will continue to set us apart from all others in the future.

The Sumas family represents the entrepreneurial, family business spirit that is Wakefern. Brothers Nick (center right) and Perry Sumas joined Wakefern soon after its formation. Nick became a member of the board and served as Wakefern's third president. Their business grew from the original small store (center left) in South Orange, New Jersey, to a publicly traded company with 26 ShopRites. Their sons and grandchildren now provide the leadership for their own business, Village Super Market, Inc., as well as Wakefern. In the top picture, standing, left to right: Robert, Jim, John P., William, and Perry. Seated, left to right: Nick and John J.

WAKEFERN
MEMBER PROFILES

The Tradition Continues...

For more than three generations, Wakefern members have upheld the traditions established by the cooperative's founders. The families profiled on the following pages represent those members who guide and govern the organization today. The future of Wakefern, and the continuation of its legacy, rests in their hands and those of the next generation of leaders, as well as those members who will join the cooperative ranks in the future. It is with them that the Wakefern banner and all of its contributions to the community will continue to make a lasting difference for years to come.

Ammons Supermarkets, LLC

David Bullard, Melissa Bullard, Peter Ammons, Megan Ammons, Ben Ammons, Debra Ammons, Larry Ammons

After decades as a supermarket executive, Larry Ammons, president of Ammons Supermarkets, became a member of Wakefern and the owner of the ShopRite of Aramingo Avenue in Philadelphia in 2000. Joining him in this new venture was his wife, Debra, and their children Melissa, Ben, and Pete. The family soon expanded their business to New Jersey with the 2007 opening of their Mullica Hill location.

Bottino's SuperMarkets

Bill Bottino, Jr.; Tom Bottino; Mark Bottino; Phil Bottino; Pat Bottino, Sr.; Jim Bottino; Maria Bottino; Jeff Bottino

The Bottinos' start in the food business came in 1977 when they opened a corner deli in Woodlynne, New Jersey. In 1996 they joined the Wakefern cooperative and began to build what is today a successful family business. The team of five brothers and one sister operate four New Jersey ShopRite supermarkets: Vineland, Upper Deerfield, Washington Township, and Millville. The Bottino family has been serving customers' needs for more than 20 years and prides itself in always keeping the customer first.

Bill's ShurSave Supermarkets

William G. Bracey, William J. Bracey II

William G. "Bill" Bracey has been a fixture in the Daleville, Pennsylvania, community since 1974 when a determined 20-year-old Bill decided to enter the supermarket business. He partnered with his father, William J. Bracey, in his first store. In 1997, an opportunity for another store came Bill's way, and he opened his Mount Pocono store. After 32 years as an independent supermarket owner, Bill joined the Wakefern/ShopRite family in 2007.

Brown's Super Stores, Inc.

Sandy Brown, Jeff Brown

Jeff Brown, the founder, president, and CEO of Brown's Super Stores, Inc., and his wife Sandy own and operate 10 ShopRite supermarkets in Philadelphia, Montgomery, and Bucks counties in Pennsylvania and Camden County in New Jersey and have been members of Wakefern since 1988. Their company's mission is to bring joy to the lives of the people they serve, and it is well recognized for its leadership and innovations in serving diverse and low-income communities, often referred to as "food deserts."

Buonadonna ShopRite, LLC

Susan Buonadonna, Melissa Buonadonna-Hernandez

Susan Buonadonna brought with her many years of supermarket executive experience when she became a Wakefern member in 2004. Today, she owns and operates two ShopRite stores in Suffolk County, New York. Her daughter, Melissa, serves as the company's district manager.

Five Star Supermarkets

Scott Capano; Ken Capano; Ken Capano, Jr.

For New Jersey native Ken Capano, Sr., and his wife, Jean, the decision to move to Connecticut and become ShopRite store owners was an easy one to make for one very important reason—family. When the Norwich Connecticut ShopRite became available in 1996, Ken and Jean saw it as the perfect opportunity to build a business with their sons and their families. The family added the ShopRite of New London in 2000 and ShopRite of Clinton in 2010.

Grade A Market, Inc.

Chip Cingari; Rocky Cingari; Dominick Cingari; Sam Cingari; Tom Cingari, Sr.; Joe Cingari; Tom Cingari, Jr.

After losing his job during the Great Depression, Salvatore Cingari bought an old school bus, loaded it with fresh produce, and became a successful grocer, calling his business Grade A Market. In 1943, he moved to his first building and his sons soon joined him in the business. In 1991 the Cingaris joined Wakefern. Today, four generations of Cingaris own and operate 10 ShopRite locations in Fairfield and New Haven counties in Connecticut.

ShopRite of Oakland

Robert Clare, Joseph Clare

With nearly 100 years in the grocery business, the Clare family has managed to combine a successful business with a warm family environment. Arthur Clare started the family's journey in the supermarket business when he opened a small store in 1928. In 1956, his sons took over the business and in 1958 joined Wakefern. Arthur's son, Thomas, opened the current ShopRite of Oakland, New Jersey, in 1972. Today, Thomas and his sons, Joseph and Robert, run the business—maintaining the family's impressive grocery legacy.

Waverly Markets, LLC

Alex Cohen, Rich Cohen, Kye Cohen,
Zach Cohen, Jordan Coen

At eight years old, Rich Cohen was a fixture in his
grandfather's market in Springfield, Massachusetts. The
Waverly Market was the inspiration for Rich's company,
Waverly Markets, LLC/ShopRite of Manchester,
Connecticut. Rich has been active in business for more
than 40 years—30 in the food industry. He and his wife,
Kye, joined Wakefern in 1999. For 11 years, two of their
four children—Jordan Coe and Alex Cohen—have been
the fourth generation in the food business. The family's
second store will open in the summer of 2010.

ShopRite of Hunterdon County

Joseph Colalillo, Jeannie Colalillo

The Colalillo family joined Wakefern in 1954 when
Joseph A. Colalillo opened a ShopRite in South River,
New Jersey. Four years later, the store relocated to
Flemington, and today it is owned and operated by his
son, Joseph, and Joseph's wife, Jeannie, who also have
stores in Clinton and Greenwich Township, New Jersey.

ShopRite of Front & Snyder

Jennifer Colligas Bond, James S. Colligas,
Suzanne Colligas

In 1960, a young ShopRite cashier, Jim Colligas,
enjoyed the supermarket industry and dreamed of
owning his own store. In 2005, his dream came
true—Jim became president and CEO of Colligas Family
Markets, owner and operator of the ShopRite of Front &
Snyder in Philadelphia, and member of Wakefern. His
wife, Suzanne, and daughter, Jennifer, joined him. Jim
brought with him more than 30 years of supermarket
experience and soon enhanced the store to ensure that
it reflected the needs of his South Philly customers.

Collins Family Markets

Larry Iaccio, Jr.; Jennifer Collins-Iaccio; Larry Collins, Sr.;
Sandy Collins; Larry Collins, Jr.; Bill Collins

Larry Collins, an experienced supermarket executive,
joined Wakefern in 1995 with the purchase of the
Front and Olney ShopRite in Philadelphia. Today, he
and his wife Sandy; brother Bill; son Larry; daughter
Jennifer Collins Iaccio; and son-in-law Larry Iaccio,
Jr., own and operate three ShopRite Supermarkets.
Two are located in Philadelphia and the third is in
Eddystone, Pennsylvania.

ShopRite of Passaic/Clifton Cuellar, LLC

Rafael Cuellar; Daisy Cuellar; Evelio Cuellar, Jr.

The Cuellars have been in the grocery business for more than 35 years. Evelio Cuellar owned President Supermarket, serving the Passaic community for decades. In 2005, his son, Rafael, sold President and purchased the ShopRite of Passaic/Clifton, becoming the first Hispanic member of the Wakefern/ShopRite cooperative. Even though the ShopRite is five times larger than his first store, Rafael strives to keep the "family" environment while providing fresh and ethnically diverse products and outstanding customer service.

Drust Markets, LLC

Kristine Drust; Don Drust, Jr.; Diane Drust; Don Drust; Enza Drust; Rick Drust

Don Drust never imagined his job as a carriage boy at a New Jersey ShopRite would lead to more than four decades in the supermarket business. But, it did. In 1997, Don and his family were offered the opportunity to become Wakefern members by purchasing the ShopRite of Meriden, Connecticut. Excited to start a true family business, the Drusts took the offer. They are looking forward to relocating to a larger, newer building and becoming the ShopRite of Wallingford.

Eickhoff's Supermarkets

Daniel Eickhoff, Geoffrey Eickhoff, Karl Eickhoff, Kristen Eickhoff Dixon, Richard Eickhoff, Joseph Eickhoff

The Eickhoff family has been operating supermarkets since 1955 when they opened their first store in Levittown, Pennsylvania. Successful business owners, they subsequently opened four additional stores in New Jersey from 1968–1993. Seeing how the Wakefern cooperative had grown and progressed over the years, brothers Karl and Richard decided to join in 1998. Today, two generations of the Eickhoffs are active in the five stores they own and operate in Burlington County, New Jersey.

Milford Markets

Harry Garafalo, Ann Garafalo, James DeStefano

Harry Garafalo's connection to the ShopRite of Milford, Connecticut, goes back to 1974 when he worked as a bagger in the original store. Skip to 2004 and Harry and his wife Ann are the owners of the ShopRite of Milford and members of Wakefern. They added a West Haven store in 2008 and look forward to adding two more Connecticut locations in late 2010. Born and raised in Milford, Harry is happy to offer his neighbors quality products at affordable prices.

Sunrise ShopRite, Inc.

Ned Gladstein and Dara Gladstein holding photos of their fathers and grandfathers—four generations in the grocery business.

The Gladsteins have been in the grocery business for four generations. In 1940, Nathan Gladstein opened Sunrise Market in Caldwell, New Jersey, with his son Irving and other family members. Irving knew the founders of Wakefern and joined the cooperative in 1951. Today, Irving's son, Ned Gladstein, is president of Sunrise ShopRite, Inc., and operates the ShopRites of Parsippany and West Caldwell, New Jersey, with his daughter Dara, who serves as director of communications.

Glass Gardens, Inc.

Terry Glass, Karen Holbrook, Irv Glass

The Glass brothers, Ben and Abe, started their family's legacy in the supermarket industry when they opened a produce business in 1938. After many successful years in business, they officially incorporated their company, calling it Glass Gardens, Inc., and opened their first store in Rochelle Park, New Jersey, in 1955. Glass Gardens and affiliated companies currently have seven New Jersey and two New York State ShopRites, which are owned and operated by Abe and Ben's sons, Irv and Terry Glass.

Food Parade, Inc.

Seth Greenfield, Jon Greenfield, Jill Greenfield, Stephen Greenfield

Although his father was in the grocery industry for more than 25 years, Jon Greenfield had his sights set on law school. When his father passed, Jon and his brother, Stephen, took over the family business—a decision he has never regretted. The family, including their sister Jill and Jon's son Seth, joined Wakefern in 1997 and today run two successful ShopRites, in Plainview and Morton Village on Long Island, New York. The family is looking forward to adding a new store in Commack, New York.

Brookdale ShopRite, Inc.

Neil Greenstein, Lesley Greenstein, Dorothy Druian (front), Mark Greenstein, Charlotte Greenstein

In 1948, Dorothy and Louis Druian opened their first supermarket in Bloomfield, New Jersey. They joined Wakefern in 1952, and over the years expanded their store, eventually relocating next to the original site in 1999. Today, the store's day-to-day operations are managed by Dorothy's daughter Charlotte Greenstein, son-in-law Mark Greenstein, and grandson Neil Greenstein.

ShopRite of Little Falls

Christian Infusino, Jonathan Tokar, Carol Tokar, Chuck Infusino

Founded by a 22-year-old Charles Infusino, the ShopRite of Little Falls began in 1946 as a corner deli in Newark, New Jersey. Charles worked diligently over the next several years, growing his business, and in 1952 he joined Wakefern. Soon after Charles moved his store from its original location in Newark to the current location in Little Falls, New Jersey, his son Chuck joined him in the family business. Today three generations of Infusinos operate the family store.

Nutley Park ShopRite, Inc.

David Infusino, Thomas Infusino, Vince Lo Curcio III

Vincent Lo Curcio, Sr., started the family business in 1932 by selling fruits and vegetables. In 1953, his family built a "superette" called Park Foods and was joined by Thomas Infusino, a butcher by trade. After the Lo Curcios joined Wakefern in 1954, Vincent, Jr., and Thomas became partners, bringing their families together to work toward the goal of providing the community with a family-friendly supermarket that offered consistent service, quality, and value. Today, three generations of the Lo Curcio and Infusino families work side-by-side in their Nutley, New Jersey, store.

Inserra Supermarkets, Inc.

Laura Inserra-Dupont; Larry Inserra, Jr.; Marie Inserra-Larsen

For more than 20 years, Larry Inserra ran successful grocery stores in New Jersey that were founded by his father, Patsy. In 1954, Larry took a bold step when he joined the Wakefern cooperative. Today, the company has grown to include 17 ShopRites in New Jersey and four in New York. Now the third and fourth generations of Inserras continue the traditions begun decades ago.

Janson Supermarkets, LLC

Harry J. Janson, Sr.; Amy Janson; Sarah Elizabeth Janson; Harry J. Janson II; Elizabeth Janson; William Janson

A native of New Jersey, Harry Janson's 40-year career in the supermarket industry led him to New York, Maryland, Virginia, Alabama, and Arkansas before bringing him close to his home state in 1998. That's when Harry, president of Janson Supermarkets, LLC, became a Wakefern/ShopRite member and built the ShopRite of Hauppauge, New York. He and his family, including his wife, Elizabeth, sons Harry II and William, and daughter-in-law Amy, manage this 61,000-square-foot location.

Joseph Family Markets, LLC

Debbie Joseph, Charles "Chuck" Joseph

Joseph Family Markets owns and operates the ShopRites of Canton and West Hartford, Connecticut. As president/CEO, Charles "Chuck" Joseph joined Wakefern in 2010 after 35 years in the industry. His wife Debbie, son Chuck, and daughter Liz join him, bringing almost 50 combined years of food industry experience to their family business. The Joseph family's vision is to be the best—striving to positively affect people with a shopping experience that provides great food for a fair price in a family atmosphere.

The Kenny Family ShopRites of Delaware

Steve Huff, Bernie Kenny, Melissa Huff, Matt Kenny, Chris Kenny, Bob Singer

Bernie Kenny is an operations expert with extreme attention to detail, a strong passion for people, and success at all levels of the supermarket industry. He founded Delaware Supermarkets, Inc., and opened the first two Kenny Family ShopRites in Delaware in 1995. Today, with four successful Kenny Family ShopRite stores in operation and a fifth in development, the future has never looked brighter. Bernie Kenny, along with three generations of the Kenny family, continues to furnish Delawareans with premier supermarkets in which to shop and work.

Kinsley's Market of Tannersville, Inc.

Christopher S. Kinsley, Jr.; Robert W. Kinsley; Doris M. Kinsley; Richard K. Jacoby; Dee Dee Kinsley-Jacoby; Christopher S. Kinsley, Sr.; Robert W. Kinsley

Robert Kinsley, president of Kinsley's Market, has worked in the grocery business for more than 50 years. As a student, Robert assisted his father, Clayton, in the original Kinsley Market. Today, four generations of Kinsleys work at ShopRite of Brodheadsville, Pennsylvania. The family joined Wakefern in 1998 and is looking forward to opening their new 95,000-square-foot store, ensuring they can meet the changing needs of their customers.

Klein's Family Markets

Howard Klein, Michael Klein, Clara Klein, Sarah Klein, Andrew Klein, Marshall Klein, Jayne Klein, Susan Klein, and Tory Klein at the Festival ShopRite ribbon-cutting ceremony.

In 1925, Maurice and Sara Klein opened a small general store in the rural village of Fallston, Maryland. Some 50-plus years later, their son Ralph, his wife Shirley, and their sons Andrew and Michael own and operate seven supermarkets throughout Maryland. A fourth generation of the Klein family (Marshall, Sarah, and Stephen) is now actively engaged in the stores' day-to-day operations. Operating as Klein's Family Markets, Ralph and his family joined Wakefern in October 2008, becoming the cooperative's 45th member.

Mannix Supermarkets

Kevin Mannix

After 30 years with Wakefern, Kevin Mannix was ready to own and operate his own ShopRite stores. For this native Staten Islander, the timing couldn't have been more "right" when two stores on the island were offered to him. Today, he owns the ShopRite of Hylan Boulevard and the ShopRite of Forest and Richmond, with a third store planned for 2012. Kevin finds it rewarding to be able to offer quality products and great prices in a customer-friendly environment to the friends and neighbors he remembers from childhood.

McMenamin Family ShopRite

Rich McMenamin, Rene McMenamin, Sean McMenamin, Bria McMenamin

Rich McMenamin brought his 40 years of grocery experience to the Wakefern cooperative when he purchased the ShopRite of Roosevelt Boulevard, Philadelphia, in 1995. A true family affair, Rich spends his days at the store alongside his wife Rene, son Sean, and daughter Bria. In 2008, the McMenamin Family opened the ShopRite of Morrell Plaza, also in Philadelphia. Together, they work to ensure that the McMenamin Family ShopRites are the preferred place to both work and shop.

Miller Farms Family Markets

Charles Miller, Marion Miller, Raymond Miller, Mary Elizabeth Duffy

Leveraging more than six decades of food industry and customer service experience, the Miller Family joined Wakefern in 2010 with the purchase of the ShopRite of Enfield, Connecticut. Miller Farms Family Markets' owner Raymond Miller and his wife Marion, along with their children Mary Elizabeth Duffy and Charles Miller, are focused on providing customers with the highest quality food, at an exceptional value. The Miller Family takes pride in bringing ShopRite back to the city of Enfield and looks forward to being a preferred employer and responsible member of the Enfield community.

KTM Supermarkets, Inc.

Joe Miller, Margaret "Maggi" Miller, Theresa Miller-Sheeler, Mary Miller, Jim Mandanci, Kathleen "Kathi" Miller-Mandanci

Joe Miller, owner and operator of the ShopRite of West Chester, Pennsylvania, joined Wakefern as a member in 1994 after more than 35 years in the supermarket industry. He and Mary, his wife and co-owner, named their company KTM Supermarkets, Inc., after daughters Kathi, Tammy, and Maggi. The Millers are focused on customer service, with Joe and Mary making sure they're on the floor every day—seven days a week—getting to know shoppers.

Perlmart, Inc.

Michael Perlmutter, Joel Perlmutter, Jim Haslett

Originally founded in the 1930s as G&P Markets by Julius Perlmutter and his brother-in-law Ben Goldstein, Perlmutter Family ShopRites/Perlmart, Inc., has grown to include stores throughout Ocean County, New Jersey. The move to ShopRite happened in 1947 when Julius partnered with his brother Seymour to open a store in Toms River and join Wakefern. Today, Julius' sons Joel and Michael, and their business partner Jim Haslett, operate the seven Perlmutter Family ShopRites.

Supermarkets of Cherry Hill, Inc.

Jason Ravitz, Brett Ravitz, Ron Ravitz, Steve Ravitz, Shawn Ravitz

As a Russian immigrant, Dave Ravitz came to this country looking for his American dream. And in 1901, he found it when he opened a small grocery store. His son Stanley joined him and together they grew their business. Looking for a way to lower prices without sacrificing quality, the Ravitz family joined Wakefern in 1984. Today, the third and fourth generations of Ravitz grocers operate five ShopRites: three in Burlington and two in Camden counties in New Jersey.

Ronetco Supermarkets, Inc.

Dominick J. Romano, Dominick V. Romano, David P. Romano

The Romano family has a long and proud history in the food business. It all began in 1927 when Thomas and Vincenia Romano started a candy store in their New Jersey living room. Their legacy continued when the family, under Dominick V. Romano's persuasion, joined Wakefern in 1956. Today, his sons Dominick J. and David P. operate seven stores in northwest New Jersey.

Saker ShopRites, Inc.

Rick Saker; Thomas Saker; Joseph Saker, Jr.; Richard Saker

The Saker family has been operating grocery stores since 1916 when Richard Saker's great-grandfather opened a "mom and pop" store in Freehold, New Jersey. Richard's father Joseph joined Wakefern in 1947, a few months after it was established, and was an active member of the cooperative. Today, Richard and family, including brothers Tom and Joe and Richard's son Rick, own and operate 27 ShopRites in central New Jersey and work tirelessly to create a "World Class" shopping experience for all their customers.

Shakoor Supermarkets

Charles Shakoor

Charlie Shakoor knows the grocery business. After all, he's been working in the industry for more than 50 years. Before joining Wakefern in 1995 as owner of the ShopRite of Old Bridge, New Jersey, he worked for other supermarket chains, as well as SRS, Inc., a wholly owned subsidiary of Wakefern. Operating this location gives Charlie the opportunity to provide great products at great value to his neighbors in Old Bridge, a community that has always treated him as one of its own.

ShopRite of Carteret, Inc.

Theresa Serluco, Leonard Sitar

Soon after John Sitar opened the ShopRite of Carteret, New Jersey, in 1954 and joined Wakefern, his young son, Len, started in the business. As years passed, this family venture grew from a small corner grocery store to today's 62,000-square-foot ShopRite. After years working at various positions, Len became president and CEO in 1995. His sister Theresa Serluco serves as chief financial officer. Len and Theresa are dedicated to continuing their dad's great work in the store and in the community.

AJS Supermarkets

Bruce Kocenski, Victoria Kocenski, Ryan Smutko, Sherry Smutko, Tony Smutko, and grandson Zachary Holzman (not pictured: Tony Smutko III)

AJS Supermarkets has a long history with Wakefern/ShopRite. Anton Smutko and his brother Frank opened Hilltop Supermarkets in 1953—the same year they joined Wakefern. In 1989, the brothers sold their stores to another ShopRite owner. In 1999, Anton's son Tony re-entered the family business, with the purchase of ShopRite of Hillside, New Jersey. Today, Tony's wife Sherry and their children TJ, Vicki, and Ryan work with him at ShopRite, ensuring that the family's supermarket legacy will continue.

Village Super Market, Inc.

Nicholas "Nico" Sumas, Perry Blatt, Laura Sumas, John J. Sumas, Jim Sumas, Robert Sumas, Ali Sumas Good, Stephanie Sumas-Tsiivos, William Sumas, John P. Sumas

Greek immigrants Nick and Perry Sumas opened the first Village Supermarket in 1937. Just under 10 years later, the brothers joined Wakefern, becoming one of the cooperative's earliest members. As the Sumas family grew, so too did their business. Today, the family, including Nick's sons James and Robert, Perry's sons William and John, and their children and extended family owns and operates 26 ShopRite supermarkets located in northern, central, and southern New Jersey and one in Pennsylvania.

Tornaquindici ShopRite

Paul Tornaquindici

As owner of two Connecticut ShopRites, Paul Tornaquindici is known for giving back to his community. He's been involved for years with local efforts, including feeding the homeless and educating students. Paul learned the importance of philanthropy and the basics of the grocery business from his father Frank, who owned Frank's Supermarkets. After years of working with his father, Paul became a ShopRite owner and member of Wakefern in 1996 with the ShopRite of Waterbury, adding a second store, the ShopRite of Bristol, in 1999.

Kearny ShopRite, Inc.

Kevin John Tully, Cheryl Ann Tully,
Richard Tully, Kristen Ann Tully

The Tully family, owner of the ShopRite of Kearny, New Jersey, have been members of Wakefern since 1948. John Tully was the first owner to put the name ShopRite on his building. Richard, John's son, joined the family business after college, and Richard's wife Cheryl has served as vice president for more than 15 years. As the president of Kearny ShopRite, Inc., Richard remains focused on the goals his father had: providing top-notch customer service, offering quality product at great prices, and giving back to the community.

ShopRite of Lincoln Park, Inc.

Larri Wolfson

Larri Wolfson, president and owner of the ShopRite of Lincoln Park, New Jersey, is a third-generation grocer. The family's start in the business began with Larri's grandfather, Raymond, who sold produce from a 1919 Model T truck, eventually opening a small store in 1932. Soon, his sons Harold and Morton joined him in the business, and they became Wakefern members in 1955. Larri started in the Wolfson family business as a young boy, becoming full-time in 1975 and taking over as owner in 1987. He was named president in 2001.

Somerset Stores, LLC

Renee Zallie, Julia Zallie, David Zallie

David Zallie, president of the ShopRite of Medford, New Jersey, has been in the grocery business with his family since his father George became a Wakefern member in 1980. David joined Wakefern in 2006, giving him the opportunity to build on the skills he learned from his father. David and his wife Renee are committed to exceeding their customers' expectations both within the store and in the local community.

GMS Zallie Holdings, Inc.

George J. Zallie, Jr.; George J. Zallie; Michael D. Zallie

George J. Zallie of GMS Zallie Holdings has an extensive 35-year career in supermarket retailing, with his family's history in the business dating back to 1956. George joined Wakefern in 2006 and today he and his sons George J., Jr., and Michael own and operate the ShopRite on Frankford Avenue in Philadelphia.

Berat, Inc.

George Zallie, Bruce Zallie

George Zallie, Sr., established the Zallie family grocery business in 1956 when he opened a corner store in the Port Richmond section of Philadelphia. His sons George J. and Bruce joined him in the business in 1973, and George's youngest son, David, became a part of the family team in 1979. The father and sons team joined Wakefern in 1980. Today, George runs Berat, Inc., with his son, Bruce. The company owns and operates eight ShopRites located in Gloucester and Camden counties in New Jersey.

WAKEFERN'S WHOLLY OWNED SUBSIDIARIES

ShopRite Supermarkets, Inc.

Dave Figurelli

When ShopRite Supermarkets, Inc., (SRS) a wholly owned subsidiary of Wakefern Food Corp., was established in 1986, it consisted of just four stores—three in New Jersey and one in New York. Today, led by president and Chief Operating Officer, Dave Figurelli, SRS includes 29 stores—three in New Jersey and 26 in New York, and is dedicated to building and maintaining shopper loyalty by connecting with customers through outstanding service and a commitment to community giving.

PriceRite

Neil E. Duffy, Howard Fruchterman

In 1995, Wakefern established PriceRite as a wholly owned subsidiary. The first store was located in Springfield, Massachusetts. Today, PriceRite operates 43 supermarkets located in Massachusetts, Connecticut, Pennsylvania, New York, and Rhode Island. Neil Duffy, formerly a Wakefern vice president, has served as PriceRite's president since 2006. Howard Fruchterman, a long-term Wakefern vice president, is senior vice president of Marketing/Merchandising for PriceRite.

NOTES TO SOURCES

Chapter One

1. Wakefern Second Annual Year Book, 1953.
2. Pia Sarkar, "Scrambling for Customers, The Supermarket Was Born 75 Years Ago. One-stop Shopping Has Come a Long Way," *San Francisco Chronicle*, 4 August 2005.
3. Groceteria.com, available at http://www.groceteria.com/.
4. Pia Sarkar, "Scrambling for Customers."
5. Robert W. Mueller, Section 2 of the Annual Survey, "Sales at New High in 1947," *Progressive Grocer*, April 1948.
6. Carl W. Dipman, Section 1 of the Annual Survey: "A Review of What is Happening in Food Retailing," *Progressive Grocer*, March 1948.
7. "Court Ruling Upholds Wakefern Stockholders' Agreement," PR Newswire, 10 August 2001.
8. Leonard Lewis, "Wakefern at the Top Despite Obstacles," *Supermarket News*, 1982.
9. David Silverberg, interview by Jeffrey L. Rodengen, digital recording, 11 June 2008, Write Stuff Enterprises, Inc.
10. Leonard Lewis, "Wakefern at the Top Despite Obstacles."
11. Glenn Snyder, "The Wakefern Shop-Rite Story," *Progressive Grocer*, 1965.
12. Samuel Aidekman, Wakefern Food Corp. Video Tape Library, Section 2: 50th Anniversary Recordings, documentation by Andrea L. Spinelli, Studio 27 Productions, 24 January 1996–14 January 1997
13. "The Wakefern Shop-Rite Story."
14. Ellen Simon, "The Biggest Little Guys," the *Star-Ledger* (Newark, New Jersey), 2 September 2001.
15. "History of Wakefern Food Corporation," Wakefern First Annual Year Book, 1952.
16. John Tully, Wakefern Food Corp., Video Tape Library, Section 2: 50th Anniversary Recordings, documentation by Andrea L. Spinelli, Studio 27 Productions, 24 January 1996–14 January 1997
17. "The Wakefern Shop-Rite Story."
18. Samuel Aidekman, Wakefern Food Corp. Video Tape Library, Section 2: 50th Anniversary Recordings.
19. Joseph J. Trout, "Cooperative Effort Turned the Tide for These Independents," *Progressive Grocer*, June 1955.
20. "Court Ruling Upholds Wakefern Stockholders' Agreement."
21. David Silverberg, interview.
22. Samuel Aidekman, Wakefern Food Corp. Video Tape Library, Section 2: 50th Anniversary Recordings.
23. John Tully, Wakefern Food Corp. Video Tape Library, Section 2: 50th Anniversary Recordings.
24. Ibid.
25. Ibid.
26. David Silverberg, interview.
27. Samuel Aidekman, Wakefern Food Corp. Video Tape Library, Section 2: 50th Anniversary Recordings.
28. John Tully, Wakefern Food Corp. Video Tape Library, Section 2: 50th Anniversary Recordings.
29. Leonard Lewis, "Wakefern at the Top Despite Obstacles."
30. Tom Infusino, Wakefern Food Corp. Video Tape Library, Section 2: 50th Anniversary Recordings, documentation by Andrea L. Spinelli, Studio 27 Productions, 24 January 1996–14 January 1997.
31. "History of Wakefern Food Corporation," Wakefern First Annual Year Book, 1952.
32. "The Wakefern Shop-Rite Story."
33. Ellen Simon, "The Biggest Little Guys."
34. John Tully, Wakefern Food Corp. Video Tape Library, Section 2.
35. David Silverberg, interview.
36. "History of Wakefern Food Corporation," First Annual Wakefern Year Book, 1952.
37. Ibid.
38. Sam Garb, interview by David Silverberg, "Statement on the

History of Wakefern," written transcript, 28 November 1966.

39. Credit report, Wakefern Food Corp., Dun & Bradstreet, Inc., 10 May 1951.

40. "The Early Years Remembered," Wakefern/ShopRite 50th Anniversary, video produced by Studio 27 Productions, 1996.

41. Joseph J. Trout, "Cooperative Effort Turned the Tide for These Independents."

42. Joe Illard, Wakefern Food Corp. Video Tape Library, Section 2: 50th Anniversary Recordings, documentation by Andrea L. Spinelli, Studio 27 Productions, 24 January 1996–14 January 1997.

43. Glenn Snyder, "The Wakefern Shop-Rite Story—Supermen of the East," *Progressive Grocer*, 1966.

Chapter Two

1. Joseph J. Trout, "Cooperative Effort Turned the Tide for These Independents," *Progressive Grocer*, June 1955.

2. Randolph McAusland, *Supermarkets: 50 Years of Progress*, Food Marketing Institute, 1980.

3. Ibid.

4. Ibid.

5. Glenn Snyder, "The Wakefern Shop-Rite Story—Shop-Rite: Supermen of the East," *Progressive Grocer*, 1966.

6. *Supermarkets: 50 Years of Progress*.

7. "History of Shop-Rite," manuscript, undated, Wakefern archives.

8. Joe Saker, "The Early Years Remembered," Wakefern/ShopRite 50th Anniversary Video, Studio 27 Productions, 1996.

9. Lynne S. Dumas, *Elephants In My Backyard: Alex Aidekman's Own Story of Founding the Pathmark Supermarket Powerhouse*, Vantage Press, New York, 1988.

10. "The Wakefern Shop-Rite Story—Shop-Rite: Supermen of the East."

11. Lynne S. Dumas, *Elephants In My Backyard: Alex Aidekman's Own Story of Founding the Pathmark Supermarket Powerhouse*.

12. John Tully, Wakefern Food Corp. Video Tape Library, Section 2: 50th Anniversary Recordings, documentation by Andrea L. Spinelli, Studio 27 Productions, 24 January 1996–14 January 1997.

13. Lynne S. Dumas, *Elephants In My Backyard: Alex Aidekman's Own Story of Founding the Pathmark Supermarket Powerhouse*.

14. Zal Venet, Wakefern Food Corp. Video Tape Library, Section 2: 50th Anniversary Recordings, documentation by Andrea L. Spinelli, Studio 27 Productions, 24 January 1996–14 January 1997.

15. Leonard Lewis, "Wakefern at the Top Despite Obstacles," *Supermarket News*, 1982.

16. Lynne S. Dumas, *Elephants In My Backyard: Alex Aidekman's Own Story of Founding the Pathmark Supermarket Powerhouse*.

17. Joseph J. Trout, "Cooperative Effort Turned the Tide for These Independents."

18. "Celebrating the Cooperative Spirit: The First 50 Years," Wakefern Food Corp. publication, 1996.

19. John Tully, Wakefern Food Corp. Video Tape Library, Section 2: 50th Anniversary Recordings, documentation by Andrea L. Spinelli, Studio 27 Productions, 24 January 1996–14 January 1997.

20. Wakefern Second Annual Year Book, 1953.

21. Ken Aidekman, notes (undated) from audio tapes of Lynne S. Dumas' *Elephants In My Backyard: Alex Aidekman's Own Story of Founding the Pathmark Supermarket Powerhouse*, Vantage Press, New York, 1988.

22. Leonard Lewis, "Wakefern at the Top Despite Obstacles."

23. Glenn Snyder, "The Wakefern Shop-Rite Story—Shop-Rite: Supermen of the East."

24. "Wakefern Food Corporation," Lehman Brothers, April 1967.

25. "Celebrating the Cooperative Spirit: The First 50 Years," Wakefern Food Corp. publication, 1996.

26. David Silverberg, interview by Jeffrey L. Rodengen, digital recording, 7 June 2008, Write Stuff Enterprises, Inc.

27. Leonard Lewis, "Own-Label Program Held in High Esteem"; seventh in the series, "Wakefern: King of the Co-ops," *Supermarket News*, 1982.

28. Zal Venet, Wakefern Food Corp. Video Tape Library, Section 2: 50th Anniversary Recordings.

29. David Silverberg, interview.

30. Leonard Lewis, "Own-Label Program Held in High Esteem"; Joel Perlmutter, interview by Jeffrey L. Rodengen, digital recording, 10 June 2008, Write Stuff Enterprises, Inc.

31. John Tully, Wakefern Food Corp. Video Tape Library, Section 2: 50th Anniversary Recordings.

32. Leonard Lewis, "Own-Label Program Held in High Esteem."

33. Ibid.

34. William Applebaum, "Super Marketing: the Past, the Present, a Projection," Super Market Institute, Inc., 1969.

35. Chuck Infusino, Wakefern Food Corp. Video Tape Library, Section 2: 50th Anniversary recordings, documentation by Andrea L. Spinelli, Studio 27 Productions, 24 January 1996–14 January 1997.

36. "The Wakefern Shop-Rite Story—Shop-Rite: Supermen of the East."

37. John Tully, Wakefern Food Corp. Video Tape Library, Section 2: 50th Anniversary Recordings.

38. Wakefern Second Annual Year Book, 1953.

39. Leonard Lewis, "Wakefern: A Leader in New Electronics," "Wakefern/Shop-Rite: King of the

Co-ops," sixth in a series, *Supermarket News*, 1982.

40. David Silverberg, interview.
41. Wakefern Third Annual Year Book, 1954.
42. Wakefern First Annual Year Book, 1952.
43. Lynne S. Dumas, *Elephants In My Backyard: Alex Aidekman's Own Story of Founding the Pathmark Supermarket Powerhouse.*
44. Glenn Snyder, "The Wakefern Shop-Rite Story—Shop-Rite: Supermen of the East."
45. Joseph J. Trout, "Cooperative Effort Turned the Tide for These Independents."
46. Wakefern First Annual Year Book, 1952.
47. "The Early Years Remembered," Wakefern/ShopRite 50th Anniversary, video produced by Studio 27 Productions. 1996.
48. Glenn Snyder, "The Wakefern Shop-Rite Story—Shop-Rite: Supermen of the East."
49. Ibid.
50. Wakefern Fourth Annual Year Book, 1955.
51. Lynne S. Dumas, *Elephants In My Backyard: Alex Aidekman's Own Story of Founding the Pathmark Supermarket Powerhouse.*
52. Ibid.
53. Joseph J. Trout, "Cooperative Effort Turned the Tide for These Independents."
54. Wakefern Third Annual Year Book, 1954.

Chapter Three

1. Leonard Lewis, "Wakefern at the Top Despite Obstacles," "Wakefern/ShopRite: King of the Co-ops," first in a series, *Supermarket News*, 1982.
2. William Applebaum, "Super Marketing: the Past, the Present, a Projection," Super Market Institute, Inc., 1969.
3. Ibid.
4. Ibid.
5. Glenn Snyder, "The Wakefern Shop-Rite Story—Shop-Rite:

Supermen of the East," *Progressive Grocer*, 1966.
6. Ibid.
7. Minutes, 28 May 1957, Wakefern Board of Directors Meeting, 1956–61.
8. Minutes, 7 November 1956, Wakefern Board of Directors Meeting, 1956–61.
9. Minutes, 19 February 1956, Wakefern Board of Directors Meeting, 1956–61.
10. Minutes, 29 April 1959, Wakefern Board of Directors Meeting, 1956–61.
11. Minutes, 19 February 1957, Wakefern Board of Directors Meeting, 1956–61.
12. Wakefern Press Release, 30 June 1958.
13. Wakefern Food Corp., "Historical Decisions, 1960–1987," years 1964 and 1965 in "Historical Highlights 1960–1987," internal documents, September 1988.
14. "History of Wakefern," manuscript, undated, Wakefern archives.
15. Glenn Snyder, "The Wakefern Shop-Rite Story—Shop-Rite: Supermen of the East."
16. Anne Buritan, Wakefern Food Corp. Video Tape Library, Section 2: 50th Anniversary Recordings, documentation by Andrea L. Spinelli, Studio 27 productions, 24 January 1996–14 January 1997.
17. Minutes, 19 February 1957, Wakefern Board of Directors Meeting, 1956–61.
18. Minutes, 9 December 1957, Wakefern Board of Directors Meeting, 1956–61.
19. "The Performers," advertising supplement, *Progressive Grocer*, 1987.
20. Minutes, 17 April 1957, Wakefern Board of Directors Meeting, 1956–61.
21. Minutes, 11 November 1958, Wakefern Board of Directors Meeting, 1956–61.
22. Leonard Lewis, "Wakefern at the Top Despite Obstacles."
23. Joseph McLean, "Report to the Board of Directors of Wakefern

Food Corporation, Progress 1961."
24. Leonard Lewis, "Wakefern: A Leader in New Elecronics," Wakefern/ShopRite: King of the Co-ops," sixth in a series. *Supermarket News*, 1982.
25. Glenn Snyder, "The Wakefern Shop-Rite Story—Shop-Rite: Supermen of the East."
26. Leonard Lewis, "Wakefern: A Leader in New Electronics," "Wakefern/ShopRite: King of the Co-ops."
27. Glenn Snyder, "The Wakefern Shop-Rite Story—Shop-Rite: Supermen of the East."
28. Leonard Lewis, "Wakefern: A Leader in New Electronics," "Wakefern/ShopRite: King of the Co-ops."
29. Glenn Snyder, "The Wakefern Shop-Rite Story—Shop-Rite: Supermen of the East."
30. Minutes, 17 February 1960, Wakefern Board of Directors Meeting, 1956–61.
31. Minutes, 28 April 1960, Wakefern Board of Directors Meeting, 1956–61.
32. Glenn Snyder, "Low-Price Merchandising Works Wonders For Nation's Hottest Co-op," *Progressive Grocer*, July 1961.
33. Glenn Snyder, "The Wakefern Shop-Rite Story—Shop-Rite: Supermen of the East."
34. Ibid.
35. Harry Castroll, Wakefern Food Corp. Video Tape Library, Section 2: 50th Anniversary recordings, documentation by Andrea L. Spinelli, Studio 27 productions, 24 January 1996–14 January 1997.
36. Glenn Snyder, "The Wakefern Shop-Rite Story—Shop-Rite: Supermen of the East."
37. Glenn Snyder, "Low-Price Merchandising Works Wonders For Nation's Hottest Co-op."
38. Glenn Snyder, "The Wakefern Shop-Rite Story—Shop-Rite: Supermen of the East"
39. "Wakefern Food Board Split on Plan to Merge 2 Supermarket

Chains," the *Wall Street Journal*, 14 February 1966.

40. "Co-ops & Voluntaries," *Chain Store Age* January 1974.
41. Minutes, 1 June 1967, Wakefern Board of Directors Meeting.
42. Dean Janeway, interview by Jeffrey L. Rodengen, digital recording, 10 June 2008, Write Stuff Enterprises, Inc.
43. Ibid.
44. Leonard Lewis, "Wakefern at the Top Despite Obstacles," "Wakefern/ShopRite: King of the Co-ops."
45. Wakefern Annual Report, 1966.
46. Glenn Snyder, "The Wakefern Shop-Rite Story—Shop-Rite: Supermen of the East."
47. Wakefern Annual Report, 1968.

Chapter Three Sidebar:
Counting on Committees

1. David Silverberg, interview by Jeffrey L. Rodengen, digital recording, 11 June 2008, Write Stuff Enterprises, Inc.
2. Leonard Lewis, "Wakefern Committees: Asset or Liability?" "Wakefern/Shoprite: King of the Co-ops," third in a series, *Supermarket News*.
3. Ibid.
4. Ibid.
5. Ibid.

Chapter Three Sidebar:
Stamp Wars

1. William Applebaum, "Super Marketing: the Past, the Present, a Projection," Super Market Institute, Inc., 1969.
2. Tom Infusino, Wakefern Food Corp. Video Tape Library, Section 2: 50th Anniversary recordings, documentation by Andrea L. Spinelli, Studio 27 productions, 24 January 1996–14 January 1997.
3. Glenn Snyder, "The Wakefern Shop-Rite Story—Shop-Rite: Supermen of the East," *Progressive Grocer*, 1966.

Chapter Four

1. Leonard Lewis, "Wakefern at the Top Despite Obstacles," "Wakefern/ShopRite: King of the Co-ops," first in a series, *Supermarket News*, 1982.
2. Minutes, 25 January 1968, Wakefern Board of Directors Meeting.
3. William Kozuszko, Jr., "Wakefern Food Corp. Historical Decisions: 1960 through 1988."
4. "Co-ops & Voluntaries," *Chain Store Age*, January 1974.
5. "The Next Century: Thomas Infusino, Chairman and CEO," Wakefern/ShopRite advertising supplement, May 1996.
6. Wakefern Annual Report, 1968.
7. Bob Gal, interview by Jeffrey L. Rodengen, digital recording, 28 July 2008, Write Stuff Enterprises, Inc.
8. William Kozuszko, Jr., "Wakefern Food Corp. Historical Decisions: 1960 through 1988."
9. "The Next Century: Thomas Infusino, Chairman and CEO."
10. Minutes, 22 August 1968, Wakefern Board of Directors Meeting.
11. Minutes, 12 March 1970, Wakefern Board of Directors Meeting.
12. "The Next Century: Thomas Infusino, Chairman and CEO."
13. Wakefern Annual Report, 1968.
14. "The Wakefern/ShopRite Story," Wakefern press release, 7 July 1970.
15. *Forbes*, 15 June 1969; Wakefern Annual Report, 1969.
16. Wakefern Annual Report, 1969.
17. Wakefern Annual Report, 1970.
18. Ibid.
19. Ibid.
20. Ibid.
21. "President Nixon Imposes Wage and Price Controls," the *Econ Review*, 15 August 1971.
22. Historical U.S. Inflation Rate 1914–Present, available at http://www.InflationData.com/.
23. Minutes, 15 October 1968, Wakefern Board of Directors Meeting.

24. Bob Mueller, editorial, *Progressive Grocer*, December 1972.
25. *Modern Grocer*, Vol. 51, No. 9, 2 March 1973.
26. The *York Dispatch*, York, Pennsylvania, 30 July 2003.
27. "How a Supermarket Chain Buys Media," *Media Decision*, October 1973.
28. Ibid.
29. Wakefern Annual Report, 1973.
30. Elaine Rose, "Can Can Sale," the *Press of Atlantic City*, 25 January 1995.
31. Wakefern Annual Report, 1973.
32. Ibid.
33. Wakefern Annual Report, 1974.
34. Minutes, 20 February 1979, Wakefern Board of Directors Meeting.
35. Minutes, 19 December 1978, Wakefern Board of Directors Meeting; Minutes, 20 February 1979, Wakefern Board of Directors Meeting.
36. Minutes, 20 February 1979, Wakefern Board of Directors Meeting.
37. Minutes, 21 August 1979, Wakefern Board of Directors Meeting.
38. Elliot Zwiebach, "New Pilot Leading Wakefern Through Era of Big Changes," *Supermarket News*, 3 August 1987.
39. Ibid.
40. Minutes, 15 November 1979, Wakefern Board of Directors Meeting.
41. Minutes, 18 August 1977, Wakefern Board of Directors Meeting.
42. Ibid.
43. "Supermarkets: Ten Years After the Break," *Chain Store Age*, December 1979.
44. Minutes, 15 May 1980, Wakefern Board of Directors Meeting.
45. "Supermarkets: Ten Years After the Break."

Chapter Four Sidebar:
Universal Product Code

1. Tony Seideman, "June 26, 1974: By Gum! There's a New Way to Buy Gum," available at

http://www.wired.com/science/ discoveries/news/2008/06/ dayintechnology/.

2. "Barcode," Wikipedia, available at: http://en.wikipedia.org/wiki/ Barcode/.

3. Minutes, 13 April 1973. Wakefern Board of Directors Meeting.

4. Minutes, 18 October 1973, Wakefern Board of Directors Meeting.

Chapter Four Sidebar:
High Kicks, Low Prices

1. Karen McAuvic, interview by Jeffrey L. Rodengen, digital recording, 29 July 2008, Write Stuff Enterprises, Inc.

2. Ibid.

Chapter Five

1. Joe Colalillo, interview by Jeffrey L. Rodengen, digital recording, 10 June 2008, Write Stuff Enterprises, Inc.

2. "Supermarkets: Ten Years After the Break," *Chain Store Age*, December 1979.

3. Ibid.

4. Ibid.

5. Ibid.

6. Ibid.

7. Ibid.

8. Ibid.

9. 1974 Annual Report, Wakefern Food Corporation, Wakefern archives.

10. Leonard Lewis, "Co-op Mirrors Policies of Chains Via System of Forced Distribution," *Supermarket News*, 17 May 1982.

11. "Supermarkets: Ten Years After the Break."

12. Leonard Lewis, "Space Crush at Wakefern Gives It Highest Turn Rate," *Supermarket News*, 17 May 1982.

13. Leonard Lewis, "Co-op Mirrors Policies of Chains Via System of Forced Distribution."

14. Ibid.

15. Leonard Lewis, "Wallkill: State of the Art in Conventional Depots," *Supermarket News*, 17 May 1982.

16. Leonard Lewis, "Wallkill: 1ˢᵗ Facility Built, Owned by Wakefern," *Supermarket News*, 17 May 1982.

17. Leonard Lewis, "Wallkill: State of the Art in Conventional Depots."

18. Leonard Lewis, "Wakefern: Highest Warehouse Turn Rate," *Supermarket News*, 17 May 1982.

19. Ibid.

20. Leonard Lewis, "Wallkill: 1ˢᵗ Facility Built, Owned by Wakefern."

21. Leonard Lewis, "Wallkill: State of the Art in Conventional Depots."

22. Ibid.

23. Leonard Lewis, "Looking Down the Road Five Years To Help 'Serve Members Properly,'" *Supermarket News*, 17 May 1982.

24. Leonard Lewis, "Wallkill: 1ˢᵗ Facility Built, Owned by Wakefern."

25. Leonard Lewis, "Looking Down the Road Five Years To Help 'Serve Members Properly.'"

26. Minutes, Wakefern Board of Directors Meeting, 16 April 1981, Wakefern archives.

27. Minutes, Wakefern Board of Directors Meeting, 18 March 1982, Wakefern archives.

28. Minutes, Wakefern Board of Directors Meeting, 19 March 1982, Wakefern archives.

29. Leonard Lewis, "Wakefern Food: A Trailblazer in Technology," *Supermarket News*, 17 May 1982.

30. Wakefern Food Corporation Historical Highlights 1960–1987, Wakefern archives.

31. "Talks Scheduled to Resume as Butchers' Strike Enters Second Week," Associated Press, 22 January 1984.

32. Bob Clare, interview by Jeffrey L. Rodengen, digital recording, 30 July 2008, Write Stuff Enterprises, Inc.

33. Murray S. Aboff, "Wakefern Denies It has Woes; Says It Won't Become Chain," *Supermarket News*, 16 September 1985.

34. Ibid.

35. Ibid.

36. Murray S. Aboff, "Wakefern Flourishes Despite Being Prime Target," *Supermarket News*, 16 September 1985.

37. Pathmark Stores, Inc. Funding Universe. Available at http://www.fundinguniverse .com/ company-histories/Pathmark- Stores-Inc-Company- History.html/.

38. Murray S. Aboff, "Wakefern Insisting It Thinks Retailing," *Supermarket News*, 30 September 1985.

39. Ibid.

40. Ibid.

41. Press release, Wakefern Food Corp., 20 November 1986, Wakefern archives.

42. Press release, Wakefern Food Corp., 20 November 1986, Wakefern archives.

43. "Wakefern's Turning Points," *Supermarket News*, 3 August 1987.

44. Ibid.

45. Wakefern "Historical Decisions: 1960–1988," Wakefern archives.

46. Minutes, Wakefern Board of Directors Meeting, 15 April 1982, Wakefern archives.

47. Minutes, Wakefern Board of Directors Meeting, 16 November 1989, Wakefern archives.

48. "Division Profile: Produce Grows Into A New Warehouse," Wakefern *Scanner*, Winter 1989.

49. Leonard Lewis, "Wallkill: 1ˢᵗ Facility Built, Owned by Wakefern."

50. Leonard Lewis, "Wallkill: State of the Art in Conventional Depots."

51. Leonard Lewis, "Wakefern: Highest Warehouse Turn Rate."

52. "Wholly Mackerel, Seafood's 'Cod' a New Home!," Wakefern *Scanner*, February 1990.

53. Kathleen DiChiara, interview with Jeffery L. Rodengen, 6 February 2009, digital recording, Write Stuff Enterprises, Inc.

54. Minutes, Wakefern Board of Directors Meeting, 21 December 1989, Wakefern archives.

55. Minutes, Wakefern Board of Directors Meeting, 21 December 1989, Wakefern archives.
56. Minutes, Wakefern Board of Directors Meeting, 16 February 1989, Wakefern archives.
57. "Wakefern Stockholders Approve New Agreement," Wakefern press release, 15 October 1987, Wakefern archives.
58. Ibid.
59. Ron Stepneski, "Store Wars: ShopRite now top N.J.–N.Y food store," the *Record* (Bergen County, New Jersey), 13 May 1988.

Chapter Five Sidebar: Wakefern's Credo

1. Minutes, Wakefern Board of Directors meeting, 16 October 1980, Wakefern archives.

Chapter Five Sidebar: ShopRite Supermarket Careers Program

1. "Supermarket Training for Special Education Students," Wakefern employee newsletter, Winter 1989.
2. "Supermarket Careers Program Receives National Recognition," Wakefern *Scanner*, Spring 1989.
3. "Two Wakefern Managers Receive Humanitarian Award," Wakefern *Scanner*, July 1989.
4. Wakefern Food Corporation, available at: http://www.fundinguniverse.com/company-histories/Wakefern-Food-Corporation-Company-History.html/.

Chapter Five Sidebar: The Legacy of David Silverberg

1. *Food Merchants Advocate* (Tarrytown, New York) December 1987.
2. *Tri-State Food News,* December 1987.
3. Leonard Lewis, "No Limit to What a Man Can Do or Where He Can Go," *Supermarket News*, 1982.
4. "Biographical Data: David M. Silverberg," Wakefern archives.

Chapter Six

1. Interview with Thomas Infusino, Chairman and CEO from "Into the Next Century: The Wakefern ShopRite Dynamic," special advertising supplement to *Supermarket News*, May 1996.
2. "News in a Minute," Food Institute Report, 25 May 1991 (citing [Newark] *Star-Ledger,* 24 May 1991).
3. "Wakefern Developing a Strategy for Growth ... Consolidates Its Perishables System," Food Institute Report, 18 August 1990.
4. Interview with Thomas Infusino.
5. Ibid.
6. "40 Years of Change," *Supermarket News*, 28 December 1992.
7. Ibid.
8. Ibid.
9. William B. Johnston, Arnold E. Packer, *Workforce 2000: Work and Workers for the 21st Century,* Hudson Institute, Indianapolis, Indiana, 1987.
10. "40 Years of Change."
11. Joel Elson, "Home & Health: Nonfood's Integration," *Supermarket News*, 28 December 1992.
12. Pathmark Stores, Inc., available at http://www.fundinguniverse.com/company-histories/Pathmark-Stores-Inc-Company-History.html/.
13. The Stop & Shop Supermarket Company, available at http://www.fundinguniverse.com/company-histories/The-Stop-amp;-Shop-Supermarket-Company-Company-History.html/.
14. The Grand Union Company, available at www.fundinguniverse.com/company-histories/The-Grand-Union-Company-Company-History.html/.
15. The Great Atlantic & Pacific Tea Company, Inc., available at http://www.fundinguniverse.com/company-histories/The-Great-Atlantic-amp;-Pacific-Tea-Company-Inc-Company-History.html/.
16. "Gristedes to Bid for Marks & Spencer Unit," the *New York Times*, 3 December 2002, C6.
17. Martha Mckay, "New Jersey's Foodtown Supermarkets Make New Supply deal," Asbury Park Press, 7 January 1999; Foodtown (New York), available at http://coop.wikia.com/wiki/Foodtown_(New-York)/.
18. James Pentland, "C&S Grocers Continues to Southward march," January 1996, *Vermont Business,* p 81; Pathmark Announces Supply Agreement with C&S Wholesale Grocers, Business Wire, 3 October 1997.
19. Steve Weinstein, "Wakefern: A Co-op that Works," *Progressive Grocer*, October 1991.
20. ShopRite, www.Wikipedia.org, http://en.wikipedia.org/wiki/ShopRite_(United_States)#Slogans/.
21. Steve Weinstein, "Wakefern: A Co-op that Works."
22. "Co-op's $100 million investment," *U.S. Distribution Journal,* September 1990.
23. Ibid.
24. *Sales Prospector,* New York, New Jersey, Southern Connecticut, May 1990.
25. *Real Estate Weekly,* 22 April 1992.
26. "News in a Minute," Food Institute Report, 25 May 1990, citing Newark *Star-Ledger,* 24 May 1991.
27. Lisa A. Tibbitts, "Wakefern's Constituent Interests," *Supermarket News,* 4 September 1995.
28. "Wakefern Developing a Strategy for Growth ... Consolidates Its Perishables System."
29. Lisa A. Tibbitts, "Wakefern's Constituent Interests."
30. Ibid.
31. *Hartford Courant* (Connecticut), 29 January 1992.
32. "Wakefern Developing a Strategy for Growth ... Consolidates Its Perishables System."

33. *Hartford Courant* (Connecticut), 29 January 1992.
34. Lisa A. Tibbitts, "Wakefern's Constituent Interests," *Supermarket News*, 4 September 1995.
35. Steve Weinstein, "Wakefern: A Co-op that Works."
36. The *Record,* Hackensack, New Jersey, 29 May 1996.
37. Ned Gladstein, interview by Jeffery L. Rodengen, digital recording, 9 February 2009, Write Stuff Enterprises, Inc.
38. Business Wire, 20 December 1996.
39. Wakefern/ShopRite advertising supplement, May 1996.
40. "Union Reaches Agreement to End Supermarket Strike," p. A29, *Orlando Sentinel,* 30 May 1993.
41. Dewey Cannella e-mail correspondence with Mary Ellen Gowin, 9 June 2009.
42. Minutes, Wakefern, Board of Directors Meeting, 17 June 1993, Wakefern Archives.
43. Lisa A. Tibbitts, "Wakefern's Constituent Interests," *Supermarket News*, 4 September 1995.
44. Ibid.
45. Sears Holding Corp., available at www.kmartmedia.com/kmart/kmart.htm#fastfacts/.
46. Mike Duff, "Supercenters Take Lead in Food Retailing: Format is the Focal Foint of Trends - Special Report," *DSN Retailing Today,* 6 May 2002;
47. "History of PriceRite Limited Assortment Stores," NationMaster website, Encyclopedia, www.nationmaster.com/encyclopedia/PriceRite#History_of_PriceRite_Limited_Assortment_Stores
48. James Sumas, interview by Jeffrey L. Rodengen, digital recording, 30 July 2008, Write Stuff Enterprises, Inc.
49. "History of PriceRite Limited Assortment Stores."
50. "Singer ShopRite Chain Now Belongs To Inserra," *Modern Grocer,* 28 November 1994.

51. "Wakefern Selects Cardinal Health as Sole Supplier of Pharmaceuticals," PR Newswire, 12 October 1995.
52. "Wakefern Food Corporation 1993 Environmental Report," April 1994, Wakefern archives.
53. Ibid.
54. "Corporate Environmental Responsibility: A Commitment to Help Solve Environmental Problems Affecting Customers and Our Communities," Wakefern/ShopRite advertising supplement, May 1996.
55. "Wakefern Food Corporation 1993 Environmental Report."
56. Ibid.
57. Ibid.
58. "Into the Next Century: The Wakefern ShopRite Dynamic."
59. 50th Anniversary: ShopRite Community Report, March 1996, Wakefern archives.
60. Ibid.
61. Ibid.
62. Ibid.
63. "Wakefern Food Corporation: Wakefern's Community Service Record and Continued Success: 1980-2000," FundingUniverse website, www.fundinguniverse.com/company-histories/Wakefern-Food-Corporation-Company-History.html.
64. "Into the Next Century: The Wakefern ShopRite Dynamic," special advertising supplement to *Supermarket News,* May 1996.
65. Ibid.
66. Ibid.

Chapter Six sidebar:
Jerry Yaguda Retires

1. "David M. Silverberg, Wakefern's President Retires," Wakefern press release, 21 November 1986.
2. "Into the Next Century: The Wakefern ShopRite Dynamic," Special Advertising Supplement to *Supermarket News,* May 1996.
3. Ibid.

Chapter Six Sidebar:
The Special Olympics

1. Letter from Ellen Giordano, Wakefern *Scanner,* July 1992.
2. SRS and Wakefern Help Sponsor Connecticut Special Olympics, Wakefern *Scanner,* July 1992.
3. "Inspiring Greatness," Wakefern *Scanner,* June 2009.

Chapter Seven

1. Joe Sheridan, interview by Jeffrey L. Rodengen, digital recording, 10 June 2008, Write Stuff Enterprises, Inc.
2. Eileen Stilwell, "The 'Chief Chihuahua' on getting good help," *Courier-Post,* Cherry Hill, New Jersey, 24 January 1999.
3. Kevin G. DeMarrais, "Chain Reaction; Competition, Consolidation, and Changing Times Are Affecting How Supermarkets Do Business in North Jersey," the *Record,* Bergen County, New Jersey, 22 July 2001.
4. Kevin G. DeMarrais, "Miles of Aisles; Supermarkets Expand in Their Quest to be All Things to All People," the *Record,* Bergen County, New Jersey, 9 November 1997.
5. Ibid.
6. Nicole Morella, "One-stop Shopping: Supermarkets Offering Many Services for their Customers," *Courier News,* Bridgewater, New Jersey, 29 October 2000.
7. Ibid.
8. Bill Sumas, interview by Jeffrey L. Rodengen, digital recording, 30 July 2008, Write Stuff Enterprises, Inc.
9. Jim Tracy, interview by Jeffrey L. Rodengen, digital recording, 29 July 2008, Write Stuff Enterprises, Inc.
10. Ken Capano, interview by Jeffrey L. Rodengen, digital recording, 3 February 2009, Write Stuff Enterprises, Inc.
11. Jeff Brown, interview by Jeffrey L. Rodengen, digital recording,

6 March 2009, Write Stuff Enterprises, Inc.

12. Irv Glass, interview by Jeffrey L. Rodengen, digital recording, 17, February 2009, Write Stuff Enterprises, Inc.

13. E-mail correspondence between Mary Ellen Gowin and Neil Duffy, 9 April 2010.

14. "ShopRite from Home," ShopRite website, available at www.shoprite.com/Cnt/ ShopRiteFromHome.html/.

15. Kevin G. DeMarrais, "Taking Stock; North Jersey's Supermarket Industry is Headed for Some Changes," the *Record*, Bergen County, New Jersey, 12 March 2000.

16. Minutes, 19 April 2000, Wakefern Board of Directors Meeting, Wakefern archives.

17. Kevin G. DeMarrais, "Taking Stock; North Jersey's Supermarket Industry Is headed for Some Changes."

18. "Big V Supermarkets, Inc. Files Voluntary Chapter 11 Petition to Implement Major Financial and Operational Restructuring; Stores Remain Open and Focused on Customer Service," Business Wire, 22 November 2000.

19. Ibid.

20. Ibid.

21. Ellen Simon, "Wakefern sues to keep shareholder from walking," the *Star-Ledger*, Newark, New Jersey, 30 November 2000.

22. Ibid.

23. "Court Ruling Upholds Wakefern Stockholders' Agreement," PR Newswire, 10 August 2001.

24. Ibid.

25. Ibid.

26. Ibid.

27. "Bankruptcy Court Confirms Plan of Reorganization For Big V Supermarkets, Inc.," PR Newswire, 27 June 2002.

28. "Wakefern Food Corp. Successfully Closes on Sale of Big V Supermarkets, Inc. to Wakefern Subsidiary," PR Newswire, 2 July 2002.

29. Ibid.

30. Kevin G. DeMarrais, "Taking Stock; North Jersey's Supermarket Industry Is headed for Some Changes."

31. Kevin G. DeMarrais, "Chain Reaction; Competition, Consolidation, and Changing Times Are Affecting How Supermarkets Do Business in North Jersey."

32. Ibid.

33. "Foodtown (United States)," Wikipedia website, available at http://www.en.wikipedia.org/ wiki/Foodtown_(Northeast)/.

34. Tom Zaucha, interview by Jeffrey L. Rodengen, 3 April 2009, digital recording, Write Stuff Enterprises, Inc.

35. Ellen Simon, "The Biggest Little Guys," the *Star-Ledger*, Newark, New Jersey, 2 September 2001.

36. Ibid.

37. Richard Turcsik, "A new look for ShopRite," the *Progressive Grocer*, 1 June 2002.

38. Tom Zaucha, interview.

39. Kevin G. DeMarrais, "Chain Reaction; Competition, Consolidation, and Changing Times Are Affecting How Supermarkets Do Business in North Jersey."

40. "Wakefern Food Corporation Selects and Deploys Hypercom Payment Terminals," Business Wire, 26 July 2001.

41. Ellen Simon, "The Biggest Little Guys."

42. Richard Saker, interview by Jeffrey L. Rodengen, digital recording, 5 August 2008, Write Stuff Enterprises, Inc.

43. Internal memo, Wakefern Food Corp., 16 January 2001, Wakefern archives.

44. Kevin G. DeMarrais, "Major Supermarkets Plan to Rattle Their Chains in 2002," the *Record*, Bergen County, New Jersey, 19 December 2001.

45. Minutes, Wakefern Food Board of Directors Meeting, 19 November 1999, Wakefern archives.

46. Minutes, Wakefern Board of Directors Meeting, 18 April 2000, Wakefern archives.

47. State of New Jersey senate and General Assembly, P.L., 1999, Joint Resolution No. 8, approved June 25, 1999, Assembly Joint Resolution No. 51.

48. Bridget Goldschmidt, "Outstanding Independent Regional Retailer: All Together Now," 15 January 2010, *Progressive Retailer*.

49. Jerry Laws, "It's a Matter of Time," *Occupational Health & Safety*, October 2003.

50. Ibid.

51. "Infusino Retiring, Colalillo to Take Reins at Wakefern," 25 April 2005, *Progressive Grocer*.

Chapter Seven Sidebar: Giving Back

1. "About Us," Feeding America website, available at http://feedingamerica.org/ about-us.aspx/.

2. Wakefern/ShopRite "ShopRite Partners In Caring" sponsorship kit, 2009, Wakefern archives.

3. Ibid.

4. "PRN Corporation Announces Launch of In-Store TV Network at ShopRite; Network to Reach Shoppers at Supermarket's Checkout Lanes in More Than 140 Stores in New York and Pennsylvania," PR Newswire, 11 October 2004.

Chapter Eight

1. Wakefern mission statement, memo, Wakefern Consumer and Corporate Communications, 12 August 2008.

2. "Wakefern Cooperative Members Celebrate 60 years of Success at Its 2006 Annual Meeting; Cooperative Announces Record Sales of $9.2 Billion Retail Sales for Fiscal Year 2005," PR Newswire, 25 May 2006.

3. "The Retail Newsmakers," *Progressive Grocer*, 1 January 2005.

4. Ibid.

5. Ibid.

6. Ibid.

7. Ibid.

8. Ibid.

9. "Liberty Property Trust to Build a Million-Plus-Square-Foot Distribution Center in Upper Macungie for Wakefern Food Corp.; New Facility to Provide 300-400 Jobs to the Region," PR Newswire, 31 March 2005.

10. "Warehouse Goes Super-Sized: New Grocery West Facility Puts its Foot Down in the Lehigh Valley," the Wakefern *Scanner,* February 2006.

11. Ibid.

12. Greg Saitz, "Working the Aisles," the *Star-Ledger,* Newark, New Jersey, 20 May 2005.

13. "Infusino Retiring, Colalillo to Take Reins at Wakefern," *Progressive Grocer* website, http://www.progressivegrocer .com/print-topstory- infusino_retiring_colalillo_to_take _reins_at_wakefern-14837.html/.

14. Food Marketing Institute, availble at http:// www.fmi.org/about/.

15. Michael Garry, "Profiles: Joseph Colalillo." *SN (Supermarket News)*; http:// supermarketnews.com/ profiles/josephcolalillo/,

16. "Infusino Retiring, Colalillo to Take Reins at Wakefern."

17. Greg Saitz, "Working the Aisles."

18. "Infusino Retiring, Colalillo to Take Reins at Wakefern."

19. "Wakefern Cooperative Members Celebrate 60 years of Success At Its 2006 Annual Meeting; Cooperative Announces Record Sales of $9.2 Billion Retail Sales for Fiscal Year 2005."

20. Ibid.

21. "Wakefern Cooperative Announces Record $9.5 Billion in Retail Sales at Its 2007 Annual Meeting," PR Newswire, 18 May 2007.

22. Ibid.

23. Ibid.

24. "Wakefern Announces Expanded Wholesale Sales Operations," PR Newswire, 29 June 2007.

25. "Wakefern Cooperative Announces Record $9.5 Billion in Retail Sales at Its 2007 Annual Meeting."

26. "New York City based Gristedes Markets Added to Wakefern's List of Wholesale Customers," PR Newswire, 2 January 2008.

27. "Wakefern Expanding Wholesale Biz Beyond ShopRite," *Progressive Grocer* website, http:// www.progressivegrocer.com/ top-story-wakefern_expanding_ wholesale_biz_beyond_shoprite- 22732.html/.

28. "New York City based Gristedes Markets Added to Wakefern's List of Wholesale Customers."

29. Ibid.

30. Ibid.

31. Fiscal 2009 Corporate Accomplishments, Wakefern Powerpoint presentation, 17 December 2009.

32. Natan Tabak, interview by Jeffrey L. Rodengen, digital recording, 11 June 2008, Write Stuff Enterprises, Inc.

33. Tom Belden, "Retailer Co-op to Buy Stop & Shops: Nine of the 10 Stores are in South Jersey"; "Wakefern Food Co-op Operates 200 ShopRites in Five States," the *Philadelphia Inquirer,* 14 July 2007.

34. "Stop & Shop Announces Southern New Jersey Store Closings," The Stop & Shop Supermarket Company, press release, 6 July 2007.

35. Maya Rao, "ShopRite in Talks to Buy 9 Stop & Shop Markets," the *Press of Atlantic City* (New Jersey), 27 June 2007.

36. "Wakefern Announces Acquisition of Ten Stop & Shop Stores," PR Newswire, 13 July 2007.

37. 2007: Year in Review, Wakefern/ShopRite Powerpoint presentation, December 2007.

38. "Wakefern Announces Acquisition of Ten Stop & Shop

Stores," PR Newswire, 13 July 2007.

39. Roseanne Harper, "Food Wholesalers/Cooperatives," *Supermarket News,* 23 July 2007.

40. "A&P Parent Agrees to Buy Pathmark Grocery Chain," Bloomberg News, 6 March 2007.

41. Ibid.

42. Michael Garry, "Profiles: Joseph Colalillo."

43. Ibid.

44. Ibid.

45. Roseanne Harper, "Food Wholesalers/Cooperatives."

46. Ned Gladstein, interview by Jeffrey L. Rodengen, digital recording, 5 February 2009, Write Stuff Enterprises, Inc.

47. Michael Garry, "Profiles: Joseph Colalillo."

48. Terry Glass, interview by Jeffrey L. Rodengen, digital recording, 3 February 2009, Write Stuff Enterprises, Inc.

49. "Klein's Joins Wakefern; Stores to Convert to ShopRite," *Supermarket News,* 31 October 2008.

50. "Klein's Family Markets Joins Wakefern Food Corp. Retail Cooperative; Seven Klein's Stores will Transition to the ShopRite Banner," Wakefern Food Corp., press release, 30 October 2008.

51. Ibid.

52. Ibid.

53. Elliot Zwiebach, "Retailers See Opportunities in Weak Economy," *Supermarket News,* 9 February 2009,

54. "ShopRite Announces an 'Economic Stimulus' Program of Its Own; Customers Purchasing ShopRite Gift Cards Receive a 10 Percent Bonus," Wakefern Food Corp., press release, 29 April 2008.

55. "ShopRite Tops Off Your Tank With Its Gas Card Giveaway; Last Week to Qualify for Free $25.00 Gas Gift Card," Wakefern Food Corp., press release, 30 June 2008.

56. Fiscal 2009 Corporate Accomplishments, Wakefern Powerpoint presentation.

57. Vincent Lo Curcio III, interview by Jeffrey L. Rodengen, digital recording, 30 July 2008, Write Stuff Enterprises, Inc.

58. Joseph Colalillo, interview by Jeffrey L. Rodengen, digital recording, 10 June 2008, Write Stuff Enterprises, Inc.

59. Joe Sheridan, interview by Jeffrey L. Rodengen, digital recording, 10 June 2008, Write Stuff Enterprises, Inc.

60. "About Us," New York City Wine & Food Festival website, www.nycwineandfoodfestival.com/2008/page.php?id=9, 9-/.

61, "The retail newsmakers," *Progressive Grocer,* 1 January 2005.

62. Allen I. Bildner, interview by Jeffrey L. Rodengen, 23 February 2009, digital recording, Write Stuff Enterprises, Inc.

63. Fax correspondence from Allen I. Bildner to Jeffrey L. Rodengen, 29 February 2009.

Chapter Eight Sidebar: Tom Infusino

1. Mark Hamstra,"Unifying Force: ShopRite has Grown to Become a Regional Power under Thomas Infusino's leadership," *Supermarket News,* 7 June 2005.

2. Thomas Infusino, interview by Jeffrey L. Rodengen, digital recording, 29 July 2008, Write Stuff Enterprises, Inc.

3. Greg Saitz, "Working the Aisles," the *Star-Ledger,* Newark, New Jersey, 20 May 2005.

4. Mark Hamstra,"Unifying Force: ShopRite has grown to become a regional power under Thomas Infusino's leadership," *SuperMarket News,* 7 June 2005.

5. Greg Saitz, "Working the Aisles."

6. Mark Hamstra,"Unifying Force: ShopRite has grown to become a regional power under Thomas Infusino's leadership."

7. Ibid.

Chapter Eight Sidebar: Joe Colalillo

1. Joe Colalillo, interview by Jeffrey L. Rodengen, digital recording, 10 June 2008, Write Stuff Enterprises, Inc.

2. Tom Infusino, interview by Jeffrey L. Rodengen, digital recording, 29 July 2008, Write Stuff Enterprises, Inc.

Chapter Eight Sidebar: Dean Janeway

1. Dean Janeway, interview by Jeffrey L. Rodengen, digital recording, 10 June 2008, Write Stuff Enterprises, Inc.

INDEX

Page numbers in italics indicate photographs.